HIDDEN AGENDAS

HIDDEN AGENDAS

Theory,
Politics, and
Experience
in the Women's Movement

ELIZABETH WILSON
with
Angela Weir

TAVISTOCK PUBLICATIONS
London and New York

First published in 1986 by
Tavistock Publications Ltd
11 New Fetter Lane, London EC4P 4EE

Published in the USA by
Tavistock Publications
in association with Methuen, Inc.
29 West 35th Street, New York, NY 10001

Printed in Great Britain by
J. W. Arrowsmith Ltd, Bristol

British Library Cataloguing
in Publication Data

Wilson, Elizabeth
Hidden agendas: theory, politics and
experience
in the women's movement.
1. Feminism
I. Title   II. Weir, Angela
305.4'2   HQ1154

ISBN 0–422–60120–9

Library of Congress Cataloging
in Publication Data

Wilson, Elizabeth, 1936–
Hidden agendas.
(Social science paperbacks; 326)
Bibliography: p.
Includes index.
1. Feminism—Addresses, essays, lectures.
2. Feminism—Great Britain—
Addresses, essays, lectures.
I. Weir, Angela. II. Title. III.Series.
HQ1154.W55 1986   305.4'2
85–31792

ISBN 0–422–60120–9

For Marge, Ben, and Laurence

Contents

Acknowledgements

I should like to thank the Editorial Collectives of *Red Rag* and *Feminist Review* for their help and encouragement in the writing of 'Libertarianism: ideas in the void', 'Gayness and liberalism', 'Thoughts on *Beyond the Fragments*', and 'Psychoanalysis: psychic law and order?'; Judith Stacey for her exceptionally careful editorial help with 'Forbidden love', also Eileen Phillips who helped with an earlier version of part of this article, which appeared as 'Romanticism: Some Notes' in *The Left and the Erotic*, edited by Eileen Phillips (Lawrence & Wishart 1983), and the late Sue Cartledge (greatly missed) who suggested, and gave much help with, another earlier version, 'I'll Climb the Stairway to Paradise: Lesbianism in the Seventies', in *Sex and Love: New Thoughts on Old Contradictions*, edited by Sue Cartledge and Joanna Ryan (The Women's Press 1983); Robin Blackburn for his help with 'The British women's movement', and Jenny Taylor for hers with 'Yesterday's heroines'.

I am grateful to W. W. Norton & Co. for permission to quote extracts from 'Heroines' and 'For Ethel Rosenberg' from *The Fact of a Door Frame* by Adrienne Rich; to *Radical America* for permission to reprint 'A reply to Selma James'; to Lawrence & Wishart for permission to reprint 'How not to reinvent capitalism: socialist welfare in the eighties' from *Silver Linings*, edited by George Bridges and Rosalind Brunt; to *New Left Review* for permission to reprint 'The British women's movement'; to *Feminist Studies* for permission to reprint 'Forbidden love'; and to Routledge & Kegan Paul for permission to reprint 'Yesterday's heroines' from *Notebooks, Memoirs, Archives: Reading and Rereading Doris Lessing*, edited by Jenny Taylor.

I am also most grateful to Gaye Tuchman and to the faculty members on the Feminist Studies Program at Stanford University,

California, for providing me with the opportunity to read more extensively and to think around feminist theoretical and political issues, however inadequately the introductory essay reflects this, and also to my students at Stanford, who stimulated my thinking and challenged many of my assumptions.

PART I ◆ Introduction

1 ◆ Women, heroines, and feminist intellectuals

'You draw your long skirts
                    deviant
                              across the nineteenth century
Registering injustice
                    failing to make it whole
How can I fail to love
                    your clarity and fury
how can I give you
                    all your due
                              take courage from your courage
honour your exact
                    legacy as it is
recognising
        as well
                    that it is not enough?'
                              ('Heroines', from Rich 1984)

Not for me! Although I never said so, I had no heroines. When other women spoke of Virginia Woolf, my mind was still on Proust; while they praised Kollontai, Luxemburg, I discovered Lenin; they retrieved women's art from its oblivion – quilts, embroidery, knitting – I was quite happy with Carpaccio and Picasso, with Jean-Luc Godard, not women's films.

My experience just never seemed to be like that of other women anyway. Yet I never quite joined the world of men. And when the women's movement burst into life I had to be part of it because I'd suffered from that half-acknowledged subordination – feeling yourself not to be there. Nothing overt or brutal about it, just silence, obliteration.

I'd always been passive and marginalized, a non-participant. Now my personal experience mattered in a way that it had never mattered in the 1960s, to CND or the Labour Party. The politics of 'The Personal is Political' helped me escape – but not so much into women's culture as into – simply – *politics*. Now I too discovered the excitement of going to demonstrations, writing leaflets, speaking in public, organizing. So, while for many women feminism began as a critique of the left and the student politics they already knew, for me, on the contrary, it made possible an active entry into socialist politics.

It also gave me a subject matter about which to write. At the beginning of the women's movement I wrote for the broadsheets and papers of the 'alternative left' and the 'underground'. I assumed that that was my destiny and never dreamt that this *samizdat* production had set me on the road to mainstream publication. Had the movement not happened I don't know whether or not I should ever have fulfilled my ambition to write, and for many women besides myself feminism has opened a space to write in new ways about new or previously unacknowledged experiences – to utter the unspeakable. Those whom the movement has enabled to write owe it a debt that can't be repaid.

Yet because of the way I came into the women's movement, and although for several years I felt quite submerged in it, my relationship to it has altered. And indeed that relationship was always rather different, perhaps, from the relationship to it of many of the women with whom I was most closely associated in the women's movement. For, while each woman brings something that is uniquely hers to feminism, so powerful were the assumptions of a shared experience, a similarity of experience (especially in the early years of the movement) that this produced its own gaps, silences, and orthodoxies.

The articles reprinted in this book are responses, ephemera – valuable for the most part only as memorabilia from forgotten moments of women's liberation. They are rooted in the particular circumstances in which they were written, concerned with the tactics of feminism, or with the tactical implications of strategic or theoretical interventions by others. What is of possible interest today is a substratum of underlying preoccupations, the 'hidden agenda', that is seldom openly stated, of which it was hard at the time even to be fully aware.

To utter the unspeakable was always even more difficult than we had supposed because this unspeakable seemed dumbly to gesture not only towards a difference from and antagonism to the male oppressor, but also to disagreements among ourselves and a consequent fragmenting back into the isolation of an unshared experience from the moment of unity and sisterhood.

In its beginnings women's liberation was consciously revolutionary, it broke with reformism, was internationalist, and aimed its attack at economy, ideology, and state all at once; was, as Juliet Mitchell (1971) described it, 'totalist'. As a liberation movement it was inspired both by national liberation movements and (but to a lesser extent, at least initially) by feminist traditions. Marxist feminism and radical feminism alike aimed to develop a theory that could explain the oppression of all women, not only of those in the capitalist West.

This was consistent with a strong emphasis on 'sisterhood'. In the early years feminists believed not only that all women shared an ultimately similar experience – one that transcended differences of race and class – but that this could be directly mapped on to feminist theory and feminist politics. Feminism sought therefore simultaneously to speak women's immediate experience and to formulate a political agenda – more, a political *vision* – for women; theory was then drawn in to act as the hinge between experience and politics.

An important feature of feminism in the early 1970s was the practice of consciousness raising. By speaking out about their individualized, private distress, women would unearth a similarity in these experiences. Many of the early writings of the movement emerged as a development of this testimony. The project of confessional writing was to demonstrate this shared oppression of women, and hence to show how the personal is political; theoretical writing developed in its turn from this: theory was the analysis of the shared oppression. Yet the very act of voicing the subjective failed in the end to cement all women in sisterhood, and the 1970s saw the development of divisions and disagreements that were formalized at the level both of theory and of political practice. In Britain the most important division in the 1970s was between socialist-feminists and radical feminists.

My interest in unearthing the articles reprinted in this book is less, however, to re-examine the established divisions than to explore what I believe to be the problematic nature of 'socialist-feminism' itself. Some of the pieces start from the position that there are certain socialist-feminist orthodoxies that need further examination, and attempt, although in a rather muffled way, to challenge these orthodoxies. Such a challenge was, and is, difficult to mount because most socialist-feminists have not perceived the views I question as 'correct' or orthodox, but, on the contrary, have perceived them precisely as *challenging* established orthodoxies – of the left in particular.

The time is appropriate for a re-evaluation of socialist-feminism because feminism and feminist theory are changing, and, apart from anything else, the established labels no longer necessarily fit the feminisms they were intended to describe. I concentrate on socialist-feminism because that is the grouping within which I have always been located, although I have always seen myself as a Marxist and a feminist rather than as a 'socialist-feminist'. I believe that to say 'I am a Marxist and a feminist' (or 'a feminist and a Marxist') is to make a statement that is different from the statement 'I am a socialist-feminist'. I also believe that socialist-feminism has changed more than radical feminism, as Marxism and socialism have moved further apart in the 'wider movement' – and that the two trajectories are related.

This introductory essay and the two groups of articles that go with it cannot possibly offer a complete re-evaluation. They can at most merely raise in a connected way certain problems and point the way to possible future developments. The essays themselves only scratch the surface in worrying at some of the ways in which British 'socialist-feminism' has, I believe, moved away from a transformative perspective.

Socialist-feminism began as a Marxist investigation of women's subordination, but the engagement of feminism with Marxism both as a body of theory and as a political practice was always tinged with ambivalence because the task feminists set themselves was to extend Marxism to explain what Gayle Rubin (1975) called the 'sex gender system'. For feminists singled out sexual experience and gender identity as that which all women experience in a similar way, and as therefore a unifying focus of the experiential. In Linda Gordon's discussion of birth control this assumption is explicit:

> 'Class differences in the nineteenth century were important in birth control, but they should not blind us to the basic similarity in women's experiences . . . . The desire for and the problems in securing abortion and contraception made up a shared female experience . . . . The desire for spaced motherhood and smaller families existed in every class . . . . The individual theory and practice of birth control stems from a biological female condition that is more basic even than class.'
>
> (Gordon 1976:70)

Effectively, therefore, for many Marxist feminists feminism was from the beginning set up as a *critique* of 'orthodox' Marxism; for example:

> 'I am utilizing the term Marxist feminist, which is now common parlance within the women's liberation movement, since in my view a correct analysis of the subordination of women cannot be provided by Marxists unless Marxism itself is transformed. The term Marxist feminist implies a commitment to, and attempt to move towards, such a transformation.'
>
> (Beechey 1977:45)

Marxist theory was judged defective because 'gender blind', and the investigation of gender soon developed a dynamic of its own that rendered Marxism not merely defective but largely irrelevant.

Marxist or socialist-feminist attempts to justify their hyphen took place, none the less, at the levels both of theory and of political organization. Theoretically, Selma James's demand in the early 1970s for 'wages for housework' led to an analysis of the relationship of unpaid domestic labour to capitalism (Malos 1980); and later to an attempt to relate capitalism and patriarchy, a relationship sometimes discussed in terms of the metaphor of marriage (Eisenstein 1979;

Sargent 1981). But whereas Marxism is a body of theory that purports to explain specific phenomena and advocates certain forms of revolutionary struggle (not necessarily armed or insurrectionary), feminism embodies many theories rather than being a single discrete theory, and, rather than being a politically coherent approach to the subordination of women, is a political commitment – or in some of its forms more an ethical commitment – to giving women their true value. It is not even possible to say that it is a commitment to equality, since some feminists have argued, both in the past and today, for separate spheres of influence, emphasizing difference and complementarity rather than equality. 'Capitalism' and 'patriarchy' are likewise non-comparable objects of analysis (Interrante and Lasser 1979).

Over the past fifteen years, then, certain themes have dominated feminist theory: the validity of patriarchy as an organizing concept in theorizing the subordination of women; the centrality of the concept of the public/private division in structuring women's lives and as a key to understanding women's oppression; the influence of Utopian views of liberation; the nature (and theories) of subjectivity and the ideological; and the fusion of sexuality and gender as the central locus of women's subordination. This is not an exhaustive list, but, in Britain at least, and to some extent in North America (Jaggar 1983; Armstrong and Armstrong 1984), these themes have been as central to socialist-feminist as to radical feminist writings.

These themes are as important as they ever were, but their theoretical development within socialist-feminism has been unsatisfactory and somehow static in recent years. By contrast with radical feminism, which has maintained the strength of its simplicity, the more complex project of socialist-feminism has developed unevenly and disconnectedly, and apart from Michèle Barrett (1980) and Alison Jaggar (1983) few writers have attempted any sort of overview of socialist-feminist theory. There has therefore been a kind of double development: on the one hand there is a recognition that we live in a dynamic world system which increasingly homogenizes, or at least bonds together, varieties of experience, so that the consumerism that shapes women's lives in the West has as its other side the devastation of the 'developing' countries: 'The underside of culture is blood, torture, death and horror' (Jameson 1984:57).

Capitalism is now a global system, and, not only in the West but all over the world it is tending to erode the 'traditional' role of women in the family, and indeed to erode family forms altogether, as it simultaneously changes the composition of the workforce, with far reaching implications for women's and men's roles therein (Elson and Pearson 1981; Smith 1984; Beechey 1985; This alone renders problematic some of the dominant preoccupations of feminist theory outlined above, for on the other hand conceptions of patriarchy and the construction of gender difference remain to a large extent unanchored to, or incompatible with, the theoretical charting of dynamic economico-political change. There has been a fairly widespread consensus that class and gender oppression come from different places and the consequence has been an inability to escape various forms of dual-systems theory. Lise Vogel (1984) has argued that this is due, partly at least, to the legacy of Engels himself, in that his conception of the property-owning family was static and ahistorical.

These theoretical scenarios were often recapitulated at the level of personal/political life, where the impact of feminism was likely to be in criticism of the behaviour of individual male leftists or 'male' forms of organization. In Britain, at least, many women seemed to want the Labour Party or the Communist Party to be organized like the women's movement, or for the women's movement to be more like a revolutionary party, and the attempt to 'marry' the two only increased the tensions. Often at political meetings feminists spoke of their political schizophrenia: 'In the women's movement I speak as a socialist, in the left I speak as a feminist.' At the very least, as Mary McIntosh put it, 'socialist-feminists go to twice as many meetings'. The word 'socialism' only added to the confusion, since the Labour Party and the trades unions were inaccurately hauled in under this banner, with little serious attempt by feminists, particularly in relation to the labour movement, to distinguish between their left and right wings.

These difficulties were most successfully articulated in *Beyond the Fragments* (Rowbotham, Segal, and Wainwright 1979). In this contribution feminism became the moral conscience of socialism and, judged in terms of the values of feminism, socialism seemed fundamentally flawed. The failures and failings of 'the left' could then be used to prove that socialism was irrelevant to women because it wasn't feminist; men had spoilt socialism, or alternatively, socialism was 'male' (Campbell 1984).

Perhaps this was almost inevitable, a translation on to the organizational level of the feminist emphasis on personal, individual change. It was not, however, helpful or creative for feminism to be set up as the conscience of the left so that it became imprisoned in a discourse that allowed it no mistakes and therefore no potential for growth. It seemed more and more anomalous to speak of socialist-feminism when socialist-feminists (along with the 'new left') appeared to see nothing positive in socialism or Marxism but spoke only of socialism's failures and Marxism's absences – first its neglect of, later its fundamental inability to elucidate, gender. Gradually, socialist-feminism became almost indistinguishable from radical feminism in emphasizing the contradiction between men and women as primary and labelling any analysis that foregrounded class and political economy as 'economistic' or 'orthodox'.

Yet if socialist-feminism moved closer to radical feminism, radical feminism had at first been akin to Marxist feminism in seeking universalistic explanations of women's subordination. Shulamith Firestone (1970) had followed Engels in seeking an evolutionary and transhistorical theory to account for the subordination of women; patriarchy in Kate Millett's *Sexual Politics* (1971) was this universal system. Radical feminists set up 'the left'/Marxist/socialism on the one hand and feminism on the other as the two poles between which feminists must orientate themselves and which, even when placed in opposition, remained mutually dependent for their discursive existence. At times this seemed as hopeless as the love of which Andrew Marvell wrote in the seventeenth century, in which lovers 'Like parallels, though infinite, can never meet'. Feminists across the board tended to see Marxism and feminism in terms of each other, but the radical feminist approach to this was not to attempt a fusion of the two, but rather to try to create for feminism an overarching, totalistic theory that was the mirror image of Marxism. Catharine MacKinnon stated:

'Sexuality is to feminism what work is to Marxism: that which is most one's own, yet most taken away. Marxist theory argues that society is fundamentally constructed of the relations people form as they do and make things needed to survive humanly. Work is the social process of shaping and transforming the material and social worlds, creating people as social beings as they create value. It is that activity by which people become who they are. Class is its structure, production its consequence, capital its congealed form and control its issue . . . .

As work is to Marxism, sexuality to feminism is socially constructed yet constructing, universal as activity yet historically specific . . . . As the organized expropriation of the work of some for the benefit of others defines a class – workers – the organized expropriation of the sexuality of some for the use of others defines the sex, woman. Heterosexuality is its structure, gender and family its congealed forms . . . reproduction its consequence and control its issue.'

(MacKinnon 1982:1–2)

To set feminism and Marxism up as mirror images of one another within a closed system means that they become mutually exclusive yet remain yoked together. Marxist method remains for these feminists the only model for feminism; male oppression (patriarchy) therefore becomes *exactly like* the power of a dominant class. The goal for feminism then reflects the goal of revolutionary Marxism: for Marxists the classless, for feminists the genderless, society must be the end result towards which we strive. This is the implicit goal for socialist-feminists as much as for radical feminists in practice, and Alison Jaggar (1983) has gone so far as to suggest that socialist-feminism is distinguished from both radical and Marxist feminism by its insistence (even more thorough-going than that of these other feminisms) on gender as a category that is both wholly socially constructed and fundamental to the oppression of women, its elimination the socialist-feminist goal *par excellence*.

Psychoanalytic theory was the key, many feminists felt, that would untangle these dilemmas. It could be used to theorize gender difference in a universalistic yet radically non-biological way. It has come to be associated with socialist-feminism partly, perhaps, because historically there has been a tradition of attempts to combine Marx and Freud, while for radical feminists Freud remained the archetypal male oppressor, so that radical feminist writings have often made rejection of psychoanalysis an important part of their critique of male-domination theory.

Yet psychoanalysis paradoxically acted as a bridge between Marxist feminism and radical feminism, for in a curious way it has facilitated an analysis of women's oppression that is equally seamless and deterministic. No matter that the cause was seen as the social construction of subjectivity rather than some essentialist male drive to power; one *result* of the emphasis by socialist-feminists on gender difference has led to:

> 'a fundamental contradiction . . . . The need to appeal to what all women have in common results in a stress on sexuality, nurturing and separation from the public world. It can result in an essentialist and self-fulfilling definition of femininity which flattens out differences of race, class and history, limiting the multi-faceted variety of women's experience.'
>
> (MacCluskie 1983:60)

This has led away from rather than towards a socialist project.

Michelle Rosaldo (1980) expressed her dissatisfaction with the universalistic theorization of gender difference in a rather different way in arguing that the 'search for origins' had been taken over too uncritically by contemporary feminists from the 'great thinkers' of the nineteenth century – from Freud, Darwin, Spencer, and Engels – for 'to look for origins is, in the end, to think that . . . our gender systems are primordial, transhistorical, and essentially unchanging in their roots . . . . Our search for origins reveals a faith in ultimate and essential truths' (Rosaldo 1980:392–93). In particular she rejected an explanation of the universal subordination of women in terms of a transhistorical dichotomy along public/private lines, the analysis that she herself and others had developed in the early 1970s (Rosaldo and Lamphere 1974). She now argued that the assumption of a universal division between domestic and public spheres simply reproduced the functionalism and evolutionism of the Victorians and their own ideology of women's place; she suggested that it would be more fruitful and less presumptuous for feminists to try to understand the *diversity* of women's experience – to see it as always distinctly located in the historical and cultural specificity of a given society.

It is possible to read this as a prescription for a return to purely empirical work, and as an argument for a completely relativistic view of gender relations in which the power differences between women and men are wiped away to be replaced merely by an exploration of the variety of 'sexual meanings' in different societies; thus a grasp of women's experience of *oppression* – the politics of gender – is lost. It may however also be read as congruent with a Marxism that looks to concrete and specific historical and political conditions and circumstances in order to develop strategies for change.

Yet although the search was on, in the 1970s, for a universal theory of women's oppression, there was always another project that potentially cut across this: women felt it imperative to try to find some way of writing that was both personal and political, that broke with, or at least questioned the barrier set up between 'theory' and 'experience'. The relationship between these two is difficult. Subjectivity struggles with abstract language; political theory strives to speak in every-day phrases. Feminists have therefore tried to find or to create a language that can reflect the lost or hidden experience of women, or articulate women's difference at the level of literature (Marks and de Courtivron 1981). Women felt they had to break with every existing tradition in order to forge a language that was wholly new:

> 'Language conveys a certain power. It is one of the instruments of domination . . . . The language of theory – removed language – only expresses a reality experienced by the oppressors . . . . Ultimately a revolutionary movement has to break the hold of the dominant group over theory, it has to structure its own connections. Language is part of the political and ideological power of rulers . . . . We can't just occupy existing words, we have to change the meanings of words even before we take them over.'
>
> (Rowbotham 1973:32–3)

In those early days Marxist discourse appeared as one possible new language, but in that respect too it has increasingly come under attack, either as too academic or as inherently male. Jean Bethke Elshtain, an American 'conservative feminist' (Stacey 1983), goes further and contrasts the anti-human language of Marx and Marxists (as she sees it) and its absence of a 'full and coherent account of human beings as speaking subjects' (Elshtain 1982) with the utterance of 'the mother'. She suggests that Marxist feminists, in replacing the 'public' and 'private' spheres with the terms 'production' and 'reproduction' have lost:

> 'the powerful and resonant themes we associate with intimate life, themes conjured up by ordinary understanding of what it means to have a "private life" or an "intimate relation" . . . .
>
> The most compelling critique of Marxist feminism's infusion of abstracted or econometric terms into the sphere of family ties and relationships would lie in a question to any mother on whether she would accept "producing the future commodity labour power" as an apt characterization of what she is doing. One's fears and love for children are drained of their meaning.'
>
> (Elshtain 1982:138)

But this argument disingenuously ignores the historical moment at which the Marxist feminist discourse Jean Elshtain so dislikes emerged. For the abstract language derived from Marxism was *deliberately* far removed from the language of feelings and intimate ties because these had been women's traditional sphere and because the Marxist feminist critique of the family sought to unmask a hidden truth of oppression, subordination, and often violence beneath the sugary ideologies of family happiness that had dominated the Western social sciences in the 1950s and 1960s; to redress a balance.

But, as the 1970s wore on, neither abstract theory nor experiential writing were so easily accepted as speaking for 'all women'. Lesbians, working-class women, and black and ethnic minority women voiced their anger with a movement that had ignored the particular oppression(s) they suffer, and dissociated themselves from the false homogeneity created by a feminist discourse that by definition then becomes white, middle-class, and heterosexist.

An outpouring of literary testimony has borne witness to the great diversity of experience to which the condition of womanhood gives rise. Many women have written in ways that challenge the boundaries between different kinds of writing as well as the 'received wisdoms' of 'white, middle-class' feminism. They testify to the multiple nature of an experience that cannot easily be reduced to concepts of patriarchy, universal victimization, or even resistance and struggle. Thus feminist discourse has become something more than an explanation of women's oppression (which therefore hopes to show us a way out of it) and is also an attempt to answer the question: what does it mean to be a woman?

The emphasis on diversity has had some impact on feminist theory and research. In women's history, for example, it has led to studies of women's varying experiences at particular times. But for the most part it has left untouched core assumptions about 'patriarchy' and the centrality of gender and its construction. The ninth 'The Scholar and the Feminist' Conference, held at Barnard College, New York City, in April 1982, the subject of which was sexuality, did constitute, however, a challenge to the ways in which feminism had understood sexuality, and an attempt to promote sexual pluralism, an understanding of 'sexualities' rather than 'sexuality', as a response to what many women felt was an essentialism and conservatism in radical feminist views of sexuality, particularly as manifested in campaigns against pornography. Many of the contributors at the Barnard Conference therefore attempted to deconstruct femininity, desire, and sexuality.

Gayle Rubin even questioned the whole way in which feminists have collapsed sex and gender together – as she herself had done in her own earlier concept of the 'sex-gender system', and suggested:

> 'that it is essential to separate gender and sexuality analytically to more accurately reflect their separate social existence. This goes against the grain of much contemporary feminist thought, which treats sexuality as a derivation of gender.'
>
> (Vance 1984:308)

She challenges this 'definitional fusion', found, for example, in Catharine MacKinnon's essay (quoted earlier) and she questions whether feminist theory can adequately deal with the theorization of sex:

'Feminist thought simply lacks angles of vision which can encompass the social organization of sexuality . . . .

It is a mistake to substitute feminism for Marxism as the last word in social theory. Feminism is no more capable than Marxism of being the ultimate and complete account of all social inequality. Nor is feminism the residual theory which can take care of everything to which Marx did not attend.'

(Vance 1984:309)

She argues, that is, for 'theoretical as well as sexual pluralism'. This brings its own problems, not least the danger of complete eclecticism, but is an important corrective to the tendency to construct a totalizing, seamless, and essentially *unchanging* theory of the oppression of all women – whose experience was also itself assumed to be unchanging – of which Michelle Rosaldo had become so critical by 1980.

It does, however, suggest the deconstruction of feminist theory – and does not that suggest the deconstruction of feminism itself? Would not the political project of a women's movement that was both unified and autonomous thereby be fatally undermined? Clearly the attempts to develop an overarching theory reflected the desire for a unified movement. As Veronica Beechey pointed out, the concept of patriarchy was used in part 'to provide a theoretical justification for the autonomy of feminist politics'. But she also argues that:

'Whether or not feminism organises as an autonomous movement cannot be deduced from theoretical arguments about the auton- omous nature of women's oppression. The decision to organise as an autonomous movement . . . is a political decision based upon a political analysis of . . . particular historical conditions.'

(Beechey 1979:67)

None the less, the loss of a comprehensive theory and the emphasis on what I have suggested is the second project of feminism: the exploration of diversity, of what it means to be a woman, may – paradoxically – undermine the very feminism of which it is such a powerful expression. 'There is a price to pay for a politics rooted so strongly in consciousness and identity. The power of diversity has as its mirror image and companion the powerlessness of fragmentation' (Zimmerman 1984:680). It is necessary to confront this tension between unity and diversity at all levels, so that the many experiences and voices that the women's movement has released from their silence may enrich a politics of women's liberation rather than fragmenting it.

No existing feminist theory encompasses this diversity, and I do not believe that it is adequate to advocate 'theoretical pluralism' either. Radical feminism, although it claims to speak for all women (as, for example, in Robin Morgan's *Sisterhood is Global*, 1984), in practice refuses diversity. Radical feminism has a clear and coherent ideology: that the 'main enemy' is 'man' and that male power operates to a large extent unchangingly – although recently some radical feminists have argued for a more historicized approach (Friedman 1982; Lown 1983). This simple and emotive analysis is very powerful and has had the positive effect of unleashing women's anger and rousing them to action. It cannot, however, account for differences between women, nor for the fact that large numbers of men are also exploited and oppressed. It tends to sink back into biologism (women being inherently superior by virtue of their maternal function) and to portray women as sharing an essential, pre-given nature rather than being socially constructed (see Jaggar 1983; Echols 1984; Eisenstein 1984).

Socialist-feminism in proportion as it has distanced itself from Marxism and emphasized its critique rather than its affirmation of the socialist project, has approximated to a pale version of radical feminism without the latter's strengths. What began as an attempt to forge a Marxist analysis of women's subordination and/or an attempt to integrate Marxism and feminism has ended as simply a feminist critique of the left – a largely negative project.

One of the few avenues of escape from this negativism has been the (as often as not inexplicit) adoption of Utopian socialist perspectives. Utopian socialism influenced Marx and Engels, despite their criticisms of it, and there has been a number of feminist Utopian writings, while radical feminism in its creation of alternative communities and services is Utopian in the sense of being prefigurative.

Utopianism therefore acts as a bridge between socialist and radical feminism. It has also acted, I believe, to some extent to hold together what I have identified as the two separate projects within feminism: the movement for political change, and the exploration of difference and what it means to be a woman. The Utopian project, in gesturing towards a future that is female, collapses women's experience and strategic vision into one.

It is customary on all sides to speak with admiration of the Utopian legacy. But I believe we should treat it with caution. Utopias are always denunciations of actually existing society, their solution always the creation of a wholly other world. They are necessarily visionary, and therefore tend not simply to ignore but actually to condemn the bridge – politics – between the world today and the envisioned world. That makes Utopianism in a sense anti-political, in that the question of power and how you get it is evaded. Moreover, the vision, contrasted with any conceivable reality, reveals the revolution as always betrayed and the actual political struggle as always a process of fatal compromise.

Utopianism, although it claims to gesture towards the future, actually seeks lost worlds of happiness, human perfectibility, a cure for all human ills. It expresses a longing for a nostalgic, imagined world of the infant, in which the self was not fractured and experience not flawed – it is about the loss of an innocent, idyllic past rather than a perfect future. And feminist Utopianism, because 'the personal is political', looks to politics for the solution to personal unhappiness, sexual discontents. But Freud's remarks on the limitations of the psychiatric cure might usefully be redirected at political Utopianism:

> 'No doubt fate would find it easier than I do to relieve you of your illness. But you will be able to convince yourself that much will be gained if we succeed in transforming your hysterical misery into common unhappiness. With a mental life that has been restored to health you will be better armed against that unhappiness.'
>
> (Freud and Breuer 1974:393)

Political change may create the preconditions for personal happiness, but cannot guarantee it. Some of our discontents, perhaps, are *not* political.

In the feminist Utopia we ourselves would be perfect, but

paradoxically in embracing a Utopian form of socialism, socialist-feminism has condemned itself to an increasing and corrosive pessimism because (and here it is unlike either Marxist feminism or radical feminism) its main object of attack has turned out to be not the oppressor without, but the enemy within. For the centrality of the social construction of gender to socialist-feminism means that it is the feminine psyche, our own subjectivity, that is faulty, our inner selves that we must obliterate and remould, if we are to come within sight of the ultimate Utopia of the genderless society. Not surprisingly, this has had debilitating consequences, and has often led rather to a resignation, an acquiescence in internalized femininity, even an exaggeration of its hold. The only alternative has appeared to be a shameless (and at least more cheerful) celebration of the kitsch trappings of conventional consumerist femininity, from sexy underwear to romantic fiction. This is not true of the whole of feminist culture, but, taken as a whole, the socialist-feminist theory of the past decade has argued itself into a depressingly deterministic position in its attempt to theorize subjectivity; the practical correlate of this has increasingly been a rather pallid reformism.

A different kind of defensiveness has surrounded the social location of socialist-feminists, who (more, it seems to me, than other feminists) have often been attacked as privileged academics or intellectuals. Socialist-feminists have had to defend themselves against anti-intellectualism, and against sneers of 'middle-class' and 'élitist' coming from male leftists who are often just as 'middle-class' themselves, or who, even if working-class, may well have access to forms of power denied women. Yet at the same time *all* Western feminists are of course immensely privileged by comparison with the vast majority of men as well as women, although the niche we have been able to carve out for ourselves within the dominant order is actually quite precarious and vulnerable. And since socialist- (and Marxist) feminists must by definition claim an awareness of all oppressions, the attempt to prioritize our own is necessarily difficult and delicate.

Socialist-feminists have therefore understandably tended to down-play or evade the (perhaps embarrassing) issue of their role as intellectuals, yet there is a good precedent for seeing the role of intellectual in a positive light. Antonio Gramsci greatly extended the whole concept of the intellectual, developing Lenin's ideas on the subject into a distinction between the 'traditional intellectual' of the bourgeois class, whose role is to 'organize' and 'hegemonize' ideas that serve to legitimate the existing order, while simultaneously claiming an independent and neutral position, above or apart from any class; and the 'organic intellectual'. The organic intellectual is developed from and identified with the exploited classes, becoming identified with their liberatory aims, and her or his responsibility is to serve the ends of fellow oppressed groups (Gramsci 1971). Although Michel Foucault (1977) has argued that in contemporary society the role of the intellectual is his own abolition, since intellectuals (by implication white, middle-class men) are useless to the masses, Gramsci did not see intellectuals as necessarily separate and apart from the oppressed.

There is a sense then in which women could be 'organic intellectuals'. At the same time, this is a position that has to be continually constructed (even more, perhaps, in contemporary consumerist society than in the Italy of the 1920s and 1930s, in the context of which Gramsci was writing) since in a media-saturated world the intellectual – in the West, at least – is more than ever the paid and tolerated dissident, the ambiguity of this position making the role always an uneasy one.

Lastly, a major problem with socialist-feminism is that in claiming that the feminist side of the 'hyphen' in socialist-feminism was always the part that was subordinated and lost, and in trying to redress that balance, socialist-feminists have lost a sense of themselves – or women's liberation – as part of a wider revolutionary project of 'human emancipation' in Marx's terms (in terms, that is, not of 'humanism', but of the liberation of all oppressed classes and groups).

A number of writers (Brenner and Ramas 1984; Vogel 1984; Armstrong amd Armstrong 1984) are now beginning to recognize the inadequacies and problems of static dual-systems theories of equal but different oppressions, and to argue for a unitary theory of women's oppression in the contemporary world where the global encroachments of international capitalism both homogenize and divide women in new ways, break down divisions between public and private, between production and reproduction, and even between 'core' and 'periphery'. As women are increasingly integrated into the paid workforce, while remaining its most vulnerable section, and while reproduction and private life are increasingly commoditized, Marxism becomes more not less relevant in a feminist analysis of this changing world. Politically, an understanding of this world involves the recognition that there is no necessary feminism that unites all women, that unity in fact can never be assumed, but must always be worked for and constructed politically. Maxine Molyneux has stated this very clearly in her account of the efforts of the Nicaraguan revolutionary government to emancipate women:

'While it is true that at a certain level of abstraction women can be said to have some interests in common, there is no consensus over what these are or how they are to be formulated. This is in part because there is no theoretically adequate and universally applicable causal explanation of women's subordination from which a general account of women's interests can be derived. Women's oppression is recognized as being multi-causal in origin and mediated through a variety of different structures, mechanisms and levels, which may vary considerably across space and time. There is therefore considerable debate over the appropriate site of feminist struggle and over whether it is more important to focus attempts at change on objective or subjective elements, 'men' or 'structures', laws, institutions or inter-personal power relations – or all of them simultaneously . . . .

These factors vitiate attempts to speak *without qualification* of a unitary category "women" with a set of already constituted interests that are common to it. A theory of interests which has an application to the debate about women's capacity to struggle for, and benefit from, social change, must begin by recognizing differences rather than assuming homogeneity.'

(Molyneux 1984:61)

It therefore follows, she argues, that 'the way in which interests are formulated will vary considerably across space and time and may be shaped in different ways by prevailing political and discursive influences'. For this reason 'it is difficult to argue, as some feminists have done, that gender issues are primary for women, at all times'.

All this may seem to have little to do with the idea of the feminist heroine with which I began. But in her poem 'Heroines' Adrienne Rich is, in fact, speaking of the tension between the imperative of identification and the recognition of difference. Not only must we recognize that our 'sisters in history', while they spoke and acted in the name of feminism, had projects and assumptions that were often very different from our own; we must also acknowledge more fully and confront the consequences of our recognition that 'feminism' today includes a wide diversity of experiences and programmes and encompasses political philosophies that are in some cases mutually antagonistic. (The very word 'feminism' has become suspect, since it lays claim to a too uncritical bond between ourselves and our forbears without making clear our recognition that they in many cases oppressed their black and working-class sisters; it has also – incorrectly – come to be associated with a view that women should not work politically with men. For these reasons I would prefer the re-substitution of 'women's liberation'.)

The idea of the 'heroine' implicitly supports a celebratory view of women. It is often said that women need heroines and (as the jargon of behaviouristic psychology has it) 'role models' – strong women to convince the rest of us that women can, despite all the odds, excel, be brave or brilliant. Yet these very exemplars recreate the outstanding, the achiever, the Artist. It is for this reason that Michèle Barrett (1982) rejects the concept of individual female 'genius' celebrated in Judy Chicago's huge art work 'The Dinner Party'. Similarly Margaret Walters (1976) has criticized Simone de Beauvoir (while paying tribute to her great achievements) for recreating her life in an exemplary fashion – as a model for other women. The whole concept of the feminist heroine carries with it an implication of identity over difference, and of *exceptional* women, of rampant individualism. It is therefore very contradictory. The identity of 'intellectual', although attacked for élitism, is actually much less grandiose, in that, in the Gramscian sense at least, it conceives of intellectuals as servants to a cause, and of intellectual activity as a collective process.

But in any case, what is required of feminism is not the creation of possible identities for women; rather in its experiential mode it ought to assist women in evaluating their own experience (and in this the psychoanalytic method may well prove helpful). The feminist heroine only embodies the 'correct' experience and qualities; the feminist intellectual represents understanding abstracted from experience.

In her recent poetry Adrienne Rich has tried to confront the relationship between identity and difference (a relationship that has implications for language, for theory, and for politics) and in one of her poems she speaks to and of Ethel Rosenberg as a woman who represents both. Ethel Rosenberg and her husband Julius went to the electric chair in 1953, for having allegedly given the secret of the atom bomb to the Russians. They were sacrificed to anti-Communism in McCarthyite America, and Ethel Rosenberg's courage was indeed that of an exceptional woman. Or perhaps it was the ordeal she faced that drew out the exceptional qualities within her.

Adrienne Rich recognizes that to try to force her into the mould of 1970s' feminism is to do violence to what she was and stood for:

'Ethel Greenglass Rosenberg would you
have marched to take back the night
collected signatures

for battered women who kill
What would you have to tell us
Would you have burst the net . . . .

If I dare imagine her surviving
I must be fair to what she must have lived through
I must allow her to be at last

political in her ways not in mine
her urgencies perhaps impervious to mine
defining revolution as she defines it.

(Rich 1984:289–90)

So the time has come, perhaps, to look beyond the labels and divisions of the 1970s, not in order to pretend that differences among women do not exist, but to understand more clearly what they are, or how they have changed. There seems to be a renewed cultural vitality in British feminism, and perhaps feminist theory can also renew itself, as it struggles to free itself from the legacy criticized by Michelle Rosaldo, and grapples anew with the global dimensions of the struggles of women.

Ethel Rosenberg, as she was about to be strapped into the electric chair, leant forward with a radiant smile and embraced the prison matron who had looked after her during her two long years in jail while appeals against the death sentence were countered by the efforts of the state to break the Rosenbergs, to barter the promise of 'life' in return for their 'confessions'. I feel it is important to remember this moment, not as simply the beautiful and courageous gesture of a 'heroine' facing death, but as a moment between two women, and that we should remember the unknown woman, the prison matron, as well as Ethel Rosenberg – the political woman embodying true sisterhood – as symbols of unity in difference.

PART II ◆ Feminist Politics and Socialist Ideas

2 ◆ A reply to Selma James (*with Angela Weir*)

Introduction

In the early 1970s Selma James made a major impact on the British (and North American) women's movement with her demand for 'wages for housework' (Malos 1980). The article reproduced here was one of a number of replies to her pamphlet *Women, the Trades Unions, and Work, or What is Not to be Done*, which had been produced for the British National Women's Liberation Conference held in Manchester in the spring of 1972. This reply was written for the following conference, held in Acton in the autumn of the same year. The Marxist feminist journal, *Red Rag*, also published a number of replies. Of these, Sheila Rowbotham's and ours were reprinted alongside the original piece by Selma James in the July/October 1973 issue of *Radical America*.

Despite the rather daunting language of this piece it is of interest because this was one of the first feminist contributions explicitly to make use of the concept of the 'reproduction of the relations of production'. Also, and more significantly, the wages for housework debate was one of the most important in the women's movement in the early 1970s, and it brought together (and into conflict) the two tendencies within the women's movement at that time: a kind of anarcho-Trotskyism very hostile towards trades unionism and any politics that smacked of reformism, and a theoretical Marxist attempt to analyse women's subordination.

A reply to Selma James

Since Selma James produced her pamphlet, *Women, the Trades Unions, and Work, or What is Not to be Done*, many women will have discussed it. We write to try to assess and to share what we have learnt from our participation in some of these discussions and where they leave us now. We welcomed Selma's paper, and the Italian paper to which it is very much a corollary, because it attempted to move beyond the arguments of a narrow feminism versus a narrow, primarily economist Marxism and tried instead to understand the objective relationships between class and sexuality in modern capitalist society. We wish in this paper to examine the responses to the paper and then to look in more detail at the analysis proffered and the strategy which is indicated – primarily, in Selma's paper, in the form of various demands.

Selma says that her pamphlet is intended to begin a discussion. Yet subsequent meetings have tended to develop as though the women's movement has *either* to accept her pamphlet wholeheartedly, accept the analysis and the six new demands, *or* to reject it and sink back into various obsessions – trades unionism; personal liberation; mindless activism. The problems Selma is raising faced the movement at its birth. We – the movement – are like a dog with a bone, worrying at one or other of these problems every so often and then burying it again in a ritual without nourishment.

Perhaps the most disappointing aspect of the discussions was the low level at which they tended to revolve around the question of whether or not to work within trades unions, or whether or not to unionize women. Those who supported trades union activism, usually members of the International Marxist Group (IMG) and the International Socialists (IS) did not even attempt to suggest – as certainly Lenin or Gramsci would require them to do – their strategy for developing higher forms of working-class struggle that would transcend the limitations of trades unionism, its bureaucratism and economism, so that trades union struggle might be relegated to a secondary position.

Given the centrality of the question of women and trades unionism it is perhaps worth re-examining the arguments. We believe these involve three levels of analysis: (1) an analysis of the social formations which produce the conditions of capitalism; (2) an analysis of the concrete operations of capitalism at a particular time, i.e. now (this must involve history), and the particular contradictions of capitalism; (3) from the above two, a strategy for women now.

Taking the first point, the analysis of the extra-parliamentary left in England – this means really the Trotskyist left – is that the crucial and determinant social formation in capitalism is the formation of the means of production and that this is located in the factory. Therefore revolutionary activity must begin by organizing at the level of the means of production. Further to this there is the quasi-psychological assumption that the grouping together of large numbers of men in large units of production will provide the subjective conditions for the realization of class consciousness and revolutionary organization.

On the second level it is thought that the particular organizations workers have evolved to *defend* themselves are the trades unions, and that therefore it is crucial to work within these 'natural' organizations of the proletariat and by a series of carefully framed demands and political education pave the way for the highest form of revolutionary struggle, namely dual power, which is created through the formation of factory committees which link to form some united confederation of workers in which quick and generalized uprisings will be the instruments for taking power. Their strategy proceeds from this analysis.

We reject this analysis and agree with much of Selma's criticism. However, we feel that because her analysis is based on a primarily descriptive/empirical account of women's relationship with the trades unions and of the nature of women's work, her paper has an insufficient theoretical basis and so in the end insufficient strategical and hence organizational directives. We wish to advance some possible lines for analysis.

Firstly, at the most theoretical level, we feel it is crucial to analyse not only the means of production but also the reproduction of the means of production, especially in terms of the reproduction of labour power, and the production of the relations of production. It is perhaps in capital's ongoing struggle not only to produce, but also to reproduce, the conditions of production – to keep its own system going – that some of its basic contradictions may be revealed.

We feel that this is the theoretical viewpoint towards which Selma, and also Mariarosa Dalla Costa in the Italian pamphlet, are both reaching, yet their analyses of women's labour still seem to be determined by the concept of 'means of production' rather than '*reproduction* of the relations of production', and thus their analyses, too, are primarily 'economic'.

In the case of Selma's pamphlet the demands reflect a more or less *ad hoc* mixture of 'material' (economic) demands, e.g. equal pay for all, and what are usually seen as more 'ideological' demands, e.g. the right to control our own bodies.

In the case of Dalla Costa, whose pamphlet is more explicitly theoretical, the problem is originally posed in terms of the haunting premise of cultural lag. (We do not especially criticize her for this, because this is the way the 'traditional' left has often interpreted the problem and she is trying to argue against it.) She says capitalism creates wage labour, and that from this women and children (and one might add the old) are excluded. Being excluded from labour these groups lose their power, and 'thus with the advent of the capitalist mode of production . . . women were relegated to a condition of isolation, enclosed within the family cell, dependent in every aspect upon men . . . she remained in a pre-capitalist stage of personal dependence.'

What seems ambiguous about Dalla Costa's pamphlet is that she appears partially to accept this vision of women excluded and thus locked in the cell of cultural and material dependency, whilst also asserting – and this is the main argument of the pamphlet – that women *do* produce surplus value. 'We have to make clear that within the wage domestic work not only produces use value but is an essential function in the production of surplus value.' We describe this as her main argument because she devotes eleven pages to her analysis of the 'productivity' of domestic labour and because she also discusses women's sexual sublimation and passivity in terms of 'productivity'. In section C she does talk about women being responsible for the reproduction of labour power, but devotes only a paragraph to it. Also, rather strangely, she finds that the cause of women's role in reproducing labour power (interpreted as disciplining husband and children) is the psychological stunting of her personality. Then this function is linked back to sexual passivity which in turn is a prerequisite or result – the causal sequence isn't quite clear – of women's exclusion from labour. To sum up, Dalla Costa is saying that women are being productive in these three ways: (1) producing domestic labour, (2) being sexually passive, and (3) being disciplinarians to children and husbands, though it is unclear whether or not she is saying that the second and third functions produce surplus value. So having 'proved' that women produce labour *qua* their role of women, women then have their own ticket to create the socialist revolution. Her final section is headed 'The Struggle against Labour' and her concluding thought seems to be that to liberate themselves from their exploitation housewives (is this synonymous with all women?) must 'recognize themselves also as a section of the class, the most degraded because they are not paid a wage'.

But who then are women struggling against, to whom then are they going to make their demands – the bosses? the government? their husbands? to all of these groups in a free-wheeling female holocaust? What is the basis of women's power if they destroy the family? Although Dalla Costa gives a Marxist analysis of women's position, and although she makes a number of acute empirical observations, all that really emerges is the demand for women to make demands in an unsystematic way: to go down to local trades union meetings and make the men demand an end to shift work so we can make love at nights, to go down to the medical students and demand that they give us the knowledge and means to have or not to have birth control, abortions, and so on. To be frivolous one might say that women are being told 'if you're going to nag, nag about the right things'. To be less frivolous one might say that although one agrees with many of these demands in themselves, they add up to no more than a mindless activism which tends to be debilitating and frustrating in the long run, and which doesn't amount to the class struggle or the possibilities of class victory.

We shall return to points about strategy and the alternatives to random demands later, but here we would just like to argue that Dalla Costa takes the wrong concept as an instrument for analysis and that it would be more satisfactory to analyse the position of women from an analysis of the reproduction of the conditions of production.

In talking about the reproduction of the conditions of production we are discussing two things: (1) the reproduction of labour power, and (2) the reproduction of the relations of production. We believe these two functions are crucial to an ongoing capitalist society and that women's position in capitalism is fundamentally defined by their relationship to these two processes. In saying this we agree with Dalla Costa that capitalism does and has excluded women from production, but we are asserting that capitalism also creates new forms of institutions and roles for women and that these can be explained by the necessity for any society to create means by which it will reproduce itself. To get to the point at last, capitalism consists not only of a new type of infra-structure, but also of a new superstructure and a new state. Rather than women's productive labour being hidden because they aren't paid a wage, what is continually hidden is women's *ideological* role in a number of state apparatuses, particularly the family, and the reasons why this role is crucial to capitalism.

Starting from (2) above, then, women are crucial in the reproduction of labour power because:

(1) They are given the total responsibility for the reproduction of children, whilst lacking the means to control in any way that process. These means are controlled by state institutions – in the case of the UK directly, since these are publicly owned.

(2) Women have the responsibility for using the husband's wage for the purpose it is intended, i.e. the material reproduction of labour power. There are two parts to this function: there is firstly buying food, clothing, housing etc., and secondly the labour of processing and maintaining them. Again, as in the case of having children, women are responsible for the wage but have no control over the means by which it is distributed.

In speaking of the wage one should also note that in the conditions of monopoly capitalism the wage is usually insufficient to cover the successful material reproduction of the wage labourer, and that two other mechanisms are often created to assist this process: (1) surplus value is often channelled away from the firm to the state and paid out again in the form of housing subsidies, health service subsidies, etc., though this in no way amounts to an equal redistribution of income. Also one might note that much of the government's money comes from taxation on the wage itself and thus the state has control over the supply of many of the minimum material necessities; and (2) women go out to work to supplement the male wage.

So women have responsibility for the material reproduction of the worker but lack control in a double sense in that they lack control over the state institutions. Women are crucial in the reproduction of the relations of production in the following ways:

(1) The care and socialization of children. It is crucial for capitalism not only to reproduce labour materially but also to ensure subjection to the ruling ideology or consent to its practice. That this be the major responsibility of women particularly during the formative learning years of a child's early life is, we suggest, a feature specific to capitalism. However, here again the state controls the educational system and while women have more autonomous responsibility in the care of children than in other functions, the state through the educational system still controls much of the ideological socialization which again is the women's responsibility. Arguably this is particularly the case at nursery and primary-school level.

(2) The disciplining of the husband – ensuring his continued ideological subjection by explicitly emphasizing her own and the children's dependence on his continuing wage.

In making these remarks we emphasize that they are likely to be more true the further down the social scale one goes – for instance sexual roles are most rigidly defined in the lower working class – and that perhaps they are most true of some black families and of immigrant workers in Europe. There the man as wage labourer is often banished from the scene altogether and women are thrown in a direct relationship with the state.

We have tried to suggest that the crucial social formations of capitalism in which women play a role are the reproduction of labour power and the relations of production and that an analysis of women primarily in terms of their 'productivity' masks the centrality of their role in reproducing the conditions of production. We want in this section to look at the present concrete operation of this role, but shall merely suggest some further possibilities for investigation since we have not done enough research to go more deeply.

It seems that the most significant factors in the present situation are high unemployment, inflation, the decreasing taxation of the very rich, the cutting of state welfare subsidies, and the full introduction of means tested social services.

British capitalism, faced with severe international competition and indeed the wage demands of the working class itself has been forced to respond in a number of ways:

(1) Automation – productivity bargaining. Capital is being concentrated in high-output, labour-saving machinery. As an example of rationalization we quote for a report in the *Guardian* (21 August, 1972) on the Covent Garden move to Nine Elms, drawing attention to the fact that it hints at a theme of a number of recent labour struggles, namely a connection between the job and life outside or around the job.

> 'Faced with the loss of the human elements which have made work in Covent Garden worthwhile . . . market workers are ready to demand compensation in traditional style: by hard wage bargaining . . . . The new market will be more like a factory than a garden . . . (and) the inevitability of the move, the well-publicized activities of property developers in shaping the new Covent Garden, and the imminent break-up of old-established employer–employee relationships have all contributed to a new mood of political awareness in the Garden.'

New investment will mean fewer jobs not more. The objects of productivity deals are wage rises in return for less shop floor control, speed-up, measured day work, higher productivity per worker and cuts in the labour force. The results are a smaller workforce, more output (product) per worker and more total product/labour cost decreasing proportionately to increased output, and increased surplus value.

(2) The 'lame duck' rationalization policy in private and nationalized industry. This has meant profitable parts of nationalized industry being sold to 'Heath's friends', while the social parts from which we all benefit are cut back – for example, the postal service – with consequent redundancies. It has meant factories and sections not immediately profitable being wiped out, because other factories and sections are producing more, usually within the same firm.

(3) Wage freezes – the £2 norm.

(4) Increasing the cost of the Welfare State – free milk in schools is abolished, prescription charges are re-established, and at the

present time rent increases are especially important. Andrew Glyn and Bob Sutcliffe point out that among many other weapons used with the purpose of increasing investment in the present economic situation the Tory government has already increased welfare charges at the same time as decreasing taxation of the very rich in an attempt to redistribute income to capital.

'The working class is also hit by reductions in social services, agricultural price guarantees, and housing subsidies, which will involve a saving of something like £500m. in 1974/5 on Labour programmes. These reductions include almost £50m. in reduced food subsidies (and therefore higher food prices) and £100–£200m. from higher council house rents. Those people below the official poverty line will escape some of the higher charges provided they submit to more means tests, and those who are very badly paid will, if they come forward, benefit a bit from Family Income Supplement which still leaves them below the poverty line. But for the working class as a whole these changes in public expenditure involve clear reductions in living standards, proportionately much greater than those suffered by higher income groups.'

(Glyn and Sutcliffe 1972)

These attacks on the working class are being backed up by legislation designed to lock the working class more firmly in their cycle of dependence upon and subservience to the ruling class. The two most important pieces of legislation are the Industrial Relations Bill (1971) and the introduction of means tested social services. Both say that same thing – if you are not officially recognized by the ruling class you have no right to challenge the existing distribution of income, nor even to possess the minimum necessary to live, a house, food, clothing. It has always been true that the ruling class decides who shall live and who shall starve; the new Tory legislation merely spells it out more crudely.

How do these processes affect women?

Welfare cuts are especially meaningful to women, who bear the brunt of them. They have a bearing too on working politically and organizing in the community. Women are, in fact, caught and crushed between two opposing economic forces: the reality of price rises and welfare cuts and the ideology of consumption and the commodity, in which they play a key role. The point about consumerism is not that the use and enjoyment of well-made and useful household objects or the desire for a more comfortable life are in themselves bad – and the women's movement must guard against the strain of puritanism that tends to imply such enjoyment is suspect – but that in this society, in the pursuit of higher and higher profits and more and more consumption, women (as the main purchasers) are offered, therefore, an ever increasing assortment of useless and unnecessary articles whilst *real* necessities – decent housing, strong furniture, safe toys – are unobtainable. It is part of the ideology of consumerism that women are encouraged to compete against one another. And there is no need to labour the point about the blatant untruthfulness of advertising.

In fact, as Selma points out, the vast majority of women can't afford the basic necessities of life for their families and themselves unless they work. Selma attempts to show how women's position is crucial in the economic situation, and she talks a lot about work, and the protest against the Protestant work ethic. It has been suggested that there is a confusion here between 'work' and 'labour' or 'wage labour'. This doesn't make the theme less important, though it indicates the degree of confusion surrounding it.

On the one hand the pamphlet expresses a deep rejection of the work ethic of our society as it is currently expressed in our daily lives. This is exemplified in mystifying demands by militants for 'the right to work' and also in the total refusal to work among sections of the youth culture ('work's too oppressive').

Most of us have been brought up with a dual attitude to work. It is portrayed to us when young as an evil necessity about which adults complain ('your schooldays are the happiest days of your life'), albeit with martyred self-satisfaction, yet children do notice how their fathers often seem lost when on holiday and become increasingly irritable and bored without their work, so that all are relieved when the holiday ends and they can return to it. On reaching adult status we are urged to find 'work you can enjoy', and it is implied that there is something wrong with anyone who can't 'buckle down to a useful job of work' ('His trouble is he doesn't like work'). Middle class and working class alike, yet in different ways, are deeply ambivalent about work, and one should not underestimate the importance of this psychology of work.

We differ, however, from Selma over her conclusions. She states her aim as follows:

'Our concern must be demands with which the Movement articulates in few words the breadth of its rejection of the oppression and exploitation of women. The tension between a local struggle and the stated principles of the Movement does not vanish, but within each local demand which mobilises women wherever they are, the struggle loses its sporadic, provincial and disconnected character.'

Can demands do this, though? What *are* demands? Demands restrict thought by tying it down to something too immediate and specific. Demands are easily misunderstood and distorted. They are already an over-simplification, and can be no substitute for an analysis or for the manifesto – a more coherent statement of aims – which could come out of that analysis. Selma does not show that her demands connect.

What then *do* we do? Before discussing positive alternatives it is again necessary to explain where and why we disagree with Selma.

The issue of work seems to be connected with what we term 'life-style politics'. We believe this is an important theme in the women's movement, but a partly submerged and unarticulated one. It represents a rebellion against the work ethic, and has also tried to offer an alternative based on co-operation (food co-operatives, communal living, non-monogamous relationships, etc.), on certain kinds of organization (such as the claimants' unions), and generally on values other than the bourgeois values of acquisitiveness (consumerism), with an emphasis on the descaling rather than the proliferation of needs (in the area of fashion the abandonment of make-up, 'hairstyles', etc., and of exaggerated cleanliness and routinization in the sphere of housework). If we need fewer possessions we need work less because we need less money and we can make what we have go further by sharing it, is one belief underlying this life style.

It is in a sense an exemplary way of life, to be differentiated on that count from the drop-out, inturned 'counter-culture' of hippies, though it has points of contact with it. Exemplary politics have been a feature of the left for a long time. Gramsci, for instance, defined this tendency as follows:

> 'there is one traditional party too with an essentially "indirect" character – which in other words presents itself explicitly as purely "educative", moral, cultural. This is the anarchist movement. Even so-called direct (terrorist) action is conceived of as "propaganda" by example. This only confirms the judgement that the anarchist movement is not autonomous, but exists on the margin of the other parties, "to educate them".'

> (Gramsci 1971)

Now we beleive that in the present situation such exemplary politics cannot be the correct ones for us, as women, to pursue, because what we have to do is not to educate the left, but to *create* it, create at least our own left-wing movement and create its relationship to the wider struggle, or perhaps it would be better to say situate ourselves simultaneously as the wider struggle and in it.

Exemplary life-style politics also emphasize the gulf between one consciousness and another. Are those who live in this new way political activists? To themselves they are; to many working-class women they are incomprehensible, bizarre, and therefore sinister. This is a familiar problem. But it does need to be restated that it really is not good enough to reject working-class women who are scared by talk of ripping off from supermarkets and don't wish to take part in even collective demonstrative public action of this kind because it is 'stealing' and they don't believe in 'breaking the law'. False consciousness maybe, but also a realistic understanding on the part of, say, a working mother of just what she would risk should she get done – her life smashed up, her kids in care, at the best interference from welfare workers or a probation officer.

Ripping off is, as a matter of fact, a demonstration akin to the absenteeism of which Selma speaks. She calls this women's refusal, their revolt. True. Yet it achieves nothing. In the first place the management of a factory can get replacements for the girls [sic] on the assembly line and usually costs for a quick staff turnover and high absenteeism so they don't suffer too much (just as supermarkets cost for shoplifting). Nor does the individual woman benefit ultimately since disaffection from work is part of a vicious circle, it is one reason why she gets married young and 'settles down' to have a family – only to have to return eventually to a similar hateful job, from which this time, because of her family responsibilities, she usually can't escape, unless indeed the second time around she takes refuge in mental breakdown, as frequently happens.

The apotheosis of unfreedom is the 'temp. typist', of whom Germaine Greer (1970) wrote as though the 'temp.' were the unfettered, roaming gipsy of our society, the truly free and ultimately liberated woman with no hang-ups about bourgeois security – when again in the long term to do temporary work is merely a recognition that a job for women is just a way of filling in time until you find a husband. To work in that way is to extend prostitution from the sphere of sexuality to the sphere of intellectual functioning.

But in any case female absenteeism can be virtually abolished by a simple rearrangement of shifts to fit in with the 'family responsibilities' of women (i.e. the fact that women have two jobs). The Peak Frean factory in Bermondsey discovered this some years ago. By introducing a nursery for babies and enabling women to fit their shifts around the family timetable, instead of vice versa, they reduced absenteeism and high staff turnover to zero, without making costly concessions.

Absenteeism, like ripping off from supermarkets, is the private, negative politics of rebellion and refusal. It is a way of saying 'no', of taking a secret revenge against the monolithic 'them' of the state. Life-style politics goes a step further in that it is a public demonstration and a way of saying 'things are not the way we want them – *this* is how they should be', and at least they are collective and not isolated. But there is more difference than a transposition of letters between reactive and creative politics. These reactive life-style politics are the politics of weakness because they proceed on the assumption that an actual revolution or transformation is impossible, and that therefore all one can do is create one's own revolutionary ghetto.

Of course we all hate work – wage labour – as it is in this society. We hate being assembly-line fodder, we hate being house-cleaning and baby-rearing fodder, we hate being pen-pushing or managerial fodder.

Yet the demand to work less is confusing because it actually could only come about in an 'affluent' society – the day surely *will* come when we work a 20-hour week – and could not be achieved, and would in any case be an irrelevant demand, in a transformed society in which this country had relinquished its exploitative relationship with the Third World.

We should like to see a society in which the bourgeois distinction between work and 'leisure' – 'spare time' as it is so significantly called – was destroyed and transcended. What we rebel against is the separation of work from enjoyment, and of home from work. Nor do we want individual men taking over some of 'our' jobs in the home while we take over some of 'his' in the office or factory. We want greater flexibility between work and home – to have our kids with us at our place of work, or to work at home; we want greater flexibility in our concepts of what is mental and what is manual labour, and also of the nature of skills. The rebellion of women against being cast all and always in the same mould of home-maker extends to every sphere. Is it necessary for any individual to spend fifty years on a production line or as a teacher? So-called experience and expertise are valuable but in our present society are fetishized and often merely an excuse for privilege.

The political struggle *does* transcend the false categories of work and play and Selma is right to say that ultimately that is at least a part of what the movement has to offer all women – the struggle for a better soceity and a belief that this is possible.

So we return at last (and too briefly) to strategy and organization. The struggle must go on at different levels. Our priorities would be:
(1) A general *ideological* struggle arising out of a development of some of the ideas we have sketched above. Instead of piecemeal struggles – for contraception and abortion on demand, free schools, etc. – and the perpetual confrontation with sexism, which often amounts to no more than lip service being paid to a situation which runs very deep, a coherent consciousness of our position as women as *essential* to the maintenance of the ideology of the capitalist state would suggest a more co-ordinated and consistent attack. This attack would not then be seen as an alternative to or as in conflict with political work at the point of production *or* in the community, whereas at present what *should*

be work connected to our position as bolsterers up of the predominant ideology too easily degenerates into merely the search for personal liberation ('my man isn't oppressive etc.')

(2) The struggle *against the state* in the community. This could be co-ordinated with the struggle in factories on an area basis. We might ask in passing what the 'community' is or can be in our society. Community feeling and community loyalty can often be initially aroused only around negative issues of felt need as slum clearance *systematically* destroys the old working-class communities and our society becomes even more fragmented. In suburbs or housing estates the men go away to work leaving a 'purdah' of young women and small children, and neither there nor at work is there a place for the adolescents, who beome the 'werewolves' of our society, nor is there a place for the old, who become its ghosts.

Yet the struggle in the community has already begun; it has to be co-ordinated and collectively directed against the state and made into a visible part of the same struggle as the struggle at the point of production.

(3) We as women need our own organization. If we do not have this we too will fall back into piecemeal and isolated groups and the women's movement will die. We have not had time in preparing this pamphlet to make concrete proposals as to what form this organization should take, so we simply suggest that it should be a priority for discussion in the movement.

A final word. This, which started as a reply to Selma but which, we hope, now exists in its own right as the beginnings of our own analysis – however sketchy at present – is heavy and will perhaps be criticized for being too theoretical. Our aim, however, is to contribute towards the ending of a false division between theory and practice. That is why we believe in a theoretical analysis as an indispensable part of action, for from the theory actions, such as we suggest, should spring.

3 ◆ Libertarianism:
ideas in the void

Introduction

This article was published in *Red Rag* number 4, in July, 1973. Like
the previous article it was a reaction to influential currents of thought
and action within and outside women's liberation at the time. My
rejection of libertarianism was particularly sharp because of my
membership of the defence group for the defendants in the 'Angry
Brigade' trial, which had taken place in 1972. The Angry Brigade
was alleged to have been a libertarian group which engaged in
exemplary symbolic acts of terrorism against property. The attempt
by friends of those accused simultaneously to mount an ideological
offensive against the repressive power of the state, by producing
publicity, giving talks, and raising money through benefit concerts
in an effort to counter media images of 'crazy bombers', and at the
same time to support a straightforward legal defence, revealed some
of the contradictions and weaknesses of the libertarian style of
alternative politics. At the same time, the whole experience was a
crash course in political reality. It permanently altered my understanding of the world; henceforth I knew that 'repressive arm of the
state' is no mere piece of academic Marxist jargon – there really is an
iron fist inside the velvet glove of consumer capitalism. During the
same period, and arising out of the same experience, some of us tried
to organize a support group for visitors to the London women's
prison, Holloway, but this was virtually impossible because of the
atomization of a group of people, relatives and friends of prisoners,
with varying needs and problems. I became convinced that the
libertarian tactic of trying to organize the most smashed and
marginalized sections of the population could not succeed, certainly
not on its own, in a political void, and that groups such as gays,

women, and welfare claimants and groups in conflict with the law (for example prostitutes and juveniles) must try to find some way of aligning themselves with the mainstream organizations of the working class and the progressive movement. Although the libertarians adopted a class analysis, they rejected political parties and trades unions; I became convinced that these were important and necessary.

Throughout 1972 and 1973 I attended a *Capital* reading group, a number of whose members joined the Communist Party of Great Britain, and at the beginning of 1973 Angela Weir and I were invited to join the editorial collective of *Red Rag*. *Red Rag* had been started by women inside the Communist Party, who had joined with some feminists who were not Party members to produce a magazine that was initially intended as a bridge between left politics and the women's movement. As a result of these experiences in 1972 and 1973, I myself joined the Communist Party at the end of 1973.

Although I still believe my criticisms of libertarianism to be correct, my judgement in this particular article now reads perhaps too harshly. Some of the actions of the early 1970s were after all very successful: the 1970 demonstration which completely disrupted the Miss World contest at the Albert Hall; the Gay Liberation disruption of the first big Festival of Light rally at Central Hall, Westminster; and the street theatre politics of many of the grass-roots groups of that period. Yet I also feel that in the anarchistic life-style politics of the time lay the seeds of the pessimistic individualism which has fed into the current rightward drift of the leftists of 1968.

Libertarianism: ideas in the void

These notes on libertarianism are concerned with a *style* of politics. The term 'libertarianism' is vague, and although some people on the left talk of a 'libertarian movement' I think others would say that there is no movement as such, but simply groups of people engaged in various kinds of political practice, though sharing certain assumptions. I am not attempting a historical analysis of why this particular kind of politics came into being at a particular time; in fact that has been done, by Henri Lefebvre and others. Nor am I attempting a definition of libertarianism; that would be impossible, because it is nebulous. I am simply suggesting certain aspects of a highly ideological politics whose ideology is undefined. Libertarians do have a political approach to which they are very strongly committed; in failing to spell it out (and perhaps this would be impossible because of its contradictions) they have been of disservice to the movements and groups they have influenced. One of these movements is women's liberation.

Cultural origins

Libertarianism has literary antecedents. From the time of the romantic movement in the early nineteenth century a significant cultural figure is that of the 'artist in revolt'. There is Byron the damned genius, who, interestingly, repudiated poetry and died fighting for a free Greece; there are the 'Bohemian' artists of mid-nineteenth-century Paris, who rejected bourgeois morality and hypocrisy; and there are the Surrealists and Dadaists of the 1920s who cultivated the irrational and the absurd, and some of whom perceived the act of suicide as the logical conclusion of their art. Today these themes reappear – in the form of political action.

The descent of the libertarians is commonly traced from nineteenth-century anarcho-syndicalists, narodniks, etc. I believe it is of more interest to locate them within the wider cultural history of previous epochs, at which I have very briefly and inadequately hinted. Libertarians owe more to Friedrich Nietzsche and Georges Sorel than to Peter Kropotkin or Mikhail Bakunin and in as much as they have turned to the writings of Pierre Proudhon and Emma Goldman (for example) this was after repudiating Marxism-Leninism, and not because they are in a line of direct descent.

Henri Lefebvre (1969) locates the birth of the 'new politics' in the student movement of the late 1960s. The reason why students should have rebelled are not hard to understand. As he says: 'Students appear privileged, but they face practical and intellectual difficulties; lack of employment opportunities and acute awareness of a static social practice which offers no perspective or possibilities . . . . They derive their sense of a marginal existence from actual social conditions which they feel justified in criticising.' He also points to the failures and abdication of the established Marxist (Stalinist) parties. Out of this gulf between organized Stalinism and individual felt oppression arose the self-organization of groups around their specific oppression. Students, along with the unemployed, women, racial minorities, were the only ones who could in fact organize in this way. They were free to do so, because the 'traditional left' hadn't bothered about them.

Just as women who have joined the women's movement have often begun by seeing through the myths about themselves, suddenly and vividly understanding how the man-made strait-jacket of womanhood distorts them, so students saw through and repudiated the great con of bourgeois 'culture'. An appreciation of 'high art' and 'European culture' is dependent on a privileged and ritualized kind of educational experience, and it too fits you into a certain mould. To recognize this comes as a shock since the private, quasi-mystical appreciation of music, painting, etc. is purveyed as being a unique personal experience (just as is love, orgasm, motherhood, for women) but is actually little more than the trappings of a bourgeois destiny.

Art for most of us is a passive spectacle. Nor do we relate only to art as spectators. In the 1960s several French writers (the 'situationists') explored a Marx who led them to a vision of the whole society as spectacle. 'The spectacle is not a collection of images, but a social relation among people mediated by images', writes Guy Debord. 'The spectacle is the moment when the commodity has attained the *total occupation* of social life' (Debord 1973). His book explores the concept of alienation, and the massified, manipulated individual he describes ends in a nightmare world with total loss of identity. These ideas have been an important influence on libertarians, who relate therefore quite centrally to Marx, albeit to the early Marx, who, some believe, was not a very good Marxist.

Spectacle and violence

If you perceive society as a spectacle, a mirror of illusion, the problem becomes how to smash through it and break out of your own alienation. (Debord, for all his exhaustive and rather literary analyses, makes no real, practical suggestions.) Nihilism, the necessity to reject everything, the whole of experience being tainted and poisoned by consumerism and competitiveness becomes part of the upsurge towards a total revolutionary position. To espouse violence becomes inevitable. The only valid response to the violence that has been done us is to destroy the nightmare.

Violence erupted spontaneously in the streets of Paris, in other capitals, and on campuses throughout Western Europe and the United States. This brought students, and workers, into direct confrontation with the state. Libertarians have tended towards direct opposition to the state because they espouse direct action; and direct action and spontaneism are bound to meet with violence.

In this opposition to the state, libertarians are drawn towards the ultimately most marginal groups in society, prisoners and outcasts, those that most strongly feel the weight of oppression from the full force of the state come against them. In the end this too can lead to a glorification of violence and illegalism and ultimately to a death trip. Victor Serge, the son of Russian revolutionaries and himself an anarchist, describes how this happened to a group he was associated with in Paris before the First World War:

'a positive wave of violence and despair began to grow . . . it was like a collective suicide . . . they had to find either money to get away from it all, or else a speedy death against the whole of society. Out of solidarity they rushed into this squalid doomed struggle, with their revolvers and their trigger-happy arguments.'

(Serge 1963)

Life-style politics

If the whole of life is a spectacle and a commodity, the political challenge also must be total. This becomes the politics of every-day life, life-style politics.

To reject 'straight' employment, to reject equally the couple with its implications of repressed sexuality and romantic, possessive 'love', to seek personal transformation through drugs, or (in the case of gay men) drag, to squat, to steal – all these become acts of violent and justified revolt, challenging bourgeois notions of property and propriety. They strike at the deepest fear, the fear of chaos. To challenge so radically the norms of society is to bring seething to its surface the deepest petit bourgeois anguish and hysteria, because of the terrible insecurities of a competitive society. 'What would happen if nobody worked?' 'They might come and squat in my house . . . .' 'The one thing I can't stand is these men dressed like women.'

Note that these challenges to privacy, to ownership, and to sexual identity have touched the same chord of petit bourgeois hostility in members of the traditional left. They themselves label such challenges petit bourgeois (just to confuse the issue); but in supporting working-class conservatism the left supports what capitalism does to the working class to divide and stifle it. Naturally working-class people cling to a 'respectability' which differentiates them from the really poor, the outcasts; and they cling to the family which has been one of their sources of strength; but respectability makes docile workers and the family instils respectability.

The importance of the libertarians resides in their having confronted these problems. What they have failed to do is to explain; nor have they grown in strength. Because they have made sacrifices and put themselves in an embattled and isolated position they have assumed that this of itself made them revolutionary. They have assumed that the extreme position must always be the revolutionary position. In their exemplary nature their politics have been those of weakness. Having rejected the authoritarian vanguard party they have had no organization or power of their own, but have taken on the state as it were single handed. Because so much remains unspoken, the way is opened to disguised leadership in the form of friendship networks and cliques (see 'Joreen' 1972), yet at the same time it would be oppressive to prevent others from making the mistakes you made.

The challenge to life styles is important, but it too may attract for the wrong reasons. For one thing it plays into a common preoccupation of our culture, the conversion syndrome. Christianity has always stressed the importance of 'being saved', and today this is as much with us as ever, in the secularized forms of psychotherapy, the counter-culture, individual self-fulfilment. Vulgarized it appeals to us on the tube ('It was accountancy for me until I discovered Smirnoff').

Life styles and the subjective

There is a similarity here to Jean-Paul Sartre's philosophy of existentialism, which stresses the importance of human choice, the importance to the individual of recognizing his real needs and desires and acting upon them with 'authenticity', the alternative being to act in 'bad faith' of which bourgeois conventions are usually an example. Existentialism, too, combines a quasi-Marxist socialism with rampant idealism. In both cases the essential act is an act of will. To choose freedom is an act of will; to smash through the mirror of illusion is an act of will. To reject your bourgeois privileges, that is, to choose to live on Social Security is somehow supposed of itself to create an actual, concrete, objective, economic position of power or solidarity with others. This it cannot do, and libertarians often end up simply creating tiny ghettoes of the new life style. They know they are very different from hippies and the apolitical counter-culture; but in the eyes of working-class neighbours they are often indistinguishable. Further, the subjective feeling of power that comes from the act of throwing off the personal yoke of convention is unmatched by any material power or basis of co-operation (and in one sense the working-class neighbours are right – they correctly see economic and material similarities between libertarians and hippies, not merely similarities of style).

This subjectivism can be very dishonest – it is easy to justify all sorts of bad feelings just because they are feelings. Practice is fragmented and confused. Some women for instance have developed an extreme form of total separatism; some support economistic demands for wages for housework, seemingly because of a false association with 'not working' (as if wages for housework could ever smash the work ethic). Repudiation of trades unions goes hand in hand with work in claimants' and prisoners' unions. An oppressive anti-intellectualism prevents proper thinking through of these contradictions, yet in libertarianism there is always an over-valuation of the power of ideas.

Libertarians connect the various parts of life which are usually compartmentalized. Yet to struggle on all fronts and with all levels of your own and everyone else's false consciousness at once can exhaust before anything lasting has been achieved. All traditional politics have assumed that alliances and working with other groups must be on the basis of compromise, but there is a purism in libertarianism that demands agreement on all aspects of life. Not only does this make co-operation impossible; it can easily become debased into a mirror image of bourgeois preoccupation with surroundings and possessions.

To say this is not to imply that libertarians are unaware of some of the difficulties, devoid of all self-criticism or incapable of change. Increasingly their insistence on grass-roots organization has led them to attempt to work in the community. Squatting is one example of this, and has certainly led to increased publicity on the issue of housing. None the less, spontaneism and the lack of or opposition to organization has meant that while some squatters have tried desperately to make alliances with local working-class residents others have violently dismissed them as the enemy because they are 'straight' (i.e. the issue of respectability versus the counter-culture again); and there appears to have been no systematic linking of the struggle of the homeless with the struggle of tenants against the Housing Finance Act (1972).

Libertarians versus Lenin

Libertarians reserve a special hatred for Lenin, yet some of his analyses may be applied word for word to the situation on the left today:

> 'The petit-bourgeois "driven to frenzy" by the horrors of capitalism is a social phenomenon which like anarchism is characteristic of all capitalist countries. The instability of such revolution, its barrenness, its liability to become swiftly transformed into submission, apathy, fantasy, and even a "frenzied" infatuation with one or another bourgeois fad – all this is a matter of common knowledge. But a theoretical, abstract recognition of these truths does not at all free revolutionary parties from old mistakes, which always crop up at unexpected moments, in a somewhat new form, in hitherto unknown vestments or surroundings . . . . Anarchism was not infrequently a sort of punishment for the opportunist sins of the working class movement.'   (Lenin 1976: 304-05)

Libertarians appear to confuse Leninism with the economism of modern Marxist parties, yet Lenin always attacked economism and workerism. They have better grounds for taking issue against his authoritarianism and puritanism, and it is in these areas that libertarianism connects with the women's movement.

The women's movement is certainly not synonymous with libertarianism, yet it too has rejected hierarchies and authoritarian forms of organization. It also is concerned with ideology, and has explored alternative life styles to break down sexism and the isolation of women with small children. It is now facing questions about the future: what should our strategy be; how do we build a movement; do we work with all women (a more feminist position) or only with right-on working-class women (as both the International Socialists [now the SWP] and the libertarians believe). How do we attack sexism?

Libertarian women have simplistic answers: 'drop by and steal something' (i.e. take what you want) and 'we want more money – we work in the home; pay us for the work we do' were two of the messages printed on stickers for the Women's Day march. This really is oversimplified and just evades the question (which as a matter of fact the left in general evades) of how you take power. Like radical feminism, libertarianism raises in an acute form certain vital questions and the very crudeness of its answers has a value in pushing individuals beyond the limits of the amount and extent of change they believed they could tolerate – which is perhaps a case of exemplary politics achieving their aim.

This year many of us on the left who have remained outside the organized parties have spontaneously turned to the study of Marx and Lenin. In this context of the search for better theory we should reject what is muddled and hasty in the answers of the libertarians, while devoting energy and attention to the vital questions they raise.

4 ◆ Beyond the ghetto: thoughts on *Beyond the Fragments*

Introduction

By 1979 I was no longer on the editorial collective of *Red Rag*, but was one of a group of women who had started a new journal, *Feminist Review*. *Red Rag* had been wholly self-produced (apart from the typesetting and printing), although in practice the design had been largely the work of the only trained artist in the group, Val Charlton. *Feminist Review* was also self-published (although the option of commercial publishing had been seriously considered) but the format was more academic and the articles longer and more explicitly theoretical or empirical. It had a paid designer, so we did not have to do our own pasting up.

Yet the preoccupations of 'Beyond the ghetto' were similar to those of 'Libertarianism: ideas in the void'. But in fact *Beyond the Fragments* was the swan song of libertarianism, and since 1979 there has been a retreat from life-style politics. Today young women and men may organize themselves into collective households from necessity; many are on the dole not because it is a feasible option nor because they want to work with the claimants' unions but because unemployment is so high; unconventional forms of parenthood persist partly because divorce rates continue to rise. These developments seem to me less ideological than the prefigurative life styles of the late 1960s and early 1970s when communal households and collective childcare arrangements were set up out of political principle. The continuation of family fragmentation and high unemployment will not necessarily perpetuate or reproduce the libertarianism of 1970; yet anarchism today is more bitter and less Utopian, but it also has more of a material basis.

'Thoughts on *Beyond the Fragments*' goes further than the earlier piece on libertarianism, however, for its hidden agenda is a critique of the whole socialist-feminist project of the late 1970s. The creation of a socialist-feminist 'tendency' had emerged as a response to the divisions within women's liberation which began to fragment in mid-decade. I was out of sympathy with the whole idea of a 'tendency', still hoping for a broad movement, more like the peace or labour movement than a vanguard grouplet. It also seemed to me that there were aspects of feminism that could only be termed 'socialist' if the latter term were extremely vaguely defined (which has of course since occurred), and I believed this the more strongly because I had just completed work on a book about women in the 1950s (Wilson 1980); that work had demonstrated to me that there can on occasion be support for feminist demands from the politcial centre, and even the right, and that feminists who are socialists cannot afford to shun these allies on principle, but should endeavour to work with them, with the hope both of securing some changes beneficial to women and of shifting demands in a progressive direction. The critique of the left in *Beyond the Fragments* also seemed very one-sided, and the idea that feminism could be set up as the model for socialism extremely problematic, given the women's movement's organizational weaknesses.

The concluding section of this article is very unsatisfactory because although some of the main problems of the socialist-feminist project have been at the level of theory, a page or so could not possibly even define the subject adequately. Many of the same issues are taken up again in 'The British women's movement', although that too lacks an adequately theoretical argument.

Beyond the ghetto: thoughts on *Beyond the Fragments: Feminism and the Making of Socialism*

What is the future for feminism – and, more importantly, for women – in the 1980s? Can socialism be achieved in a country such as Britain, unique in its situation of decline from imperial heights towards possible de-industrialization? More immediately, how are socialists and feminists fighting one of the most reactionary governments Britain has seen in the twentieth century? If we look at the Labour Party, the Marxist left, and the women's liberation movement we find confusion, fragmentation, and disarray. The 'left' (defined very broadly indeed) has lost a lot of ideological battles recently. At the same time, although the backlash (which was inevitable and should always have been anticipated) against feminism is beginning, it is in itself quite contradictory. It might be stronger had the women's movement not made important inroads in the general consciousness over the past ten years. Yet in the situation in which feminism does have some strength and some successes to build on, we find an abandonment of feminism within some sections of the women's movement itself. Amongst socialists, too, there is a spirit almost of defeatism. Surprisingly few socialists seem to see the Tory victory as a comdemnation of right-wing Labour Party policies; more often it seems to be read as a mysterious spirit of reaction that has willed the populace to the right.

These are some of the large and difficult problems examined, either explicitly or implicitly, in the pamphlet *Beyond the Fragments*, written by three socialist-feminists (Rowbotham, Segal, and Wainwright 1979). What follows should not be read as a reply to their pamphlet, but rather as an attempt to raise problems they do not raise, and to question assumptions they do not question. I am not expressing a definitive position or view (and I am certainly not expressing a *Feminist Review* position), but trying myself, equally as much as the authors of *Beyond the Fragments*, to reach towards a reassessment of my political situation. Unlike them, I do not feel that any 'answer' can be offered at the moment. A more radical reappraisal of the successes and the failures of the progressive movement of the last ten years is needed before we can know what the next step should be.

Beyond the Fragments

Beyond the Fragments: Feminism and the Making of Socialism is the development in written form of talks given by Sheila Rowbotham and Lynne Segal and introduced here by Hilary Wainwright. Her introduction, written in the run-up to the general election (1979) at which Mrs Thatcher was elected prime minister, describes the disheartening experience for socialists of having their politics entirely marginalized by the traditional two-party system and the media. This appears as the starting point for the project of the pamphlet as a whole; if the left is so weak and disorganized what form of socialist organization could regenerate it and make the 'fragments' of the alternative left movement more cohesive? Sheila Rowbotham in the longest section of the pamphlet, *The Women's Movement and Organizing for Socialism*, particularly develops the theme of the contribution feminism has to make to the 'making of socialism' while Lynne's brief, clear section at the end explains why after years of struggle in the 'libertarian' left and in local struggles of the women's movement she has joined the small, nationally based Marxist group Big Flame (a group partly modelled on, or at least influenced by, the Italian groups Lotta Continua and Avanguardia Operaio). These prioritized community struggles and supported struggles at work that sprang from the factory floor rather than being masterminded and controlled by union bureaucracies. Lynne feels that Big Flame did offer, unlike the libertarians or the feminists, a national network and a national perspective on local struggles. Sheila's section on the other hand marks her definitive rejection of the 'revolutionary party'. While both, therefore, are engaged in the attempt to relate their personal experience to their political practice, they have reached different conclusions in terms of what form of *organization* is best able to express and forward their political aspirations.

Hilary's introduction really simply *states* the issue of organization as crucial and as the problem to which we should address ourselves. It is *assumed* that an effective revolutionary organization would be the answer to the current fragmentation of socialism and socialist practice in this country. Following from that: 'this pamphlet . . . is intended to begin a discussion of the limits of traditional principles of revolutionary organizations, in the light of the advances and insights made by recent movements, starting with the women's liberation movement'.

Already there are problems here. While I would not deny that the organization of political movements is an important issue, it is not the only or necessarily the most pressing problem. Historically, the revolutionary left in Britain has been small. One response to this (I am not sure why) has been to see the perfect organizational form as the solution to lack of numerical strength. *Beyond the Fragments* appears to share this perception of an orgnaizational form as the panacea, whereas I believe that appropriate forms of organization will only be reached after a much more far-reaching evaluation of the successes and failures of the past ten years.

And then, the new organizational forms of the women's movement should be, but are not, subjected to careful evaluation. It is not enough to say that consciousness-raising groups and small campaigning groups and self-help groups have been, at times, inspiring and successful. We need also to look at attempts to create national organizations for national campaigns, such as the National Women's Aid Federation and the National Abortion Campaign. Their successes and failures are never so much as mentioned, which seems astonishing. Besides, it is surely important to assess the way in which the women's movement has utilized, alongside its 'new' use of small groups as a central organizing focus, perfectly traditional campaigning methods. We have marched, lobbied, and written to MPs as trades unions and traditional pressure groups have been doing for many years; and why not.

Lynne's section is in itself an admirable summary of what 'libertarianism' meant in the late 1960s and early 1970s. She reminds us that it stressed autonomy and rejected 'vanguard' forms of leadership, that it meant living out your politics in your daily life and organizing around your own oppression. It had a rich appreciation of the political nature of the bourgeois state and of a variety of areas where 'ideology' operates very clearly – women, youth, racism, and the alienation of the consumer society. This was at a time when the organized left groups were still locked in economism, limited, it seemed, to struggles about wages that never raised questions about the state, the oppression of women, or the quality of life.

Sheila's section is hardest to summarize. Her argument develops out of an account of her own political history within what may loosely be called the new left, her brief connexion with the International Socialists (now the Socialist Workers Party), and her much longer and still ongoing involvement in the women's movement. She attempts to describe the *process* of an evolution as a socialist away from a belief in the Leninist conception of the 'revolutionary party' and towards the 'new' forms of organization in which the women's movement has participated, and she also stresses the importance of 'prefigurative' life styles, ways of leading one's life that pre-figure socialism and a society where men and women are truly equal. What she seems not to recognize is the extent to which hers is not the experience of all feminists, nor of all socialists for that matter, and the account is littered with references which I suspect would mean little to those not already in the know – IMG, Stalinism, Leninism, Eurocommunism, for example, all appear without explanation, and while it might be argued that the pamphlet is addressed to the left, who *will* understand these terms, that is one of the very things I find depressing about this pamphlet – it is the left talking to itself yet again. It particular, it is a pity that the Leninism that is attacked is never defined but used more as a blunt instrument with which to knock out male Marxists. However, the implication of what is being said seems to be that the Leninist conception of revolution and of the revolutionary way of life denies all feeling, denies tentative process, and leads itself to a coercion and suppression of that very mass of the working people it claims to represent. These are familiar criticisms of communism and, however correct, I truly don't think they can be said to contribute any sort of *new* insight into the problems of the left.

This summary is inadequate, but then the pamphlet itself wouldn't claim to be the exposition of a logically perfect argument. Here, anyway, are three socialist-feminists asking questions that have tormented women on the left for the past ten years. They are asking these questions very much from within that conglomeration of politics, sectarianism, hippie life styles, and hard, quite traditional, and often effectively reformist, struggle at the grass roots that has constituted the world of the alternative left since 1968. This world has been an absorbing one for many feminists. It has given many of us, especially if we have been somehow outside the confines of the family, a space and a refuge. As both space and refuge it has always held a tension between its pioneering, innovative, and spirited confrontational challenges to the *status quo*, and its contrary tendency towards ghettoization. And within the wide spectrum of the alternative left there exists a further tension between the organized revolutionary socialist (Marxist) groups and the whole range of nonaligned socialist movements, including socialist feminism. This alternative left, that is, holds within it the tension of 'libertarianism' versus 'Leninism'. And there is of course another tension, and that is the relationship of feminism to socialism.

I'd like to develop three themes arising out of this discussion. The first is to break out of the questions the pamphlet actually poses, to question what is taken for granted: that organization is the vital question, and that socialism and feminism go together in an unproblematic way. The second theme is the nature of feminist writing and its relationship to academia and to the left. The third is a theme I feel lurking unexpressed within the pamphlet, and that is the *political* relationship between men and women. These themes are all far too big to be dealt with in one short article and I don't see this contribution as more than a very small part of an ongoing debate.

The value of history

As Lot and his wife fled Sodom and Gomorrah Lot's wife looked back at the conflagration and was turned into a pillar of salt.

Today we live in the twin glare from two great conflagrations: the Russian revolution and Hiroshima. It is true that when we look back over the plain and see the smoke rising from the cities 'as the smoke from a furnace' we are not taking the measure of our escape, since it is by no means clear that we have escaped, if indeed that was our aim. We are, more likely, taking measure of what has been destroyed.

In the 1930s socialists still drew faith and inspiration from the mere fact of the Russian revolution. The Utopia could after all be built on this earth. After 1945, not only was this belief in the socialist future on earth destroyed, or partly destroyed, by the revelations of all the fearful excesses and repression carried out in the USSR while Stalin was in power (and before and since as well), but the *scientific* nature of socialism became suspect because the progressive faith in science characteristic of many communists in the pre-war period had been undermined. If science could create the atom bomb, then it could not be unproblematically progressive.

Hilary Wainwright, in blaming the British *left groups* for the way in which socialism has in Britain become 'so sterile and so dead to most working class people', neglects a whole wider history and is already making the mistake for which I would criticize the pamphlet as a whole. She ascribes too much importance to the Marxist left in this country, objectively speaking, and by casting Marxism not only as the starting point but also as the parameter of the discussion fatally subordinates feminism to socialism and also contains it within the ghettoization of the left.

It seems strange to discuss contemporary feminism so persistently in the context of the history of socialism. As socialists we have to understand the past of our own movement, its many bitter disappointments and failings must be examined even as history also has a role to play in the celebration of what has been great and creative in the socialist tradition. But in the end we (socialists and feminists) must say 'enough is enough'. We cannot look back forever. In the end we must lay aside our anger and grief at the way the revolutionary movement has treated us and wounded itself. If we look back too often at the betrayals we will have wept so much that all that will be left of us too will be a pillar of salt from our tears. Speaking bitterness is one thing, but the recital of wrongs ought surely to lead to a catharsis that would *release* us from the past; and I cannot but feel that the large part of Sheila's section of this pamphlet, devoted to a restatement of familiar wrongs and a catalogue of the bullying tendencies of the traditional left, is obsessive. We do *know*. What is never mentioned is the history of the feminist movement and what we might learn from that.

Although the dinosaur of capitalism lurks menacingly in the background throughout *Beyond the Fragments*, to read the pamphlet is on the whole to enter a world in which *the* enemy is the democratic centralist party. Crudely defined, democratic centralism is the form of political party organization developed by the Bolsheviks and adopted – at least until recently – by Western European Communist and Trotskyist parties as well as in socialist countries. It consists of a hierarchical structure which is intended to be democratic because it provides channels for the interaction of the views of the majority at the roots (at the level of the local cell or branch) and the leadership and central decision making body, which is, in theory at least, the national congress to which democratically elected delegates are sent. Debate and discussion are encouraged, but minorities must abide by the decision of the majority, once this has been arrived at by democratic means. This form of organization has been increasingly criticized (and not only in the West) for not operating democratically in practice, and also for its whole notion of leadership, held in itself to be an élitist concept. Just as the leadership of the party is its vanguard, so the party itself is to be the vanguard of the working class. This has been a much disputed issue, but while it is of relevance to feminists within socialist groups in so far as these groups have or have not seen their role as giving leadership to the women's movement as well as to (say) the trades union movement, it is not of direct importance to the women's liberation movement which has always rejected the very idea of leaders and of any close knit structure. So the posing of Leninism as so central for feminists I find rather odd.

Feminism and socialism

How can feminists participate in the making of socialism? is the question put in this pamphlet. At first reading the question appears unproblematic to socialist feminists. But is it? In exploring the question of the relationship of feminism to socialism, I am doing so as a socialist and a feminist, yet for me the connexion remains far more difficult than it appears to be for the authors of *Beyond the Fragments*.

It seemed to many of the new generation of feminists after 1968 that the faith of the 'old' feminists in constitutional reform had been proved illusory. This led some women towards the view that a capitalist society cannot give all women equality, although it *may* provide a few privileged women with something approaching it. Constitutional reform proved unable, for example, to deal with the dependent status of the 'non-working' wife, although feminists after 1945 attempted to resolve the contradictions of her position by legislative means. In a way the obvious alternative for feminists *was* to look to socialism, and especially was this the case for women such as Sheila Rowbotham who were active in the new left of the 1960s.

Although there were in Britain a number of women's organizations and groupings of feminists who for years worked together across the established political boundaries, the 'new' women's liberation movement emerged from and has always been defined in relationship to the new left. As early as 1966 Juliet Mitchell was starting her critique of women's position from an assessment of the *failure* of socialism to produce equality for women (Mitchell 1966), and throughout its own history the women's liberation movement has paid far more attention to the history of socialism and socialist women than to the history of feminism (a point Sheila acknowledges in a footnote, but does not develop).

But the women's movement did not come wholly out of the student movement and the new left. It also grew out of an incoherent and only gradually developing sense of injustice and oppression amongst many women, many of whom were neither socialists nor politically active. There was, too, the influence of the American women's movement. And the celebrations of fifty years of the vote for women in 1968 did seem to act as some sort of catalyst. Yet how much have we ever really examined the history of feminism? We admire the suffragettes, and socialist-feminists heroize Sylvia Pankhurst. But do we really understand, for example, why it is that a 'bourgeois' feminist movement was able to use ultra-revolutionary tactics verging on terrorism in pursuit of a wholly constitutional reform (the vote) whereas we, while proclaiming our devotion to revolutionary socialism, have never engaged to any significant extent in 'illegal' actions. I am not suggesting that we should start to burn letter boxes or flood the Albert Hall organ, but the paradox does seem worth thinking about. Do we understand the mutations of the feminist movement between the two world wars, and why feminists such as Vera Brittain supported Stalin's family code, or why feminists after 1945 supported a traditionalist view of motherhood?

The 'new' women's liberation movement resolved a twin, partial rejection of two traditions, the old feminism and 'Stalinism' (what was seen as the distortion and perversion of revolutionary communism and socialism under Stalin's dictatorship), both of which had 'failed' women, by emphasizing its newness. It was new and different from the 'bourgeois' feminists in Britain because it rejected constitutional change and reformist politics; it was new and different from traditional socialism because it rejected the straitjacket of the organized left parties, who equally abjured it. Part of its fervour came from this 'born again' quality, and Sheila calls for a fidelity to this spirit of 1968, to that sense of *anything* being possible, and to that appreciation of the immediacy of experience. But we can't go back.

It was precisely because that spontaneity had its own problems and because it was recognized that the surge of energy could not last forever that some women were attraced to left groups.

But whereas a relationship, or the absence of it, with the bourgeois feminists never caused women's liberation much lost sleep, our relationship with the left has always been charged with painful ambivalence. On the one hand we could never get away from it, since it was, like us, 'revolutionary'; on the other, Stalinism always knocked us backwards. When we rejected the left it didn't go away; when we entered its embrace it either hugged us till our bones cracked, or else didn't even notice, in which case our agonizing and our sacrifice (perhaps) of principle had been in vain.

Some feminists joined the Communist Party, but the politics for which the Communist Party stood have never made much headway amongst feminists. The Communist Party views revolution as a mass movement, impossible unless it is supported by a majority. This has led to compromises, alliances, and cautious tactics which have often seemed to other revolutionaries to be a betrayal of revolutionary ideals. I believe this raises, for feminists and socialists alike, the question of how far compromise is possible, and how far reforms are a step on the way to a socialist society and how far they actually hold back the revolutionary process. Communists, seeing revolution as a long process rather than as an explosive moment, have taken a kindlier view of reforms than have other revolutionaries, and while it would not be true to say that communists believe that reforms can of themselves bring the revolution, they have seen reforms as steps on the road to socialism.

The women's movement on the other hand has adamantly rejected 'reformism', certainly in its rhetoric, and although it has in practice fought for, or to protect, a number of reforms, the more uncompromising stances of Trotskyism have been more attractive to contemporary feminists. Although the interventions of actual Trotskyist groups in the women's movement have often been crude, the Trotskyist fidelity to notions of revolution and militancy have made an impact. Trotskyists have also, amongst other things, been critical of the Soviet Union and their denunciations of Stalin have always included a denunciation of his legislation on the family, abortion, and other issues relating immediately to women. The position of women in the USSR and in Eastern European countries is an important one for socialist-feminists in the West, since those countries claim to be socialist and the position of women within them may therefore be an indication of what women may expect from socialism. One negative aspect of these criticisms, all the same, has been that if all socialist countries are to be denounced then the whole idea of socialism becomes Utopian, and the conspiracy of capitalism (or patriarchy) so awful that defeat, pessimism, fatalism blanket us again. Sheila summarizes these aspects of Trotskyism well:

> 'Within Trotskyism the desire to return to the molten heat of the early Russian revolution has all the intensity of the need for survival itself . . . in an eerie way the heroic conscience only comes to exist as the opponent of the bad man.'
>
> (Rowbotham, Segal, and Wainwright 1979:36)

There were two ways in which Marxism influenced the women's movement. After a few years of activity and campaigning in the movement, many women felt the need to relate feminism more specifically to a general theory of politics and class struggle. A number of Marxist feminist study groups sprang up and this was a return to Marxism in a different, more theoretical and less tainted way. In some respects this was very useful in giving women a more general understanding of the nature of capitalism, of class struggle, and of women's relationship to the class structure. Yet Marxism has not been able wholly to explain the subordination of women even within capitalism. Not only have socialist-feminists had to take on board all the theoretical problems of Marxism as well as those of feminism, but increasingly other bodies of theory have had to be explored and attempts made to relate them to Marxism as we have tried to explain and understand the 'oppressor in our heads'. The most familiar of these bodies of theory is psychoanalysis, which has sometimes been described as a theory of patriarchy. One result of the attempt to unite these disparate bodies of theory has been an abstract theoreticism to which Sheila makes passing reference.

The second way in which Marxism imposed itself on the women's movement was by raising the choice of whether to belong to a Marxist group/party or not. This is substantially the question to which *Beyond the Fragments* is addressed. Essentially four choices were/are open to Marxist feminists. You could remain 'nonaligned'. You could join the Communist Party. You could join a Trotskyist or neo-Trotskyist (which is how Sheila describes the International Socialists) group. Or you could associate yourself with libertarian Marxism. This drew inspiration from a number of sources, from Herbert Marcuse, from Wilhelm Reich, from R. D. Laing – who brought a 'revolutionary' approach to questions hitherto perceived as purely psychological – and from the writings of urban guerilla movements and Mao Tse Tung.

At one time the Communist Party had a certain amount of credibility within the women's movement. Communist women did not (contrary to the prevailing stereotype of 'left groups') take any 'party line' into the women's movement. For one of them (myself) to say that probably in itself casts doubt on its truth in the minds of some women, so great is the distrust of the bogey Communism, even in countries such as Britain where it is weak. But since there was, and still is, debate and disagreement within the Communist Party on the position of women and the nature of their oppression it would have been objectively difficult for us to have had a 'line'. Yet if communist women did share a view on given political questions, wasn't that *really* a 'line' and wasn't it disingenuous to pretend that it wasn't, to try to be a feminist like any other in the women's movement while being a communist in some other part of one's life? Wasn't this tantamount to a position which held that women's oppression was purely 'ideological' and bore no relationship to the class system and the economy? The position of communist women illustrates in other words the 'paralysing split' for socialist women as they tried to connect feminist practice with socialist politics.

But, leaving these political differences aside, the real drawback for many feminists to membership of the Communist Party or Trotskyist parties and groups was that their commitment to feminism was never trusted. It was therefore more natural for many feminists either to remain nonaligned or to associate themselves with libertarian Marxism, which gave greater emphasis to community groups in struggle, such as squatters, the claimants' unions, radical newspapers, self-help projects and life styles. Lynne suggests that these sprang up spontaneously and were not anarchist in inspiration, but, whether consciously or not, these groups have shared with anarchism an emphasis on the small autonomous unit as a structure, linked in a loose federal way, an emphasis on the importance of sexuality and personal relations, and the attention to life styles to which Sheila draws our attention. Similarities to aspects of the women's movement are obvious.

The effect of these different and *incompatible* influences on the women's movement is seldom discussed. The combination of rousing calls to unite against imperialism, with the working class, in the crisis, and aspirations to live out socialist, non-sexist lives in the present must be partly to blame for what Sheila describes as a 'paralyzing split' between socialist organization and the organizational forms of the women's movement. It's more, though, than an organizational tension, it's a tension about politics at every level for feminists who are also socialists. And add to this the efforts spent in campaigning for quite small reforms and the picture becomes even more contradictory.

What has happened to women who do join left groups? Many women *and* men have had to struggle to come to terms with being either inside or outside a left group. Such is the state of the left that neither the autonomous movement nor any of the groups is weak enough finally to be dismissed; yet none is strong enough to impose its solutions as wholly credible. To be in *or* outside a left group can seem equally wrong; and it feels at times as if Hilary and Sheila are trying to wrest a solution from a situation that does not actually offer one. True, the libertarian left is more *like* the women's movement than other left currents; that does not make it more *right* as a road to socialism.

To align yourself with a particular section of the left is never the end of the story for feminists. For some women the important thing becomes not to develop and strengthen feminism but simply to take it into the left – essentially in a way what Sheila seems to be proposing for libertarianism – as a weapon to change the left. Some women have left in disillusionment with this tactic, or because the left can perhaps never make feminism central enough to satisfy a feminist; others have been sucked into 'the party' and have effectively left the women's movement so that, continuing to think of themselves as feminists, they have increasingly defined that in 'party' rather than in feminist terms.

For these and other reasons the autonomy of the women's movement has always been of central importance. The autonomous women's movement does not simply represent an organizational principle. It also represents a difference and a distance between feminism and organized political groups. So when Sheila says that she sees 'the growth of new forms of organizing within the women's movement as part of a larger recovery of a libertarian socialist tradition', while I am sure there is no intention to undermine the principle of autonomy, there does seem to be a danger that in collapsing together the problems of feminism and socialism we will bypass a number of unresolved questions about the differences between what feminists and what socialists want, and about different kinds of *power* that are being sought. In concentrating, too, on organization, these authors render unproblematic the question of the aims of the women's movement, which seems to me to raise knotty problems.

Those of us who are both feminists and socialists feel that feminism must have a relationship of some kind with socialism, since the kinds of social change the women's movement has demanded and worked for are not wholly compatible with capitalism. Feminism is a radical and progressive force and we do share many of the aspirations of socialism. Yet there remains a dimension to feminism which separates it from socialism. Socialists do not necessarily share the feminist aspirations of feminists, as is all too clear from the experience of the socialist countries and the experience of Western feminists in the left and the labour movements of the West.

More importantly, in the present context, the question of Leninism and Bolshevik forms of organization is a question of how to take power. Leninism is one theory of how socialists take power, or how the working class takes power. The libertarian form of organization seems to imply that the transition to socialism comes about gradually by the growth of spontaneous grass-roots centres of struggle, which are simultaneously socialist in themselves and a form of opposition to capitalism. Though gradualist, they are saved from reformism since they operate outside the traditional structures of power.

But do feminists aim to 'seize power'? I don't know that we have decided what kind of power we want and whether we can discuss power in the same terms as those used by socialists. In some of its campaigns the women's movement has expressed if not a wish for, say, state power, at least a wish for access to the resources that power would give us. At the same time feminism has been a radical critique of power relations. So there is an ambiguity here.

Certainly we cannot resolve these problems by making our priority *their* (socialists') regeneration by the addition of *our* values. To do this would be objectively to subordinate feminism to socialism, and to neglect the problems within feminism, which is neither homogenous nor problem free.

Lot's story did not end when his wife was turned into a pillar of salt. Subsequently he hid in the mountains with his two daughters. They made him drunk, and each in turn went to him in his cave and conceived a child by him so that their tribe should not die out. We, like Lot's daughters, are the daughters of necessity, and like them we have to make the best of an actual situation, however misbegotten the results. They felt they had no choice but to turn to the father. So socialist-feminists are trying to deal with the real situation of an authoritarian and capitalist society. But perhaps Lot's daughters should have gone off and founded a lesbian commune or had daughters by AID.

While Sheila describes both the creative aspects and the shortcomings and disadvantages of the practices of the women's movement with some wonderful flashes of insight there is no sustained analysis of how we have and how we should operate now and in the future. Despite her disclaimer she tends to idealize the women's movement and there is no real suggestion that the organizational forms of the women's movement are themselves problematic or in need of reconsideration. There is no mention of the fact that there has been no national women's liberation conference since early in 1978, and that revolutionary and radical feminists are implacably hostile to Marxism and socialism. Yet they *are* feminists, and we can't simply wipe them out by claiming feminism as part of socialism. There is no consideration of the multitude of women we might dismiss as 'reformist' or 'liberal' but who do share many of our views. How might we bring them within our movement? To ignore that problem is again to ghettoize feminism within left sectarianism. Rather than posing the question of how forms of feminist organization can come to the aid of socialism, thereby improving *it*, I feel we should be addressing ourselves to the problem of how *we* are to be better organized. Simply to take the practice of consciousness raising and feminist therapy to men will not answer these questions. Our own movement is in dire need of developing and strengthening. Only if we are strong (as a women's movement and not just as part of the woolly mass of the libertarians) are the Leninists *or* the libertarians going to take notice (not to mention the capitalist state . . .). Male domination and sexism have always been just as much a problem within the libertarian left as within Marxist groups. Moreover the socialist humanism of the new left of the 1950s and 1960s ultimately posed *dissolve* feminism within the general humanist struggle. The humanism of the new left of the fifties and sixties ultimately posed the male/female relationship as the humanist *solution* to the alienation of a sick capitalist society (Wilson 1980). But the struggle of the contemporary women's liberation movement has been to differentiate itself out from other radical struggles.

Lastly, the weaknesses of the libertarians tend to mirror those of the women's movement. Its tendencies towards fragmentation, individualism, and a ghettoization within a form of life-style politics that cuts it off from most people can't be denied. Like the women's movement it lacks the strength of an organization *through time* which is important for any movement since it permits the passing on of knowledge and the accumulation of experience. This educational and affirmative aspect of organizations is one that is very little discussed yet surely it is important. We need alternative traditions and history as well as alternative life styles. And Sheila tacitly acknowledges this to be a problem for the women's movement.

Feminism and academia

A lot of energy has gone into the attempt to develop a feminist theory that would link feminism and socialism. I shall not attempt to summarize that project here (but see Beechey 1979 for a review of some of the literature). In part this has been an attempt to grapple with the subjective feeling, voiced by Sheila, of being 'split' between one's feminist convictions and one's socialism. One solution to this feeling is simply to acknowledge the split. Pat Arrowsmith, for example, has stated that she feels there is *no* relationship between her work for Troops Out, that is her support for the Irish struggle, and the fact that she is a lesbian, her sexual politics (Birch *et al.* 1979). Many socialists in the women's and the gay movement have however tried repeatedly to relate the two. Attempts to understand women's labour in the family and state welfare provision in terms of the general workings of capitalism are these days likely to be labelled functionalist. To explain the form of the family and the mechanisms used to support it in capitalist society in terms of the 'needs' of capital and the efforts of a planful capitalism to secure its 'needs' by giving the family the 'function' of reproducing the working class – producing new generations of workers, and refuelling the current generation – is held to give insufficient place to both working-class struggle and to the complexity of the structure of both the individual human being and the family. I don't actually think there was ever any intention of denying the complex and contradictory nature of what constitutes the family, just as it was always explicitly stated that the creation of the 'welfare state' was a complex and contradictory process. In any case the alternative, which seems to be virtually to deny causality and the dominance of any one 'discourse' over any other seems philosophically questionable as well as a political dead end. More importantly for the purposes of this article, the arguments now caricatured as functionalist made possible a link between feminist struggles around family and sexual relationships and the socialist struggle around the means of production. Louis Althusser, the French Marxist philosopher, was important to feminists because he saw the family as the site of ideology and not as some natural sphere outside capitalism, which for many years had been the view of the traditional left.

What is the alternative? In an extraordinary article in *m/f* no. 3, Diana Adlam demolishes a number of attempts to link Marxism and feminism at the theoretical level yet ends with a wholly voluntaristic assertion of the existence of socialist-feminism as a 'coherent political force'. One is reminded of one of those paintings by Magritte in which a hugely heavy granite egg hangs miraculously in mid-air. We could all defy political gravity if we only had to say something for it to be.

As Sheila points out, the more usual alternative has been effectively to perceive two spheres, the sphere of waged work (production) and the sphere of the family (reproduction) and to leave them as virtually separate spheres for men and women. This 'dualism' is found in the work of Juliet Mitchell and in a number of other writers (see some of the articles in Eisenstein 1979). Sheila suggests that the two spheres are bridged by ideology and by the state, and I would agree with that. But feminist theory has moved in a different direction.

As time has gone by the search for the theory that would answer our questions about how the 'oppressor in our heads' is created has assumed an ever more conventional academic form. Marx, strucuralism, Althusser, Lacanian psychoanalysis, semiotics, have all been taken up and (it would appear) dropped again when, like last year's shoes, they proved too uncomfortable to wear. The doyennes of intellectual fashion castigate unmercifully those unfortunate enough to have been caught hobbling along in their cast offs. The latest piece of intellectual *haute couture* from Paris is paraded in the full knowledge that it is beyond the reach of most of us. Or, to change the metaphor, the dreadful heresies of humanism, functionalism, historicism, idealism, sociologism, and so on, are hunted out with inquisitorial zeal. And anyway, how much do these changing intellectual fashions really signify? The cult of Althusser, after all, was started by precisely those theoreticians who now most savagely dismiss him.

I have no wish to attack all theoretical work or to be anti-intellectual. On the contrary. But it does seem that the attempt to develop a theory of women's oppression (if I may be excused for putting it in that way) has taken an unfortunate turn. The reversion to Freud is opening the way to the reactionary position of 'equality in difference' and 'complementarity' between men and women. Some women are ceasing to question the sexual division of labour and are arguing that all we need is for women's labour in the home to be (somehow) more highly valued. These positions have been argued, for example, by Ann Oakley in *New Society* (23 August, 1979) although not in her case, as it happens, from an explicitly Freudian standpoint. [I now feel that Ann Oakley is making a rather different argument. E. W., 1985] Articles by Parveen Adams, alone and with Jeff Minson, and by Mark Cousins in issues of the periodical *m/f* argue that 'sexual difference' does not imply 'sexual division'. Nor, they argue, is there such a thing as a unitary 'woman' – we are all bundles of contradictory atoms and impulses. The idea of the unitary self is a fiction. Leading on from this there is no such thing as 'women's oppression' in any unitary sense. This may be logically correct in the perfect world of Mind; it is politically dubious, to put it mildly, when the Tory government is starting to argue that women should be in the home as a cloak for their spending cuts and unemployment.

It is not possible within the confines of this article to mount a comprehensive critique of the positions being taken up (whether explicitly or not) by some of the feminists who have become interested in psychoanalysis, nor to argue through the questionable logical and political implications of their work. In questioning or, it may appear, attacking, the use made of psychoanalysis by some feminists, I am not denying the importance of the questions they raise. The concept 'patriarchy' is indeed unsatisfactory, as Diana Adlam argues. To raise the question of the construction of the subject (how we come to believe in ourselves as coherent individuals with a 'personality') and to argue that it is contradictory is interesting. Yet in atomizing the individual and demolishing the very possibility of an oppression that is coherent, the way is being opened to strange political consequences. To assert that the construction of sexual difference is *the* problem for feminists, and to become absorbed in psychoanalytic explorations of the creation of difference between masculine and feminine is not surprisingly leading back into justifications of the *status quo*, is leading back to the positions shared by postwar liberal feminists and psychoanalysts who believed that women and men, with their differentiated natures, *should* inherit different spheres. This may not have been the intention of the theorists, but it is the objective result, or one of the results, of their work. And I believe we can – and should – judge theory in terms of its political results. (We all argue, as again Diana Adlam does, that theory and politics cannot be separated, but often this means no more than that theoretical work is justified *as* a form of political practice.)

To blame Marx and Engels for all this may be unfair. It does seem amazing, though, that after ten years of the new feminism we are (some of us) moving back towards the positions held by Vera Brittain and Eva Hubback in 1950. We should remember that women in the 1950s *tried* 'equality in difference' and it didn't work. In fact it was one of the preconditions of the women's liberation movement.

Have feminists then been mistaken in adopting an academic or semi-academic form of writing and a predominantly theoretical approach to the attempt to unravel their own oppression? Although the women's liberation movement has stressed the importance of the experiential, feminist writing has tended to take an academic and theoretical form. Even Betty Friedan (1963) and Germaine Greer (1970), in books we tend to remember as 'popular', were quite academic in their use of theory. All the feminist writers since the second world war, from Simone de Beauvoir onwards, have drawn on and written critiques of a wide range of theoretical literature. Most went over the Marxist and Freudian ground before the birth of the contemporary women's movement. The typical form for modern feminist writing has been the part academic treatise, part polemic, a hybrid form with a number of disadvantages. It has been partly dictated by publishers who saw only a restricted market for most feminist writing, yet who in encouraging the academic slant perpetuated the restriction of the audience. The academic content weakens the immediate political impact of the polemical appeal, while the political argument may strain the academic material.

Women's writing has, though, tried to find a place for the more open expression of emotion as a valid part of *political* discourse. Sheila Rowbotham, especially in *Woman's Consciousness; Man's World*, explored how it might be possible to relate the political to the personal in the way she wrote. In *Beyond the Fragments* the attempt to describe a process seems to me less successful. It results in an Alice-Through-The-Looking-Glass-like wandering away from the direction that looks like the right one in order to get back there in the end, a rather oppressive circularity and repetition. In *over* personalizing political experience or intuition, in other words, Sheila seems in danger of caricaturing her own response, or even of caricaturing a kind of femininity.

But how *do* you avoid the jargon of conventional political and academic writing without becoming woollily 'feminine'? How *ought* feminists to write? The main alternative to polemical academicism has been a 'creative writing' approach which, while it has (so far) explored certain women's dilemmas has had limited political impact. Kate Millett is the best-known feminist writer to have made the journey from academia to creative writing and that project has not been without its hazards, for such writing easily becomes hyper-subjective and often self-indulgent.

Women and men

There seems to be another theme latent within *Beyond the Fragments*. How are women who are not separatists and who do not see men as the enemy to work politically with men if they are not in a political party? Membership of a party or a trades union does after all solve the problem at a practical level. Engagement in political (or theoretical) work with men can be a rewarding as well as a frustrating and sometimes enraging experience. Sheila says, rather wistfully, 'despite its creativity, feminism, by definition, expresses the experience of one sex. It is necessarily partial'. And the implication of this is that perhaps feminists would like to find ways of sharing the creative and inspiring aspects of feminism with men. It does seem a pity only to use it as a weapon against them. Women who enjoy heterosexual relationships have sometimes felt this as contradictory to their feminism, or as at least raising a dilemma. There is a dilemma for the woman who, perhaps, has found that it is the father of her children who has been her best ally in caring for those children, rather than any 'sisters'. There is a dilemma for women who may have experienced just as much hostility and frustration in political relationships with women as with men. Sisterhood doesn't rule okay, unfortunately. The existence of socialist-feminism expresses at some level a feminist willingness to include men, to work with men, to welcome men as both comrades and lovers. In questioning the nature of socialist feminism I am not arguing that women should not work with men. I think it important that we do find ways of working with them, and that we reassert what after all is the case, that feminism is not simply talking about the wrongs of women, it is also talking about a better way of life for men, women, and children.

And yet on the other hand there are problems in the political perspective of a reconciliation between women and men. 'Leninism' is not, as Sheila seems to suggest, the only barrier between politically active men and women. We cannot assume that feminists will always prioritize the same issues as (male) socialists, for instance. Nor, where the interests of women appear to contradict those of men, can we rely on a more Utopian, socialist-feminist perspective to reunite them.

Conclusion

It is always easier to raise questions than to resolve them. I have used *Beyond the Fragments* as a take-off point from which to begin an exploration of some of the problems of feminism that I find more interesting and relevant than the (to me at least) rather stale arguments around Leninism and spontaneity. It may be that *Beyond the Fragments* is addressed primarily to the left rather than to feminists and that in questioning its relevance to feminism I have missed the point. Yet the rather too reassuring vision of feminism it offers the left, must I think be questioned. To say this is not to imply that the problems are all within feminism and that the left need not set its house in order, since that clearly isn't true. But for me the immediate questions for the women's movement – and for the left for that matter – are not organizational. Organizational problems reflect it seems to me deeper uncertainties about the direction in which the women's movement and the left should be going. Nor do I feel that unless it enters into a symbiotic (and I use the word in a precise and non-pejorative sense) relationship with libertarian socialism, feminism will be, as Sheila fears, left in its own ghetto. Politically, feminists have to make alliances with *various* groups, using the word 'political' in a traditional sense. Politically too, women have to confront the antagonism of men and fight the political battles in relationships and attitudes, using the word 'political' more as in 'the personal is political'. And here libertarian socialism cannot help them.

First things first. Where are we going in the women's movement? What sort of power do we seek? In what way do we wish to make our mark on the world? Do we want a share in the world or do we simply want 'women's sphere' to be given greater value? Or do we want to break out of those dichotomies altogether?

We need to be very aware of the fluidity of feminism, which has historically adapted itself to a wide variety of political views. We need to know to what extent it is our own fault that modern feminism is in some ways so narrow, when the aspirations it expresses reach so wide and find sympathy with so many.

Life, as Diana Adlam puts it, with its 'teeming immediacy' *is* fragmentary. There *is* no magical politics that will unite all our aspirations into one grail. Our lives as socialists and feminists express the most acute political and moral tensions. We must confront them rather than trying to wish them away.

5 ◆ How not to reinvent capitalism: socialist welfare in the eighties

Introduction

This article was originally a talk I gave at the penultimate (1980) Communist University of London – an annual summer event organized by the Communist Party throughout the 1970s – at a period when their student membership was fairly high. The talk was one of literally hundreds I gave in the years following the publication of my first book, *Women and the Welfare State* in 1977. The particular focus of this version of my 'welfare state talk' was an early critique of the concept of 'Thatcherism'. It therefore represents an Ur-version of some of the arguments developed in 'The British women's movement'.

How not to reinvent capitalism: socialist welfare in the eighties

That the election of Margaret Thatcher's Tory administration in May, 1979 represented a major political break in the history of postwar Britain is widely accepted, by left and right alike. The Thatcher administration has clearly abandoned the consensus politics adopted in 1945 as part of the Keynesian 'postwar settlement' and has settled for the discipline of the dole queue and the bankruptcy court. In Thatcher's Britain the weakest go to the wall. The world economic situation and the concomitant apparent end to détente have created a political situation that is one of profound crisis, a crisis by no means unique to Britain. But just as the solutions of the Tory government are unique to Britain, so also is the response of the British left.

This response has been one of profound pessimism and a deep

sense of defeat. Hilary Wainwright, for example (Rowbotham, Wainwright, and Segal 1979), in her introduction to the first edition of *Beyond the Fragments* wrote of her amazement that the British working class *could* have voted a Tory government into power. Paul Corrigan (1979) likewise expressed astonishment: 'I believe and I think most of us acted on the belief that the case for massive state involvement in both welfare and in the economy had been irrevocably won amongst the hearts and minds of most working people.'

These responses seem to me exaggerated, and lacking in historical perspective. There is indeed a crisis. Many on the left, however, are arguing that this crisis is not simply a crisis of British and international capital, although it is that; it is also, they argue, a special kind of political crisis for the British left since the rise of a new radical right has enabled the Tories to capitalize on what is seen, according to this argument, as a massive and general lurch to the right.

In the following pages I shall argue that this analysis is overgeneralized, that the desperate search for 'new' forms of struggle – which has been the response of the left – is confused, and that the whole discussion has lacked any historical perspective. I shall particularly look at welfare, since it is around disillusionment with the welfare state that a good deal of the discussion has centred. A brief historical reprise is necessary to locate the current anxiety surrounding the very concept of state welfare intervention, once regarded as an unproblematic keystone of socialism.

The pursuance of full employment policies, reforms in the health and education field, and the implementation of the Beveridge Report received widespread support in the years following the Second World War, and tended to be equated with socialism. Whatever the actual influence of the Fabians (Hobsbawm 1968) these reforms, over-reliant as they were on formal legal rights and parliamentary fiat, came to be seen by a later generation as 'Fabian'. During the 1950s there was no properly developed Marxist approach to welfare provision. The Marxist left was in retreat during this period, and took up positions similar to those of the Labour Party; welfare provision was seen as supplementing and supporting the 'working class family'. Such an approach was bound to find it hard to deal with social problems thrown up within the family, such as divorce and delinquency; and indeed on the left these were perceived either as an 'effect of capitalism' or as entirely outside capitalism, in which case the appropriate remedies were simply those offered by capitalist welfare: social casework and psychotherapy based on vulgarized versions of Freud – the personal was definitely *not* political for Marxists.

At this period many feminists too hitched their star to Labour Party Fabianism. Many of them seemed to feel that the Attlee welfare state had secured basic provisions for women within the family (Brittain 1953). There were, it is true, attempts to improve the economic status of women within marriage, but although this offered some challenge to the power of men as the owners of wealth, it did not question the organization of the family into a breadwinner and dependants; simply it required that the wife as a dependant be better rewarded (Wilson 1980).

With the rise of the first 'new left' new forms of struggle and the beginnings of a renewed interest in a non-Stalinist Marxism began to develop in Britain. Philip Seed (1973) has described how some CND activists moved out into community struggles in the early 1960s; he mentions housing (squatters) and the plight of Gypsies as two areas that were contested during this period. Towards the end of the decade the claimants' unions were formed, and in 1970 *Case Con*, a magazine for radical social workers, was started.

At first the radicals who were involved in these struggles relied simply on moral indignation to explain their actions, and in a sense they were struggling for the rights within a welfare capitalist state which had been promised but denied them or those for whom they fought. Pressure for the reform of the laws relating to homosexuality, divorce, and abortion during the 1950s and 1960s also operated on assumptions of gradual change within capitalism (Weeks 1977; Greenwood and Young 1980). There was no satisfactory explanation for the failure of the welfare state to deal with the problems it had promised to solve. But Marxism did offer an explanation of the persistence of inequality and poverty. And, since the radicalism of the 1960s had brought a renewed interest in problems of consciousness, of subjectivity and ideology, and was resolutely anti-economistic, this neo-Marxism promised to contribute as well to an understanding of those problems of personal life that the sexual liberation movements began to tackle.

Marxist theorists of the welfare state in the early 1970s were trying to find some coherence in its conglomeration of disparate benefits and services, and they began to perceive an ideological pattern of repression and control. The radicals who engaged in this debate (the social workers and social work teachers, for example, who initiated *Case Con*) were also themselves *workers* within the welfare state. Social workers mediate welfare provision in a highly ideological way, and are the bearers of very explicit state notions of how families and individuals should behave, who should receive discretionary benefits and on whom the punitive elements in welfare should fall. They also constantly confront the bureaucracy of the welfare state on behalf of their 'clients'. They see, in other words, both the most reactionary effects *and* the most ideologically unified parts of the welfare state.

Although, therefore, there was always an understanding that the idea that there is something unitary called the 'welfare state' is an illusion (this notion of 'the welfare state' is itself a powerful part of capitalist ideology) it is not surprising that the characteristic Marxist analysis of the welfare state to come out of their experience was one that emphasized the *intentionality* of the capitalist welfare plan, especially at the ideological level. The organizing principle of the welfare state came to be seen, particularly by Marxist feminists (Weir 1974; Wilson 1977), as the regulation of the domestic life of the working class, and indeed the recreation and preservation of family life and the nuclear family.

It is not really true, as some critics have suggested, that this analysis drew: 'a direct line . . . from the capitalist state through the monogamous reproductive family to the oppression of individual women' or that: 'by such a route the economic oppression of women in capitalism is equated with a form of sexual behaviour, popularly defined as "repressive" – that is, the form of monogamous reproductive sexuality in which women's active sexuality was not represented except by a series of prohibitions' (Coward 1978b: 12). On the contrary, the Marxist feminist analysis of the welfare state always made clear that women were subject to contradictory pressures.

It was also clear that the social casework literature of the 1950s, far from wishing to 'repress' women, exhorted them to *be* sexual. But the Marxist feminist analysis did seek to demonstrate a certain coherence, and to demonstrate that the welfare state cannot be fully understood unless we understand how women and the family get to be constructed by welfare provision. Marxist feminists therefore emphasized the many policies that welfare capitalism does have for the family. This was not the same as saying that the welfare state *alone* determines the situation of women. Nor was it the same as saying that the capitalist welfare state is one giant conspiracy.

The critique of the Marxist feminist analysis has tended to emphasize a latent conspiratorial aspect of it, or the 'left functionalism' whereby the needs and plans of capital are alone held to determine social change. This critique, however, had its own political imperatives. Its emphasis was on class struggle as the motive force in securing welfare provision for the working class (Corrigan 1977). But as Mary McIntosh has pointed out (McIntosh 1978a; 1978b) the 'class struggle' approach is really only the other side of the coin of 'left functionalism' since it is simply stressing the 'needs' of the working class rather than the 'needs' of capital. And although it would be incorrect to perceive the welfare state simply as a smooth running plan for the reproduction of the labour force, it equally cannot be explained as purely the result of class struggle. For one thing it is necessary to distinguish between different kinds of welfare provision. The education system, for example, has indeed come about partly as a result of demands by the organized working class. But there has never been any working-class demand for social work, which has in some ways developed in antagonism to the efforts made by the working class to develop their own systems of mutual support and self-help. And even when welfare provision has come about in part as a result of class struggle its form may still be oppressive. The 'class struggle' approach also singularly ignores the way in which concessions won by the working class in the area of welfare have quite often worked against the equality of women.

Today, discussion of the welfare state on the left is dominated by the reality of the massive cuts, the general attack on the welfare state, and the economic and political crisis. In response to this new situation it is possible to discern several different theoretical approaches, each of which carries with it certain political implications. The Conference of Socialist Economists State Group (1979) has recently published *Struggles over the State*. This book explains the British recession, in the context of the world economy, in a fairly orthodox way: while the tendency of the rate of profit to fall is not an inexorable law and there are counter-tendencies, capital *is* constantly engaged in the attempt to maximize surplus value, and the current crisis is a crisis of profitability. The CSE State Group also points out that the public expenditure cuts and the restructuring of state provision began under the Labour Government in 1976, when for the first time since 1945 the expenditure cuts involved cuts at the absolute, not simply at the relative level. At the same time Denis Healey and Roy Jenkins launched a 'major ideological campaign against state expenditure'. This period saw the imposition of cash limits and the building of a new consensus 'which establishes that state expenditure is an unproductive burden on the rest of society'. The overall effect, the CSE Group argues, is 'to maintain long-term ideological domination and effective day to day control, so that the long term interests of capital in general are furthered'.

The strategy most fully discussed by the Group to combat this situation is the Alternative Economic Strategy (AES). But they argue that this must be seen as including struggle against the state form and not just as a strategy for the management of capital. (For a short account of the AES, see CSE London Group 1979.)

Another group originally associated with the CSE, the London Edinburgh Weekend Return Group, has written *In and Against the State: Discussion Notes for Socialists*. This emphasizes the fundamental contradictory nature of the state and the negative subjective experiences both consumers and state workers have of it. It discusses both the struggles of workers 'inside' the state, and the grass-roots struggles of groups such as parents, patients, teachers, and tenants, and the importance of linking the two. At the same time, an essential part of the group's analysis is that: 'the state . . . treats us as individual citizens, families, communities, consumer groups – all categories which obscure class'. And, while bringing material benefits to the working class, the state has 'pushed the oppression and fragmentation implicit in state organization deep into the texture of society' (London Edinburgh Weekend Return Group 1979).

Yet – although I share their belief in the importance of grass-roots struggles – in emphasizing this form of struggle without any real organizational form that would draw different struggles together, the group does tend to set up anew the 'mystifying' groups of citizens with rights as individuals which it earlier accused the state of having set up in an atomizing way to mask the class nature of the struggle. This danger – that the class is again atomized into a conglomeration of pressure groups with narrow sectional interests – they do not confront.

Then there are several writers who have developed an approach which is to be distinguished from the CSE approaches by its greater emphasis on ideology and on a new, reactionary consciousness within the working class itself. Paul Corrigan (1979) claims that, at the last general election, 'not only was there a distinct vote against the welfare state and the experience of nationalization, there was also a vote against the trade union movement'. Martin Jacques (1979) also argues that the general election result marked not only a break in government but also a break in popular attitudes: a major realignment of class forces occurred, he suggests, in May, 1979, and a radical break from the previous Labour government, because even if Healey and Callaghan *did* descend into monetarism and mount an attack on state intervention, this was done in a merely pragmatic way; they did not, like Mrs Thatcher, attempt to break with the past thirty-five years.

Martin Jacques correctly sees the preconditions for the change in British politics in the whole history of the postwar period, when short-term measures failed to deal with Britain's continuing underlying economic decline. During this period, the Labour Party conducted no positive defence of the welfare state, and was indeed party to its gradual erosion.

Peter Leonard (1979) develops a rather similar argument within the specific context of the welfare state. His is an interesting and detailed examination of right-wing welfare ideologies and he shows how various strands in this ideology could coalesce into something very repressive.

A number of women have also developed feminist approaches to welfare. Hilary Land, for example (Land 1975; 1976a; 1976b; 1978a; 1978b; 1978c; 1980), has sought to demonstrate how state social security systems subordinate women to men, in the interests of men, within marriage. Mary McIntosh (McIntosh 1978a; 1978b) has argued from a rather different perspective that feminists should explore 'the way in which capitalism subordinates women, even though we acknowledge that women's oppression antedates capitalism', and she asks the question: 'What part does the state play in establishing and sustaining systems in which women are oppressed and subordinated to men?' She argues that effectively the modern capitalist state does support a specific form of household: the family household dependent upon a male wage and upon female domestic servicing. This analysis also points to a central contradiction in British capitalism: that between the family form and the wage form (Barrett and McIntosh 1980).

Feminist hostility to the family wage is rightly widespread, and is shared by the work of the Socialist Feminist Social Policy Group. Their work represents in other aspects an application in the area of social policy of the work of Barry Hindess and Paul Hirst and their associates (Cutler et al. 1977; 1978), and is influential in some sections of the left.

A number of feminists have been attracted by the work of Hindess and Hirst because of the primacy it allows the ideological, and in particular its recent emphasis on feminism. Yet ironically the Hindess and Hirst reaction to feminism was initially to dismiss it as unamenable to Marxist discourse; and although they have subsequently expressed support for feminist politics, Paul Hirst at least appears now to have evolved to a position which many feminists must find contentious, even were they to accept his authority to tell us what to do. He now believes:

'It is precisely by supporting and extending ordinary women's aspirations and actions *in* the family that modern feminism can have most effect *on* the family . . . . If feminists wish to improve women's lot in contemporary capitalism, rather than wait for some completely socialist social system . . . they must adjust their politics to the place of the family in capitalism . . . . By committing itself to a narrowly anti-familialist ideology modern feminism could all too easily alienate itself from the majority of women.'

(Hirst 1981a)

In any case it seems strange that feminists should have felt they needed the theoretical support of writers such as Hindess and Hirst, since feminist writings have never been narrowly economistic but have always emphasized the ideological and the political, and their complexity, and the complexity of women's subordination.

Feminsts influenced by Hindess and Hirst have tended to take exception to the work of Marxist feminists who investigated the effect of the capitalist welfare state on women in capitalist society. They have sought, for example, to disprove that the state is 'homogenous in oppressing women by reinforcing their dependence on men and their confinement to the traditional sex roles of the nuclear family' (Bennett, Heys, and Coward 1980:186). These authors argue, in fact, for an absolute plurality and non-homogeneity of discourses of social policy. Yet Mary McIntosh is surely right to argue that, since we live in a capitalist society (but I suspect that for the followers of Hindess and Hirst the distinction between capitalism and socialism has become effectively as meaningless as the distinction between reform and revolution which they explicitly repudiate), it is necessary to analyse and understand the *specific* ways in which the state in a capitalist society influences and shapes the lives of women. For state intervention does have considerable intentionality. Plans for welfare provision in capitalist society are many and various. Indeed, the obverse side of this multiplicity of plans is contradiction and struggle. So, for example, there are attempts to secure the unequal family and reinforce certain child care practices, discourage 'idleness', and so on, but the multiple plans that are made are often not internally consistent because of the conflicting pressures they attempt to mediate.

In a recent article, members of the Socialist Feminist Social Policy Group criticize the feminist groups 'Rights of Women' (ROW) and the Campaign for Legal and Financial Independence. These latter groups have advocated the disaggregation of tax and social security, arguing that men and women living together, whether married or not, should be assessed as separate individuals and not as some spurious unity. Bennett, Heys, and Coward (1980) criticize them on the grounds that many and more far-reaching changes are needed – nursery provision, the breakdown of the traditional sexual division of labour at work and in the home, and so on. But what feminist would dispute this? ROW has never suggested that the reform of the tax and social security laws are more than one possible campaigning focus, or that such a campaign would constitute a total strategy for women's liberation (such a proposition is manifestly absurd). More strangely, having criticized the narrowness of what they misperceive as the ROW approach, Fran Bennett and her co-writers have themselves only the narrowest of solutions to offer. The main strategy they put forward is a 'socialist incomes policy' (see also Campbell and Charlton 1978; and Campbell 1980).

Each of the above political analyses of the 'crisis in welfare' has certain implications, and in some ways they are all quite close together. Most of the writers whose work has been briefly (and, I am aware, inadequately) sketched in above cautiously endorse the AES, although with varying degrees of reserve. All have assumed that the policy of massive cuts must of course be reversed and a policy of positive social investment campaigned for. All emphasize that, seen as a purely economic strategy, the AES is not enough: the key to its progressive implementation is to make it part of a political struggle for socialism. All writers advocate 'new' forms of struggle in opposition to the Tories and as part of the development of resistance and a new 'popular politics' of the left. 'New' forms in this context mean grass-roots community struggles and the forms of resistance developed by such movements as women's liberation and the Anti-Nazi League.

None of these writers fully confronts the problem posed by party politics. The problem of the Labour Party looms but isn't dealt with openly; nor do any of these Marxists consider the relevance of the Marxist party or 'left group'. What, for example, is the logical conclusion of the CSE Group's emphasis on the continuity of policies between the Callaghan/Healey government and the present Tory administration?

Martin Jacques, on the other hand, strongly distinguishes between Labour and Tory governments. His analysis is made rather controversial by his insistence that the crisis consists of two 'linked' but presumably separate, or at least separable, breaks: the recession, and 'Thatcherism'. In saying this he detaches Thatcherism from the crisis; no longer is it simply a response to the recession but has developed an absolute autonomy of its own, in which case its appearance needs further explanation. For it is not clear *why* social democracy should be in crisis at all unless it is because it has failed to deal with the threat of recession and the economic cycle of boom and slump.

His emphasis on monolithic Thatcherism is in fact a displacement of the problem of the Labour Party's failures, and the contribution these made to the Tory election victory. In any case, he attributes too much importance to one election victory; although the long term loss of support for Labour must be a serious problem. That long term problem, however, is clearly *not* due to something called Thatcherism. After all, the Tories were returned to power in 1979 after a period during which the Labour Party was rapidly abandoning its remaining tenuous commitments to socialism and was seeking to be the party of 'responsible government' rather than the party of the working class, while prime minister Jim Callaghan was more often likened to Stanley Baldwin than to any hero of the left.

Martin Jacques's definition of Thatcherism is also open to question. He includes within it not only the assault on 'scroungers' and on the 'power' of the trades unions but also a variety of movements – Mrs Whitehouse and her National Viewers and Listeners Association; the Festival of Light; and the anti-abortion lobby. Here he seems on rather weak ground, for none of these movements could be called popular in the common sense use of the term. In the case of abortion in particular it is clear that a majority of the population favours liberal abortion laws; a resurgence of general reactionary moralism and anti-liberalism on 'moral issues' is far less well established than hostility to the trades unions and to aspects of the state. In this respect Great Britain offers a sharp contrast to the United States, where there clearly is a massive right-wing backlash orchestrated by fundamentalist Christianity

Nor is Thatcherism entirely coherent when it comes to its ideology of women and the family. This is an ideology, moreover, fully shared by Jim Callaghan and large sections of the Labour party, including some on the left of the party, such as Frank Field.

The implication of Martin Jacques's analysis is that the only alternative to Thatcherism is a populism of the left. He argues for a wholly *new* vision of socialism, combining collectivism, intervention-ism, and democratization. Like Peter Leonard he emphasizes new forms of struggle and the idea of 'democracy' rather than the role of a left party.

The tactic of a 'socialist incomes policy' put forward by some of the feminists discussed earlier in this article might seem rather separate from, as well as much more limited than, these calls for a 'new vision'. It is, all the same, consistent with them, stemming as it does in part from a disillusionment with the failures of traditional trades union tactics, especially since these have not done all that much to help women. Beatrix Campbell, for example, suggests that incomes policies in the mid 1970s did help to bring women's earnings closer to men's, although in saying this she appears to fail to take into account the impact of the Equal Pay Act (1970) (see Weir and McIntosh 1982). Her confrontational polemic against male trades unionists appeals strongly to women and does pinpoint a major problem for women in the trades union movement (and outside it). But it does not therefore follow that an 'incomes policy' represents the best strategy to equalize the earnings of women. Beatrix Campbell greatly oversimplifies the whole problem by presenting it as a case of greedy, short-sighted, and economistic wage bargaining by men versus the demands of women workers for better working conditions, shorter hours, and so on. She also collapses together a whole range of different issues affecting the position of women in the labour market, amongst them the maintenance of wage differentials, the 'dual labour market', part-time work for women, and the family wage. To argue for an 'incomes policy' as the complete, and necessarily the best, answer to all these problems, which surely require a variety of strategies, seems simplistic.

Furthermore, the 'socialist incomes policy' for which both she and Fran Bennett and her co-writers argue is not clearly defined. What after all *is* an incomes policy, and what is wrong with free collective bargaining? To argue for free collective bargaining as a principle is simply to defend the legal right of workers to negotiate the terms of reward for their labour, a legal protection we surely do not wish to lose. We might all agree that the planned redistribution of wealth and the reorganization of work are desirable goals. But everything depends on when and by whom an incomes policy is implemented. Should we co-operate with an incomes policy produced by the present Tory government? What do you think about the incomes policies pursued by previous right-wing Labour governments, and those that would certainly be introduced by a party of social democracy?

Incomes policy might be a necessary tactical measure for a left-wing government to take. This does not make it an adequate or even a particularly relevant strategy for feminists concerned more broadly with social policy. Women should be arguing for a much wider range of more specific and far-reaching changes. The bargain for which Fran Bennett and her co-writers argue – incomes policy in return for an extension of the 'social wage' – was in fact precisely the strategy of postwar social democratic governments. This strategy has repeatedly failed to redistribute wealth and simply to dredge it up now does nothing to promote the feminist cause.

Lastly, what kind of alliance is being suggested? Are these writers suggesting that the feminist movement should support right-wing governments against the trades unions? Beatrix Campbell well expresses the frustrations of women faced with the indifference displayed by the unions to the inequality and exploitation of women both in the labour market and in the home. But is the answer really to support the TUC leadership and the right wing of the Labour Party?

The call for a 'new vision' of socialism has been raised in *Beyond the Fragments* (Rowbotham, Segal, and Wainwright 1979) as well as by many writers within 'the left' – and the issue has frequently been raised very specifically in the context of discussions of social welfare provision. *Beyond the Fragments* calls for autonomy and lays stress on prefigurative alternative forms of collective organization. It attacks the whole idea of the Leninist party.

One reason this sort of position has attached itself to discussions of socialist welfare is because (as I suggested at the beginning of this article) modern welfare capitalism has been confused with socialism. As the CSE State Group puts it:

' "Statism" has been identified with the working class struggle and the construction of socialism. Such an identification is not merely created by the capitalist media, it has been nurtured and fostered within the labour movement and the working class by the belief that state-regulated capitalism, and a capitalist welfare state *is* socialism – the ideology of social democracy.'

(CSE State Group 1979:123)

I share with all the writers discussed above the belief that 'economism' in welfare is not enough. That is, we do not want more of the same, but *control* over the means of production and over resources. Socialists must also challenge the bureaucratism of the welfare state we have. The *form* in which welfare comes must be challenged (one of the major lessons of the women's movement). I also share with some of these writers the belief that grass-roots struggle and the labour movement must be linked; the labour movement must take on board issues and demands relating to welfare. The provision of child care and the lessening of unsocial working hours for men as well as for women are important here.

These writers all claim to incorporate the demands and vision of feminism. This brings consciousness and subjectivity to the fore and an emphasis on how we *experience* our daily oppression. Arising out of this comes an emphasis on ideological struggle, and here the major problem as defined by most of these writers is how to rekindle mass support for the welfare state and for socialism.

I share these concerns and endorse much of the emphasis. Yet I also have serious doubts and reservations about some of what is being said.

The role of feminism in the construction of socialist welfare policies must indeed be a central one. So far, most 'radical' or 'progressive' writers on welfare policy have had at best an 'additive' attitude to feminism: they take the position of women to be yet one more thing that we need to incorporate into our demands, or a separable or separate area of struggle. But feminist welfare demands would alter *everything* about welfare – they are *central* to any truly progressive reorganization of social welfare. The way or ways in which the family gets constructed in modern capitalist societies needs to be addressed much more centrally by the left. The problem of the social relations of the waged and the unwaged and how the state links them, tries to preserve already existing links, and tries to secure the redistribution of the wage, is central to contemporary feminist analyses but has yet to be fully understood by the left at large and the trades unions. It is never enough to argue simply for 'more of the same' when it comes to welfare. The left must fight for welfare provision that does not rely on the unpaid work of women and does not sustain the present unequal family; it must abandon the whole notion of the family wage (Barrett and McIntosh 1980), and the division of society into rigidly separated categories of wage earners on the one hand and dependants on the other.

The left must also address more consistently the many problems thrown up by contemporary 'family life' and its breakdown, thus confronting complex issues of individual and collective need. Support for self-help groups, which while not socialist themselves raise issues pertinent to socialism (as well as helping many individuals to survive, which is more important) must become more than a gesture. Issues of violence against women, and of income support and housing for women, to take only a few examples, have suffered from *theoretical* neglect by the left, and are still often not seen as 'really' political. Yet sexual and love relationships, 'family life', *are* the terrain of power struggles and *are* therefore political. A different but related problem is the way in which our subjectivity, constructed in the family, structures our view of the 'world outside', including politics: our political views, views about 'public life', are formed in the 'private world' of the family.

It is here that I begin to diverge from most of the writers under discussion. They appear to believe that the right has understood the irrational undertow that links these private and secret emotions to political attitudes and has exploited this vein of irrationality; and that the left needs somehow to tap this highly emotional source of support as well.

But is the rhetoric of populism the best way to do this? For populism is extraordinarily ambivalent. As Raymond Williams puts it:

'The habitual assumptions and strategies of populism – a mobilization of the existing resources of "the people" against a native or alien ruling class – have an honourable record. At the same time, we have seen, in the twentieth century, a "populism" of the right, superficially similar, in which a version of "the people" is effectively mobilized, in periods of social crisis, as a way of altering the character of class rule or of foreclosing socialist solutions.'

(Williams 1977:86)

This populism of the right, which Stuart Hall (1979) has named 'authoritarian populism', has been attempted to be mobilized in Britain in recent years, although not I believe as successfully as Martin Jacques imagines.

Whether or not it has been mobilized, I doubt whether some ill defined kind of 'counter populism' can be mobilized against it, and populist calls for a 'new vision' have too often been emptily rhetorical. In the first place, for populism to become progressive it seems to me that very special circumstances are required. For example the threat of Fascist attack and the reality of full-scale war against Nazi Germany did unite large sections of the British population behind a social democratic vision of a better postwar Britain. But more often populism relies, I believe, too much on various emotional and often very irrational responses which contain more latent reactionary implications than progressive ones. Some of these are: nationalism (with its ever-latent racism, certainly in Britain, heartland of Imperialism); reactionary visions of woman-as-mother (or think of the ambivalent symbolic significance of Eva Perón, madonna and whore rolled into one); and the 'little man's' hatred of 'them up there' – of big business and central government.

As Raymond Williams himself points out (Williams 1977), the empty 'residual rhetoric' used by the Communist Party of Great Britain in the early 1950s, appealing to a vague notion of 'the people', was ultimately patronizing. In a sense the 'first new left' of the 1950s also relied on a populism that collapsed different problems and different forms of social need into a culturalism that implicitly validated that rhetorical entity 'the working class family' amongst other things (Wilson 1980). I do not, in fact, believe that the conditions exist at present for some united progressive movement around a notion of the 'people' to come into being, nor do I see how such a movement would retain an insistence on the specificity of various forms of exploitation and oppression which has been one of the main gains of the 1970s for progressive politics.

So, while it is clearly of the greatest importance to build alliances and form links so that isolated struggles become more coherently directed, the way in which populism has been discussed in this debate makes it seem as if the priority is seen as the building of a more coherent 'ideology' of populism, and it is this that needs to be questioned.

Peter Leonard argues for the populist vision of a 'democratized' welfare state, a democratic populism to set against 'authoritarian populism'. Issues of control *are* vital; but the invocation of 'populist' and 'democratic' tell us remarkably little. What, for instance, would constitute popular democratic control of a school: control by parents; control by teachers; control by children; or control by the local authority?

There is, as it happens, a contradiction between populist rhetoric and the emphasis on grass-roots struggles, which do after all arise out of the specificity of the social needs of various groups. And although I believe that the welfare state, or some aspects of it, do still command a rather passive kind of popular support, this might be converted into more active enthusiasm by a programme of detailed proposals for change. These would confront the issues of: *how* welfare provision is to be organized across the range of situations it has to meet; *what* social needs are to be met and what the priorities of a left government would be; and *how* it is to be financed. Such a programme would build up to a 'wider vision' in a more real and realistic way than generalized rhetoric can ever do. Of course, the creation of a left policy programme would entail much debate and work, especially given the disagreements there would inevitably be (of which the feminist dispute around incomes policy is one example). But it would be more convincing than the general call to Utopia. When confronted with the call for a wholly new vision of socialism we should bear in mind Sebastiano Timpanaro's warning: 'Whoever speaks of a socialism that must be "reinvented wholly anew" winds up inventing something very old: capitalism' (Timpanaro 1975:261).

Part of the 'new populist vision' calls for political organization in a form untainted by centralized state power as traditionally conceived, either within monopoly capitalist societies or in socialist countries. However, while the Bolshevik concept of the democratic, centralist party with absolute secrecy and unquestioning obedience is inappropriate in the contemporary situation, some kind of organizational principle (a political party) is still needed if struggles are not to remain inchoate and confused. The dismissal by the authors of *Beyond the Fragments* of *any* unifying principle to bring grass-roots struggles together does effectively amount to the well trodden path of syndicalism and libertarianism. And the past decade has demonstrated the shortcomings of this tradition as surely as it has demonstrated the weaknesses of economism.

The politicizing as well as the orchestrating and co-ordinating role of the political party needs re-emphasis in this context, and there are still good arguments for that party being a Marxist – a Communist – party. The political party cannot be replaced by a simple reliance on nonaligned, autonomous groups, whose links even with other pressure groups and community groups are by no means assured and whose links with trades unions may be even more tenuous.

Socialism could not come about in such a way. But nor is socialism to be collapsed into social democracy, which is what the 'new vision' for the most part amounts to. Social democracy is bound to seem reassuring and therefore attractive to many so long as the present government maintains its current policies; we must remember that it has not sustained support when in power. We must remember too that the 'old' vision of socialism was never put into action. Our welfare state has never been socialist – it didn't redistribute wealth; it didn't make women equal; it didn't house and educate people in the way that had been hoped.

Perhaps in fact what is needed is something simpler, something less pretentious, something more small scale than the glorious vision. Perhaps we should be talking not about the final goal but about the next step: what we want tomorrow, or now.

6 ◆ The British women's movement (*with Angela Weir*)

Introduction

'The British women's movement' brings together some of the themes of the earlier articles in this section. Although written in 1984 it reflects a long-term unease about the way in which socialist-feminist politics seemed to be evolving in the late 1970s and early 1980s. The article was published at the same time as a pamphlet (Fine, Harris, Mayo, Weir, and Wilson 1984) which addressed similar problems in the context of the general crisis within the British left. Both pamphlet and article were quite intensively discussed and proved controversial, arousing strong feelings both for and against.

Our main thesis should not be controversial, although it may not have been clearly enough spelt out. It is simply that the development of capitalism is at present eroding women's position in the 'traditional', 'breadwinner/homemaker' (Davis 1984) family, while at the same time women are increasingly drawn into the labour market in circumstances that make the majority of them very vulnerable. By the same token, differences in wealth and status *between* women appear to be widening. We argue that *in this situation* the strategy of the women's movement, which has always ultimately been based on a concept of women's unity in the face of male oppression, may have to be revised to the extent that class and race differences are sharpening and alliances with groups of men become increasingly necessary. We therefore dissent from what has, we believe, become a consensus view within socialist-feminism. This consensus view casts the trades union movement in an historically crucial role in excluding women from the labour force and in reinforcing the unequal family system primarily through demands for a 'family wage' (Alexander 1976; Phillips and Taylor 1980; Barrett 1980; Cockburn 1981; Taylor 1983; Brenner and Ramas 1984). Even if that was to some extent the case (and the historical record does not present a clear-cut case either way) it does not therefore follow that unremitting denunciation of trades unions is an appropriate feminist tactic today.

Feminist critiques of trades unionism and the feminist use of psychoanalytic theory are normally discussed separately, but are linked by a hidden problem with which this article does not adequately deal: that socialist-feminism has come to distinguish itself from other feminisms by its attempt to link theories of subjectivity and gender construction with analysis of modes of production, capitalism in particular, and has especially emphasized the social construction of gender in historically specific relations of production and reproduction: 'Socialist-feminism . . . offers a combination of class and gender as explanatory of patriarchy' (Assiter 1985). This has produced a form of dual systems theory that we, and some other feminists, find problematic (Brenner and Ramas 1984; Vogel 1984). We question the whole concept of 'patriarchy' (Ehrenreich and English 1979; Interrante and Lasser 1979); we also question whether women's subjectivity is inevitably constructed along stereotypic lines in the way suggested by some theorists (Chodorow 1978). But it is precisely the discussion of gendered subjectivity in a separate box from discussion of women in the labour process that reinforces a tendency towards dual systems, and minimizes awareness of the extent to which conditions both at work and in the family are changing rapidly.

The preoccupations of 'The British women's movement' are similar to those of 'Beyond the ghetto' and the two articles are, to some extent, opposite sides of the same coin: an argument against the attempt to create a homogeneous socialist-feminism, together with, in this case, a positive argument for a *socialist* strategy for women that is progressive, incorporates feminist demands, and is capable of attracting the support of a broad section of women. But it is precisely because we do regard feminism and socialism as separate and in some sense incommensurable movements that we support the existence of an autonomous women's movement, and feel that its present decline is a serious setback for women. We also believe that the cry on the left in recent years: 'the women's movement has so much to teach socialism' is misconceived. The relationship between the two projects can never be a one-way street; socialism has positive lessons for feminism as well as the other way round; and feminism may just as easily become as narrow a sectoral movement as the labour movement is alleged to be.

What has become clearer since 1979 is the extent to which many socialist-feminists have been caught up in what we perceive as the rightward drift of the 'new left' of 1968. While many disagree with this view, others share it, and it is clearly important that there should be continued discussion about the role of feminism in relation to the trades unions, the Labour Party, and the progressive intelligentsia. The discussion has been initiated independently elsewhere (Armstrong and Armstrong 1983; 1984) and some feminists are now trying to produce a unitary theory of women's oppression in global capitalism, and at the same time to substitute a more materialist analysis of women's subordination – by exploring the biological parameters of the female condition – for the rather idealist emphasis on psychology characteristic of much socialist-feminism (Brenner and Ramas 1984; Vogel 1984; Lewis 1985).

The British women's movement

A complete overview of British feminism would require a book rather than an essay. Within the context of a brief history of the movement we therefore aim in this article at an assessment of the developments within one section of the movement, socialist-feminism, since the second half of the 1970s. It will become clear that we are critical of much that now attracts the admittedly vague label of 'socialist-feminism'. We wish to shift the ground of the debate, and hope to reinfuse socialist-feminism with some of the political sharpness it had in its early days, but which has now, we feel, been lost. Ours is undoubtedly a minority view within the broad spectrum of the left intelligentsia and of feminism, but since the women's liberation movement in contemporary Britain is, and always has been, a loosely connected movement of groupings of women activists with a variety of political priorities and theoretical positions, any assessment of the movement by individual feminists must necessarily be partial. We hope that readers will share our view that this partiality does not invalidate our critique. Our criticisms are not intended as a destructive exercise, but arise precisely because we share with many socialist-feminists a sense of the urgency of the problems facing women today. The present time is one of intensified class struggle nationally, and of great danger internationally. In this threatening political climate it becomes more, not less important to locate women's continuing subordination as central, and to reassert that no political strategy that does not start from this assumption can achieve real or lasting change for the vast majority, women and men, black and white, either in the developing world or in the 'imperial heartland'.

The British feminist movement in its renewed form in the early 1970s was originally known as 'women's liberation'. In the word 'liberation' were encapsulated both the notions of 'sexual liberation' in circulation in the 1960s and also the inspiration that Western radicals, and particularly the youth and student movements, drew from the national liberation struggles of developing countries, above all of Vietnam. Because, however, of the particular history and role of the British labour movement and the existence of a non-Marxist Labour Party as the parliamentary arm of the working class, the relationship of feminism to the organizations of the working class took a specific form in this country. British feminists did not have to relate to, or react against, large Communist parties as was the case in France and Italy. On the other hand they were closer to the labour movement than appears to have been the case in the United States, where a mainstream women's organization (the National Organization of Women) had been founded in the middle of the 1960s at the same time as women were becoming politically involved in single-issue radical protest movements such as the Civil Rights Movement and the protests against the war in Vietnam.

The women's movement in Britain did not get going until the end of the 1960s (the first National Women's Liberation Conference was held at Ruskin College, Oxford in 1970). From its earliest moments, therefore, it felt the influence both of the European revolutionary student movement and of the feminist theory that was already coming out of the United States and which was more strongly based on a critique of male radicalism.

Because of the circumstances of its inception, women's liberation in Britain was far more closely identified with socialism than had been the feminist movements of the nineteenth and early twentieth centuries. Juliet Mitchell, for example, is simply typical of a general attitude in her dismissal of the 'old suffragists' in *Women's Estate* (1971). Many feminists in the early years of the movement hoped that feminism would drag the labour movement and the working class further in the direction of socialism as well as feminism, and that a feminism that was wholeheartedly socialist could be forged. Although, therefore, those hostile to the movement – whether in the media, the labour movement, or the political parties – liked to label women's liberation as 'middle class', the feminists themselves wholeheartedly rejected reformism and 'bourgeois feminism'.

In its early years the British women's movement sought to create a relationship with, and exert a feminist influence on, the trades unions. Examples of such campaigns were NJACWER (National Joint Action for Women's Equal Rights) which organized a demonstration in favour of equal pay following an important strike of women machinists at Fords, Dagenham. The night cleaners' campaign followed in the early 1970s, later the Working Women's Charter, set up in 1975, and feminists also supported a number of women's actions, for example the occupation and subsequently the setting up of a co-operative at a leather garment factory in Fakenham, Norfolk, in 1972 and the strike at Trico's windscreen-wiper factory in West London in 1976. One of the more recent, and most visible, examples of this kind of approach was the work of the National Abortion Campaign, which culminated in a TUC-backed march for abortion rights in 1979.

The relationship of feminists to the left and the labour movement was none the less always ambivalent. In the early 1970s the Labour Party hardly seemed an option for the new generation of revolutionaries who were more likely to be attracted either to what was usually called libertarianism – a form of Marxism influenced by anarchism, rejecting formal party political structures and hence suspicious of Leninism, but extremely 'vanguardist' ideologically – or else by one of the Trotskyist groups that briefly flourished. A third option was the Communist Party of Great Britain. To begin with this was viewed with the general distaste felt towards traditional left parties, but it did succeed in recruiting both from the women's movement and the intelligentsia in the mid-1970s, partly because it became more open to discussion of feminist ideas than other left groups. These were the years of the great success of the Communist University of London, which provided an important forum for the development of ideas often imported from Italian 'Eurocommunism' at a time when the 'broad left' dominated the National Union of Students.

It is often suggested that, partly as a result of this leftism, and by contrast with the movement in the United States, British feminism has had no 'mainstream' voice, and has therefore been easily marginalized. Certainly there was little interest in the early years in the advancement of women in existing political structures, or in business, whereas in the United States a more developed concept of civil and of individual rights may have helped some women at many different levels of society, including blue-collar workers and women from ethnic minorities, to make inroads on male bastions of privilege at work and in mainstream politics. On the other hand, this very success has led to a backlash such as has not been experienced in this country, where there is in any case no fundamentalist religious movement on anything like the same scale as in North America to fan its flames.

The British women's movement was influenced less by American campaigns for equality in the boardroom and on the assembly line than by the radical feminist literature that had already emerged from the United States by 1970. Kate Millett's *Sexual Politics* (1971) and Shulamith Firestone's *The Dialectic of Sex* (1970) were important because they sought to theorize the belief that the primary social and political contradiction in all societies is that between men and women, and that women's subordination arises from male power, known as 'patriarchy', the 'patriarchal order', or sometimes 'patriarchal relations'. Feminists who hold this view are known as radical feminists, or sometimes in Britain, revolutionary feminists, and in the early days of the movement they tended then to characterize socialist-feminists as essentially non-revolutionary, since, they alleged, socialist-feminists did not believe in the existence, or certainly not in the primacy of male power, but believed on the contrary that the subordination of women arose simply as a result of capitalism. On the other hand, at least some British radical feminists subscribed to the view that capitalism is also oppressive (Chester 1982), and would describe themselves as anti-capitilast or as socialist; but they tended to view male organizations of all kinds, whether of the ruling class or of the male working class, as equally oppressive, and as institutions of male power.

It is not actually the case that socialist-feminists (or all socialists for that matter) view women's subordination as an 'effect of capitalism', although this position was characteristic of Marxist thought in the 1950s and 1960s. The CPGB abandoned this position under the impact of women's liberation, but the Revolutionary Communist Group was still arguing the 'effect of capitalism' thesis in the mid-1970s (Adamson, Brown, Harrison, and Price 1976). But earlier Marxist writers, notably of course Engels, never argued this, and radical feminists never understood or seriously tried to come to grips with what was actually the position of most socialist-feminists in the 1970s.

In the early years of women's liberation, however, disagreements about the nature and causes of women's subordination had not hardened into antagonistic currents, and it would probably be true to say that in the beginning all socialist-feminists were radical feminists and all radical feminists were socialist-feminists; or rather that the two strands had not yet separated out as distinct currents: 'in the beginning you said you were in women's liberation, you called yourself a feminist' (Chester 1982). There was a belief that 'sisterhood' – an experience of oppression common to all women, black or white, working-class or middle-class – would unite all women and transcend our differences. These differences were recognized, but the recognition paled by comparison with an optimistic, and what may now appear a naïve, faith in women's common interests and experience.

The political expression of sisterhood was the attempt to create a loose, federal, national, women's liberation organization, its basic unit the small local group, and an insistence that women's liberation was an umbrella movement, a 'broad church' that could accommodate every kind of feminism. Initially this appeared as a source of strength. There was the flowering of a sophisticated body of theory and many different kinds of intervention – from the setting up of refuges for battered women to the development of lesbian and gay groups in trades unions; from campaigns to defend existing abortion legislation to the establishment of women's studies in the academy; from direct action against porno bookshops to the burgeoning of flourishing feminist sections within commercial publishing.

Yet the belief in sisterhood also made the confrontation of clashing feminist political positions difficult and bitter. As early as 1974 sisterhood was under considerable stress. The presence or absence of men in the Women's Liberation Workshop in London, the relevance or otherwise of left parties and groupings and the importance or otherwise of a Marxist analysis, the position of men in Women's Aid and in the National Abortion Campaign – almost every campaign threw up these disagreements. The presence of large contingents of men, many of them from the CPGB, on the 1975 International Women's Day march in London enraged many women; soon it became impossible for women's liberation to organize unifying events on this day. There was bitter resentment when the Socialist Workers Party decided to concentrate on the abortion campaign and entered local NAC groups in large numbers. Radical feminists felt that socialist-feminists were 'selling out' to men and accused them of not believing in an autonomous women's movement (although most of them did). Socialist-feminists could not accept the divorce of women's oppression from all other oppressions, and continued to believe that in a class society and in a situation of the global aggression of imperialist capitalism and the existence of national liberation struggles women had to form alliances with other exploited and oppressed groups to free themselves and their sisters. They could not accept the attack on all men as equally violent, which came increasingly to dominate the radical feminist analysis. At the last National Women's Liberation Conference, held in Birmingham in the spring of 1978, this particular issue caused violent disputes, and since then there have been no national conferences of the women's liberation movement. Effectively the women's movement had split.

Since then, numbers of campaigning groups have continued to do their work; they can no longer be said to be part of an ongoing national political organization. Feminism survives as a body of thought, and as an inspiration to many men as well as women; its political muscle must surely have been weakened by its nonexistence as a *national* movement. Later we shall examine some of the attempts that have been made to substitute other organizational forms for a women's movement as such.

We propose to concentrate on developments within socialist-feminism since that period. This is not to deny the importance of radical feminism. Indeed, we shall argue later that in recent years radical feminists have taken over the activist energy of the women's movement. None the less we regard its analysis, however immediately compelling, as inadequate and ultimately mystifying. The assertion that the subordination of women is the simple effect of a monolithic 'male power', always asserted through coercion and violence, has generally led to a transhistorical analysis:

'In the intimate world of men and women, there is no twentieth century distinct from any other century. There are only the old values, women there for the taking, the means of taking determined by the male. It is ancient and it is modern; it is feudal, capitalist, socialist; it is caveman and astronaut, agricultural and industrial, urban and rural. For men, the right to abuse women is elemental, the first principle, with no beginning unless one is willing to trace origins back to God and with no end plausibly in sight.'

(Dworkin 1981:68)

This fundamentalist rhetoric is the vehicle for a grotesquely oversimplified and utterly pessimistic vision of the human experience, and one that offers no political solution. Some left-wing men, however, have capitulated to it (Livingstone 1984), perhaps partly because it is congruent with other developments in 'post-Marxism'. The particular emphasis on male violence, while important, has also tended to feed the re-emergence of an ideology that asserts not only women's difference from men, but their superiority. Such an ideology resembles that of sections of the nineteenth century movement, when biological notions of difference led to a conservative emphasis on women's sacred role in the home, and as guardians of moral purity.

Perhaps partly because of this easily grasped ideology, however, radical feminism has increasingly appeared more forceful than socialist-feminism. Originally the very concept of women's liberation gestured, as we stated earlier, towards the experience of the common revolutionary struggle of men and women. The gradual substitution (never formulated as a definite decision by the movement) of 'feminism' indicated an insensibly changing perspective, as the movement moved towards a more restricted, more 'realistic', and less 'revolutionary' orientation.

In the early 1970s many feminists set up Marxist and *Capital* reading groups, and the first Socialist-Feminist Conference was held in Birmingham in 1973. At that time the main disagreements centred on the issue of alignment or nonalignment with left political groups. Leninist conceptions of the party and the political vanguard were hotly contested issues, but there appeared to be a general acceptance of the Marxist critique of capitalist society. At this period there was a resurgence of interest in Engels's work on the family and the origins of women's subordination, and at the same time the recognition of absences in Marxist social analysis gradually led to the development of a position which argued that the subordination of women in the twentieth century, both in the developing countries and in the West, resulted from the complex interaction of capitalist relations of production with institutions of male power. By the later 1970s, however, it was becoming clear that socialist-feminism itself was not a single coherent tendency within feminism. Some argued for a distinct socialist-feminist current; others, more in the 'broad left' tradition, still hoped for a 'women's liberation movement' that would be, or at least could develop into, a mass movement of women, not a narrow socialist sect.

In the event, specific socialist-feminist groups were set up with their own newsletter, *Scarlet Woman*. Inspired partly by the experience of Grunwick, a long struggle by Asian women workers for trades union recognition, and by the Anti-Nazi League, anti-racist and anti-fascist work became an important focus for their activity. The last Socialist-Feminist Conference, in 1980, dealt with the relationship between women's liberation and the third world struggle, the situation in Northern Ireland, and the position of black women in Britain. Despite the differences between organized socialist groupings which always tended to dominate socialist-feminist conferences, this was an early attempt to explore differences among women from a class perspective.

However, until the last two years there have been few black women in the movement. White women with higher education and professional occupations dominated all sections and perhaps particularly the socialist-feminist current. This had little appeal for black women or for working-class white women, who had in any case little access to these political worlds.

Today, one of the most significant changes is the number of black women who are organizing on their own behalf, as part of the resurgent black struggle in this country. This has raised in a new form the issue of separatism posed first by radical feminists. Black feminists have criticized as racist the attempt by white feminists to erect a unitary theory of women's subordination (Carby 1982; Amos and Parmar 1984).

Black feminists have also rejected the radical feminist insistence that women should never work politically with men or in 'male' organizations, since this would be divisive in terms of the struggle against racism. We feel it would likewise weaken feminism if black and white women were never able to work together politically, and if women's liberation fragmented into discrete interest groups in which everyone fights for their own corner. Any gains made in this way are likely to be partial, and at the expense of other oppressed groups, rather than the ruling class.

Such an approach, while it may appear to give due priority to black women, would also have the incidental effect of letting white women off the hook. Racism is a white problem, but we do not believe that it can be understood or fought against by whites alone (and of course in practice the opposite is more likely to be the case). 'Racism awareness training' for white women, although it may be a useful ideological tool, cannot be a solution to racism unless one has an extraordinary belief in the powers of self-healing and the dominance of psychology as a determinant of racism. We believe that a theoretical basis, if not for unity at least for a much needed political co-operation among different groups of women, can be most accurately and concretely developed in the context of class analysis. Far from obliterating differences Marxism provides the most effective tool for understanding what is often a gulf between the experiences of black and of white women. It seems to us impossible to address racism or to understand our relative positions in society unless we do confront this country's imperialist past, its position in world trade today, the role of the multinationals, the significance of national liberation movements, the operations of the industrial reserve army, and the coercive role of the state.

The position of lesbians within feminism has also been a contested one, although the lesbian community contains many more black and working-class women than the women's movement itself. Lesbians made themselves present politically in the women's movement from an early stage. In 1971, at the Skegness National Women's Liberation Conference, they not only demanded the right to a hearing, but were instrumental in ousting the Maoist grouplet that was then attempting an organizational take-over of the movement. It was important that the intervention against the Maoists was headed by lesbians who were also socialists, since at that time this had a more unifying effect than radical separatism would have done. Nevertheless, radical feminism as it developed offered a political analysis of lesbianism that was in welcome contrast to then dominant explanations in terms of neurosis and inadequacy – usually backed by vulgar Freudianism, and often quite acceptable in socialist circles.

In the mid-1970s by contrast lesbian relationships were often perceived by feminists as a solution to the problems of sexual relationships with men, and were sometimes advocated in a moralistic way. Since feminist analysis emphasized the central role of sexuality in structuring female subordination it was not surprising that lesbianism became an important preoccupation; nor was its centrality as a political practice surprising, given the anarchistic emphasis within the movement on personal solutions and alternative and prefigurative relationships and life styles. Clearly the oppression of lesbians is one of the most significant aspects of female oppression, since the threat of being labelled lesbian, and thus deviant, is used to police all women; but the way in which it was discussed within the women's movement was sometimes voluntaristic and based on a possibly mistaken notion of the extent to which sexual desire is alterable at will. Yet, rather strangely, while lesbianism became part of a possible life style, and while lesbians wrote extensively at the experiential level, they were astonishingly absent at the level of socialist-feminist theory, as we shall see when we discuss psychoanalysis.

During this period the Marxism that influenced socialist-feminism was itself evolving. The resurgence of interest in Marxism in the late 1960s was contradictory. On the one hand it arose out of dissatisfaction with traditional liberal and conservative explanations of social inequality, and particularly with functionalist sociology and the ideology of consensus, 'pluralism': the idea that different interest groups in Western societies compete on more or less equal terms and non-antagonistically. On the other hand, it was equally critical of the socialism of the Soviet Union and Eastern Europe. It began as a critique both of bourgeois society and of the economistic stagnation of Marxist theory in the 1950s and 1960s, of the reformism that, it was felt, had everywhere stultified the left.

Louis Althusser and Nicos Poulantzas were perhaps the two most important theoreticians of the attempt to steer a regenerated Marxism between the Scylla of Stalinism and the Charybdis of social democracy. Ellen Meiksins Wood (1983) has argued that their work, and that of others, such as Ernesto Laclau, has had as its objective the theorization of the political perspective of Eurocommunism: the extension and gradual transformation of bourgeois democracy until it becomes a new and less statist form of socialism, the means to this end a system of alliances in which the working class is displaced from its traditionally central role in class struggle and replaced by an idea of 'the people'. As she herself notes (and we raised this issue above in relation to separatism) the concept of alliances is a crucial one within socialist politics.

Yet the neo-Marxism of the 1970s increasingly sought the causes for the failures and shortcomings of struggles for socialism in both East and West Europe less in a failure to create such alliances than in the theoretical roots of Marxism itself, while the (male) working class was not simply displaced politically, but was denounced morally.

In Britain the popularizers of the deconstruction of Marxism at the political level were Barry Hindess and Paul Hirst. By the second half of the 1970s they and their disciples were arguing that Marxism was an epistemological theory which purported to describe: 'a distinct realm of concepts and a distinct realm of objects, existing outside the realm of objects but knowable by them' (Coward 1978a). Such a theory, it was suggested, naturally privileges its own explanations, and is inevitably dogmatic and intellectually anti-democratic. Class, they argued, can no longer be an index of political struggle; it is necessary to free Marxism from harmful concepts such as mode of production, the contradiction between the forces and relations of production, and the determination of the economic in the last instance. All that is then left is a series of wholly discrete 'social conditions of existence' and these can be analysed only in relation to specific practices. By the late 1970s the way was clear for the re-emergence of that very same sociological pluralism which had been rejected by Marxists a decade earlier.

Rosalind Coward, in a number of challenging articles, suggested that women were marginalized within socialism not accidentally, because of male prejudice, but necessarily, because they were marginal to the central contradiction between the forces and relations of production that constitutes class struggle. Moreover, by freeing attention from the study of modes of production and transferring it to the study of specific practices, sometimes called discourses, feminists would be able to embark on a proper study of the social construction of gender differences. This implied the real possibility of women's liberation without socialism, and the old distinction between reform and revolution became redundant for women.

She argued (Coward 1978b) that previous socialist-feminist attempts to trace the relationship between capitalism, the family, and women's oppression were mistaken in their methods, and that to understand the construction of gender difference, we should:

'look at the conditions of existence of transformations of the definitions of sexuality in various discourses. But these trans-formations do not directly reflect any of these conditions, they are produced within the work of the discourse itself. Thus the struggle for power within discourses becomes an issue of political importance for the women's movement.'

(Coward 1978b:22)

To ask: 'What is a discourse', 'Where does one discourse end and another begin?', and 'What are the elements of the transformations that are produced within the work of the discourse and what are these processes?' is rather like the small boy asking the emperor why he has no clothes. In the name of freedom from dogmatic Marxism, no answers to these questions are offered, and the author is free to posit and prioritize whatever relationships strike her as relevant. This is the *auteur* theory of political economy. Cause and effect have not been banished – in fact causal relationships are seen everywhere and every human practice may become the object of discourse analysis. Epistemological agnosticism cannot discriminate between the weighty and the trivial; it refuses to privilege that which can be altered from that which cannot. The highly contestable assumption of this approach has been that basic socio-economic relationships are structured like a language, a view which fails to note that the former are subject to quite different material constraints from those which govern the latter. Economic scarcity and the requirement of material production pose us with options quite different from those which confront a person framing a sentence. Within the promiscuous and agnostic world view of the discourse analysts there can be no way of establishing social or political priorities, and hence no prospect of elaborating a genuinely emancipatory strategy. The result is a political relativism which cannot be progressive.

The indeterminate implications of discourse theory have undermined the feminist journal *m/f*'s ability to challenge, and distinguish itself from, either mainstream socialist-feminism or radical separatism. The critique provided by *m/f* has not supplied very strong grounds upon which to criticize radical feminism. The *m/f* authors argue that 'discourse theory' challenges radical feminism on the following grounds: (1) it challenges essentialist notions of human nature or sexuality and asserts that gender difference is socially constructed; (2) it therefore suggests that men and women may work together to challenge existing forms of gender, and recreate themselves in more equal relationships.

The major difficulty with this challenge is that it leaves out the problem of *men* and, incidentally, of heterosexuality. If, as Rosalind Coward has suggested, the 'struggle for power within discourses' is the political issue for the women's movement, then is it not odd and requiring of explanation that in all these different discourses it is men who have the power? Rosalind Coward has herself made this point (Coward 1981). If one denies all Marxist attempts to explain a relationship between male power and successive forms of production and reproduction, male power appears as an irrational monolithic system which does not look amenable to the kind of piecemeal feminist social engineering that forms *m/f*'s main policy plank. That is, at any rate, how it can look in the radical feminist analysis. The alternative *m/f* view rejects the seamless notion of patriarchy, but since it has no historical materialist basis for explaining the dominance of men, the problem of male supremacy in history is simply conjured away.

In fact, discourse theory has encouraged an individualism that has increasingly ignored collective political action. In arguing that the personal is political the early women's movement was not suggesting a *laissez-faire* approach, or 'do your own thing'. Quite the reverse – personal struggle to alter your way of life was believed to be a product of, and carried out in relation to, a political movement of women and to be a political challenge to a society where male power and privilege were hegemonic. The kitchen and the hearth were to be turned into battle fronts, not left as isolated discourses where life might be more rationally and harmoniously ordered. Moreover, taken seriously, discourse theory 'deconstructs' the individual subjects and portrays them as at the mercy of 'power'. Thus the work of Michel Foucault contributed to the strengthening of political and theoretical positions that were deconstructive of Marxism in moving away from any idea of the primacy of the economic and towards a metaphysical notion of the superordinate networks of power, the source of which is never specified.

Gradually a view now gained credence that tended to equate all Marxism with a dogmatic caricature. In theory, a distinction continued to be made between Marxism as an open, at times contradictory, and unfinished body of theory, and what is known as 'dogmatic Marxism'. Ernesto Laclau and Chantal Mouffe (1981), for example, have invoked an early Marxism in which the 'primacy of the political' is still allowed, but this Marxism is but vaguely delineated by comparison with the economistic and utilitarian dogmatism of the whole Marxist tradition from the time of the Second International onwards. (Lenin is partly but not ultimately exempted from this.)

Even more striking is the opposition set up in more recent work, by Barbara Taylor, between the 'vision' of Utopian, Owenite socialism and the 'utilitarianism' of the Marxist tradition from the late nineteenth century onwards. In these texts formal obeisance is made to the virtues of classical Marxism (before, in a sense, it was contaminated by working-class politics and before the working-class movement became more powerful); yet the impression remains of its moral and political insufficiency. For example, *Eve and the New Jerusalem* (Taylor 1983) constitutes an eloquent plea for a reassessment of the Owenite Utopian socialists, particularly in terms of their attitude towards the liberation of women, superior, she argues, to that of later Marxists. She argues that the Owenite *vision* (a crucial word) 'of a society freed from the deformations of both class exploitation and sexual oppression' was at a higher level, morally and politically speaking, than the later Marxist project, and that 'those who later abandoned that ambition in the name of science and proletarian revolution did not thereby raise the socialist project onto a higher terrain, but contracted it around a narrow programme that left little space for women's needs or women's demands' (Taylor 1983:286).

However, her own detailed discussion of the Owenite communities and of Utopian socialist politics in the years before 1840, approximately, leaves some doubt as to just how much in advance of some later Marxists the Utopian socialists were. Collectivized housework was part of the Owenite plan, but it appears that it was still to be done by women or sometimes children. This is only one example, and certainly women were very much 'on the agenda' in the Utopian movement. But Barbara Taylor herself acknowledges the force of Engels's strategic objections to Utopian socialism; she notes that Engels was critical of the Utopians' attempt 'to emancipate all humanity at once' rather than 'a particular class to begin with'. Marx and Engels, as she points out, condemned Owenism as 'Utopian', as a 'fantastic dream' of socialism that was doomed to failure, because it depended on rational benevolence and practical co-operation to prevail against the greed and self-interest of emergent capitalism. The Owenites believed in 'the natural harmony of human needs, [which] would be realised through the peaceful suppression and replacement of all disharmonious ideas and institutions (Taylor 1983:xv). Marx and Engels, on the other hand, believed in scientific socialism, that is, in a revolutionary strategy based on a 'scientific assessment of the balance of class forces', rather than on 'optimism of the will'. In their view, Owenism could not succeed because it did not understand the inevitability of class struggle and the nature of class antagonisms in capitalist society. Barbara Taylor goes on to say:

> 'Nonetheless, if the Owenites' *strategy* was thus fatally flawed, their *aspirations* were still to be admired . . . . This concession was by no means a minor one. Yet over the years it has been largely forgotten, and what has remained in its stead is an increasingly rigid distinction between "primitive", idealist Utopianism and the scientific politics of proletarian communism – a distinction which acquired increased popularity after 1880 as organized (male) labour emerged as a key protagonist in the arena of national and international politics.'
>
> (Taylor 1983:xv)

A contrast is here implied between a Utopian vision that could encompass the liberation of women, and a male, working-class politics that could not. This distinction is enunciated more clearly in a brief essay by Barbara Taylor, in which she states:

> 'The Owenite emphasis on the universal, trans-class character of "male supremacy" (their term) disappeared to be replaced with dogmatic assertions of sexual equality within the proletariat, calls for sex unity in the face of the common class enemy, and a repudiation of organized feminism as bourgeois liberal deviationism. The vision of a reorganized sexual and family existence which had been so central to Owenite thinking was increasingly pushed to the far side of a socialist agenda whose major focus became an economic revolution which would automatically liberate the whole of the working class.'
>
> (Taylor 1981:159-60)

Barbara Taylor at once acknowledges that this is 'something of a caricature since so many staunch sexual egalitarians were to be found in the ranks of later Marxist organizations' but her conclusion remains that this was a suppressed discourse, a marginalized problem, and emphatically not part of Marxist orthodoxy.

Barbara Taylor's implied contrast between early Utopians and later Marxists is misleading in several respects. The small groups of Utopian socialists experimented with an interesting mixture of good and bad ideas, and we are certainly in Barbara Taylor's debt for the marvellous account she gives of them. But in their own time they had little or no wider political influence: thus the British Radicals or Chartists of the period failed even to support female suffrage. When one variety of Utopian socialism, that associated with Proudhon, did acquire influence within the early workers' movement, this influence was used to oppose improvements in the civic rights of women. The early Marxists, by contrast, were far more open to the pressure of feminist ideas and women's issues. Engels's writings on the family and Bebel's *Socialism and Woman*, however inadequate or problematic from the vantage point of contemporary feminism, did commit the largest and most influential Marxist parties to support for women's rights. A remarkable group of socialist and Marxist women used the space so created to press for organization and agitation on women's issues. And often it was those keenest on Marxism and revolution who also raised women's issues: Clara Zetkin, Alexandra Kollontai, and Sylvia Pankhurst being notable examples. It has long been customary to decry the economism of the orthodox Marxism of the pre-1914 Second International. Yet the fact remains that the German SPD had a women's movement with 175,000 members in 1914 and had introduced the first motion calling for the enfranchisement of women in the Reichstag in 1895. The SPD was formally committed to crèches for working mothers, equal pay for equal work, the education of women, relaxation of the abortion laws, and availability of contraceptives. The women's journal *Die Gleicheit* (Equality), edited by Clara Zetkin, advocated proletarian revolution, anti-revisionist Marxism, women's rights, a new household regime in which boys would be encouraged to do housework, and an education for girls that would encourage them not to confine themselves to traditional 'female' roles. With 124,000 subscribers in 1914, *Die*

Gleicheit was one of the widest-selling socialist journals of the time. Despite the great influence of Utopian socialist ideas on the French workers' movement it remained strikingly backward compared with the more orthodox Marxists of Germany, Austria, Russian, Finland, and elsewhere. The French Socialist Party had fewer than 1,000 women members in 1914 and did not support female suffrage (Evans 1977).

Barbara Taylor does concede, in passing, that 'all the new socialist organizations continued to harbour some feminists and to support them' but the impression remains that women and women's issues were marginalized within the early Marxist movements. The reality was more complex and interesting than Barbara Taylor allows. The early Marxists by no means always supported their feminists; on the other hand, women's issues did loom quite large for them. Clara Zetkin and Rosa Luxemburg not infrequently encountered hostile or patronizing behaviour from their male colleagues while they themselves were opposed to the more radical socialist-feminism of Lily Braun. The orthodox Marxists were not insensible of the need to project an image of the socialist future; indeed one of the most influential visions of a socialist future was that elaborated by Bebel in *Socialism and Woman*, a work that contained a not dissimilar mixture of reactionary and progressive notions to that found in the early Utopian socialist writers. It could be objected that the everyday politics of the socialists and Marxists accorded little importance to women's issues other than those concerned with the vote or civic equality. There would be some truth in this, but then this was also true of the non-Marxist and non-socialist women's movements at that particular time.

In a different context Ann Oakley has pointed out the importance of Utopianism in feminist fiction, and especially of all female Utopias:

> 'This kind of all female world is a necessary vision because it is the only strategy which allows women to become the model for humanity . . . . [Joanna] Russ once said there were no men in her feminist Utopia because a truly equal two-sexed society is unimaginable.'
>
> (Oakley 1979:394)

The appeal of *Eve and the New Jerusalem*, however, is actually rather different: rather than presenting a vision in which 'the future is female' it presents a socialism from which class antagonism has been wiped away. In addition, and even more importantly, antagonism between the sexes appears as unimportant and is replaced by the co-operative enterprise of progressive women and men, often of petit bourgeois origin, in the building of a sex-egalitarian society. It is only working-class men (the men of the men's tailoring unions) who display real hostility to women in attempting to banish them from the union and from the trade.

E. P. Thomspon (1976) is right to suggest that to place the 'scientific' (utilitarian) over against the Utopian is to close off wide areas of political debate. Much of the implied criticism of the working-class movement seems to stem from the fact that it was engaged in day-to-day political struggle with the attendant compromises, disappointments, and failures. We feel none the less that it is a mistake for feminists to seek refuge in a vision of Utopia if this involves not only the abolition of necessity but also the abolition of politics. Besides which, as a reading of William Morris's own Utopia, *New from Nowhere*, demonstrates, one person's Utopia may be another's prison house; we do not look forward to a future in which women dressed in Pre-Raphaelite teagowns happily confine themselves to domestic work because this has been given the 'recognition' and 'importance' it deserves.

While we are critical of Utopian socialism it does retain a moral radicalism which is capable of mounting a sharp critique both of capitalism and of male supremacy. A more alarming trend within socialist-feminism is the tendency to counterpose feminism to Marxism to the unintended benefit of a new construction of social democracy.

Michèle Barrett, for example (1984a) has recently suggested that Marxism, strictly construed, may be incompatible with feminism. Using Marx's 1843 article 'On the Jewish question', she argues that feminism is a movement of political emancipation and that Marx opposed political emancipation. Feminism, she says, is 'based on a notion of equality' whereas Marxism is anti-egalitarian in the sense that Marx argued for revolutionary politics and 'human emancipation' rather than for sectional emancipation under capitalism. This is inaccurate on two counts.

Firstly, it is not the case that Marx, or later Marxists, opposed political emancipation or civic rights for oppressed or exploited groups. Marx certainly did not oppose extension of the suffrage to the working class though he believed that in itself access to the vote constituted only 'political emancipation'. Equal rights were desirable, since they furnished a more advantageous starting point and terrain of struggle, but they would not in themselves produce substantive social equality or emancipation. Marxist parties, as we have noted above, supported votes for women, although there were, of course, disagreements over whether it was right to support extensions of the vote to women without universal suffrage, that is, prior to the abolition of property or educational restrictions.

The second erroneous implication of Michèle Barrett's argument is that feminist demands can be subsumed under the concept of 'political emancipation'. Clearly Marx did not anticipate the modern feminist critique of women's oppression, nor did Engels even in his most 'feminist' work; moreover both exaggerated the trend towards equality of rights in bourgeois society and failed to understand male supremacy in the working class. But the modern critique of women's oppression has always sought to distinguish itself from the bourgeois discourse of merely political equality. 'No Liberation without Revolution and no Revolution without Liberation' was the slogan of the 1973 women's liberation march. Feminist theory has sought to probe the deep socio-economic roots of women's oppression, just as Marx sought to uncover the deep socio-economic roots of capitalist exploitation. Thus the formal structure of the Marxist argument for social emancipation, and its contention that merely political or civic equality would be quite insufficient to encompass it, are congruent with feminist analysis. The experience of the women's movement in the 1970s and 1980s has certainly confirmed that reforms in the civic and juridical field do not, on their own, achieve the equality that is sought.

The retreat from radical anti-capitalist perspectives was in part due to the advent of a right-wing, Tory government and the perceived failure of class politics in Britain. In response to this situation a political strategy emerged, most notably in the pages of

Marxism Today, the theoretical journal of the British Communist Party, which argued for a new, popular, electoral consensus incorporating feminism, conceived as a movement for women's rights.

Briefly the argument to support a social democratic position runs: there is no evidence that class struggle will lead to revolution. Indeed, such an approach is 'economistic' and denies the importance of 'the political'. It led to the defeat of the working class prior to the First World War, and to the rise of fascism and the Second World War. Closer to the present day, it has created the conditions for the growth of right-wing ideology and practices (known as 'Thatcherism'). The task of the 'democratic radicals', building on the work of Antonio Gramsci in particular, is to throw out the reductionist baggage and 'rather to conceive of society as a complex field in which the multiplicity of subjects must be recognised and accepted'. This in turn gives rise to a very different notion of alliance, a 'Copernican revolution' in Marxist theory in which this multiplicity of subjects must be politically unified in a 'vast system of alliances that are continuously redefined and renegotiated, with an organic ideology to serve as cement for the new collective will' (Laclau and Mouffe 1981).

Translated into the terms of contemporary British politics, this new political theory is used to justify the creation of a new mass electoral alliance around the Labour Party, analogous to the Popular Front, which will pose as its 'central political task the democratization of the economy, civil society and the state' (Bloomfield 1984).

The main proponent of this thesis, put forward in the 'Labour's lost millions' debate, is Eric Hobsbawm, whose two most recent articles appeared in the October, 1983 and March, 1984 issues of *Marxism Today*. Such an alliance, Hobsbawm argues, could appeal to all women 'across class lines', and would recognize that the 'situation of women could neither be explained nor resolved simply in class terms'. In fact, Jon Bloomfield has two sorts of movements: 'people's movements', which include women, youth, senior citizens, and ethnic minorities; and 'the working class movement', consisting, presumably, only of waged workers who do not fall into the above categories, and are therefore, we must infer, not 'people'. Women have thus been totally banished from class relations, albeit they may re-enter the political stage as constituted people-subjects. What that entry might materially mean no one has said – although in fact this line of argument paves the way for the re-emergence of a conservative ideology of women, which would implicitly banish many of the original demands of the contemporary women's movement as too *avant-garde*, and as out of touch with the 'mass of women'. Significantly, it is only Paul Hirst (1981a) who has had the intellectual honesty to state as much openly.*

One of the most amazing aspects of the 'Labour's lost millions' debate is that despite the importance given to drawing women into the debate, no male writer has given the slightest inkling of what actual policies for women a new, popular, democratic alliance would fight on (let alone for blacks, who in any case are hardly mentioned). In this context the consistent critiques that Eric Hobsbawm and others have made of 'left' tendencies in the Labour Party is alarming, for as Doreen Massey, Lynne Segal, and Hilary Wainwright (1984) have pointed out, it has been the left in the Labour Party that has fought for resources for women, set up women's committees, and tried to expand the provision of day care.

No doubt this silence on policies for women is partly due to male prejudice and ignorance, but more fundamentally we argue that to pose 'democracy' as the cement for what Ernesto Laclau and Chantal Mouffe have called the 'new collective will' cannot lead to a coherent strategy for women. What is more likely is that women's demands will be treated as just one set among many sectional demands, which will be negotiated with a pragmatic eye on the opinion polls. By implicitly rejecting the importance of an alignment with the working

---

* The book review in which he put forward this position led to the resignation from the editorial group of *Politics and Power* of almost all its women members, including Beatrix Campbell and Rosalind Coward (Coward 1981). Despite their disillusionment with the lack of feminism of the 'new', 'radical' politics as exemplified in the practice of the *Politics and Power* editorial group, the women editors are critical of Paul Hirst and others *only* on feminist grounds, and do not appear to countenance the possibility that Hirst's views on women might actually be logically consistent with his general political position. The problem is therefore defined as one of male chauvinism only, rather than of male chauvinism in the context of a general drift towards populist social democracy.

class, this new direction of socialist-feminism would increasingly lay itself open to absorption into social democratic structures.

In arguing that there is no necessary relationship between women's oppression and class oppression, some socialist-feminists themselves have perversely undermined the whole *raison d'être* of socialist-feminism. Today, as a result, the politically most militant feminist ground is usually occupied by those women who adhere to the radical separatist tradition. Radical feminist groups have determined contemporary feminist debates on male violence, lesbianism, pornography, and, indeed, on such issues as peace and race, to which traditionally socialist women gave more emphasis. Indeed socialist-feminism is now generally in a 'tailist' position, both to the mainstream socialist movement and to radical feminism. It is literally no person's land, and it is therefore not surprising that whatever controversy and debate remain have removed largely to academic feminist circles. Michèle Barrett recognizes this when she writes:

> 'Feminism in its non-socialist forms is immensely more powerful and influential than we are. The political resonance of feminism lies in the women's peace movement, in women's culture and literature, in women's increased public visibility in the media – and none of these can be captured for a distinctively socialist-feminist perspective in any easy way. Indeed it seems to me that our most pressing political project should be to try to win back what is effectively lost ground for socialist-feminist ideas in the women's movement.'
>
> (Barrett 1984a)

But what are these ideas? In recent times socialist-feminists have devoted most of their energy to attacking the organizations of the working class and the most important body of socialist theory, Marxism. Why then invoke socialist-feminism at all? It has become no more than what Michèle Barrett herself called in earlier days merely a statement of 'ethical goodwill' (Barrett 1980).

These developments are also apparent in the relationship beween feminism and the trades union movement at present. The undoubted male chauvinism of sections of organized labour, and their general failure to prioritize the interests of women members, have led some feminists to question the relevance of trades union organization for women and the centrality of working-class movements in the struggle for socialism (Phillips and Taylor 1980; Cockburn 1981; Cockburn 1983).

This is not to say that all feminists working within trades unions take up similar positions. Indeed, it may be that socialist-feminism as a theory sometimes diverges from the concerns of feminists whose major area of political work is in the unions. At all events, some socialist-feminists who have written about paid work and the unions have argued that the trades unions are 'male' in their methods of organization and that they represent 'male' as against female interests, indeed even, in Beatrix Campbell's words, that the labour movement is a 'men's movement' (Campbell 1984). A fairly strict dichotomous set of relationships has now been constructed along the following lines:

MALE ATTRIBUTES	FEMALE ATTRIBUTES
Hierarchical organization	Decentralized, open organization
Concentration on pay	Concentration on ancillary conditions, hours, conditions of work
Neglect of the social wage	Emphasis on the social wage
Belief in importance of strike action	Emphasis on other forms of industrial action, for example occupations and work-ins

There is little actual evidence that these differences do fall along biological sex lines, and the arguments are usually an extrapolation of work that has been done which shows the very different terms and conditions of male and of female work. It is argued that specific sex differences dominate the terms and conditions of the labour market and that consequently women have interests which are different and on occasion antagonistic to those of male workers. The feminists who put forward these arguments have not so far commented on how these sex-specific differences are affected, if at all, by race-specific characteristics. Indeed a similar argument in relation to race would be likely to be denounced as racist.

There are a number of problems with such an approach both at a theoretical and at a strategic level. At a theoretical level it fails to explain why women's labour takes a particular form other than its being a consequence of being female; in other words the relative position of women and men in the workforce is seen as an *exemplum* of male/female power relationships in general, which is a circular argument to say the least, and it also assumes that the interests of ruling-class and of working-class men necessarily coincide in relation to women. Particular difficulties arise in explaining tendencies that do not demonstrate this power relationship; for example, although as Irene Bruegel has argued, individual women may be more at risk of unemployment than individual men in the same situation, it may also be that women are unemployed for shorter periods of time and that overall there has been a shift towards women's employment, while the number of unemployed men continues to rise (Bruegel 1979).

At a policy level, the approach outlined above has led to increasingly open conflict between current 'left' demands in the trades unions, and what are held to be feminist policies. Two issues, the importance of manufacturing jobs, and the importance of free, collective bargaining, illustrate this conflict.

The Alternative Economic Strategy, which has been adopted by most sections of the labour movement as an alternative to the Conservative government's (and the previous Labour government's) monetary economic policies, argues, as part of its programme, for an expansion of jobs in the manufacturing sector. The AES is susceptible to several different interpretations, and we do not wish here to enter into a general debate about its practicability or otherwise, or whether it can or cannot be seen as a form of socialist transition strategy. We do wish to take issue with feminists (Hunt 1981; Coote 1981; Phillips 1983) who have criticized in particular the whole idea of the expansion of the manufacturing sector, on the grounds that it is of little relevance to women, since women, it is said, work primarily in the service sector, and therefore an increase in manufacturing would not create more jobs for women. We believe this argument to be dangerous and misleading for several reasons. It completely ignores the loss of women's jobs in manufacturing. In 1968 over half of all employed married women were in manual jobs; by 1981 this had fallen to one-third. The decline in manufacturing has meant that there are fewer jobs for the poorest women, and the increasing size of the service sector has not offset this. It is also in manufacturing that relative pay has declined most rapidly. For example, women sewing-machinists earned 98 per cent of the average wage for full-time women workers in 1968; now they receive only 76 per cent. In the same period, although overall the number of women with jobs has been rising, the proportion of women in part-time work has increased from 34 per cent in 1968 to 44 per cent in 1981. The effect of this has been to increase differentials between women workers and also to tend to cancel out the effect of women's earnings on the incomes of the poorest families. Thus in 1968 a family in the richest 10 per cent was approximately three times as well off as a family in the poorest 10 per cent, but by 1981 they were five times as well off (Joshi 1984).

Whatever the sex differences between men and women in the labour market – and we do not wish to underestimate these – it is simply wrong to suggest that women workers occupy some separate sphere and that their position can be understood and improved without analysing their relationship to general developments in the relations of production, particularly responses to tendencies of capital accumulation and the industrial reserve army.

Feminist critics of the AES have also tended to underemphasize the degree of exploitation of women in the private sector of the service industries, where the lowest-paid female jobs occur. It seems that the tyranny of old-style paid domestic labour (being a servant in a private house) as the only occupation for millions of working-class women is now being replaced by a new *demi-monde* of service for exploitative employers who rely upon poverty wages and degrading conditions to maintain high profit margins. In many areas we cannot talk about 'jobs' at all. What is being created is a casualized lump labour force – often drawn from the most exploited sections of the community, the immigrant groups – without protection or organization. These are also the employers who stand to make most out of the Tory policy of privatizing the public services. It is sad to note that although one of the first campaigns of the women's movement was for night cleaners, now, with large scale privatization of cleaning services, barely a word is mentioned on the subject in the feminist press.

There is nothing intrinsically noble about this private sector. The only groups it serves are private companies who escape the necessity of capital investment by exploiting the most vulnerable sections of labour. One response to these conditions, of which feminists are not unaware, has been to criticize trades unions for failing to organize and protect such workers. While there are certain steps that unions could take as well as important changes in trades union legislation that should be fought for (Weir and McIntosh 1982) it will still be almost impossible to organize workers in these conditions. This has nothing to do with the male chauvinism of the trades unions (although we certainly do not deny that this exists), it is an intrinsic difficulty. Rather than engage in the Sisyphean task of hoping to organize or control the employment of labour in such twilight zones, it will in the long run be in women's interest to argue rather for an expansion in the economy and equal entry to the most secure and best-paid jobs. What women urgently need is access to the better jobs in the mainstream of the British economy, not casualized work on its margins.

The arguments against free, collective bargaining have been put most forcefully by Beatrix Campbell in a series of articles (Campbell and Charlton 1978; Campbell 1980; see also Tomlinson 1984). Although she now appears to have abandoned her earlier assertion that an incomes policy is the answer to women's low pay, she still insists that women's low pay is a product of collective bargaining. In fact the periods of incomes policies, even the £6 flat rate during the period around July, 1975, did not make an appreciable difference to male and female earnings, and the convergence that was appearing had tailed off by 1975. More significantly, as demonstrated by the data we have cited on the effect of the decline of the manufacturing sector on women's jobs and earnings, women's average earnings relative to men are at least as likely to be affected by general trends within the economy as by some pre-given sex difference.

To assess the direct impact of collective bargaining on differentials the most instructive comparison is between the earnings of men and women workers who are covered by collective agreements and those who are not. A study quoted in *Women's Low Pay* (Thomson, Mulvey, and Farbman 1977), based on the New Family Survey, suggests that those covered by collective agreements earn more than those not so covered and that the earnings differential is greater for women than for men. Manual women workers covered by a collective agreement, including wage boards and councils, earn 18.6 per cent more than women not so covered, while for non-manual women employees the differential is 28 per cent. The figure for manual male workers is 12.2 per cent and that for non-manual male workers slightly negative.

The antagonistic relationship that has been set up between feminism and the trades union movement has been paralleled by a changing socialist-feminist analysis of the family. The early women's movement of around 1970 took as its question how the family was constituted within capitalism. What feminists then searched for was the mechanism or form of articulation between the family and its structures and the relations of production. This endeavour led to a number of different paths of enquiry: the domestic labour debate, the role of the state, particularly in the provision of welfare services, and the family wage discussion.

Many of these studies had as their starting point Engels's analysis in *The Origins of the Family, Private Property, and the State*. Engels's predictions that capitalism would emancipate women from their subordination within the family had patently, it seemed, not been fulfilled. Although women had entered into production, the family was flourishing, and wives and mothers still occupied a subordinate position. Feminists tried to explain this in a variety of ways, but two main trends in the argument have emerged. The first has increasingly seen the structures of relationships within the family itself as autonomous from the relations of production, and from one another. The second has treated the family as an autonomous structure within capitalism (but see Barrett and McIntosh 1982 for a more challenging approach).

The genesis of the first approach may be found in Juliet Mitchell's original essay in *New Left Review*, 'The longest revolution', written in 1966 (Mitchell 1984). In this she argued that the family must be analysed in terms of its component structures and functions. These, she said, were: production, reproduction, sexuality, and the socialization of children, a list based on Talcott Parsons's functionalist analysis of the family. In this essay Juliet Mitchell was much influenced by the work of Louis Althusser, and it was in part a study of ideology. Later, both feminists and others on the left began to concentrate on this area of ideology in response to perceived failure: why had the revolutionary fire of 1968 gone only so far before burning itself out? Why was sexual desire so 'unreconstructed'? The apparent failure of materialistic explanations prepared the ground for a study of the construction of subjectivity and of sexuality that increasingly removed these to a separate sphere.

Juliet Mitchell's work also pioneered the feminist reappropriation of psychoanalysis (Mitchell 1974), for it was natural that what began as an enquiry into ideology should look again at psychoanalysis. Althusser himself had been influenced by Jacques Lacan, and – perhaps paralleling a rather romantic view of sex and love – sexuality was increasingly seen by women as the 'core' structure of feminine identity.

The debate on psychoanalysis has been a highly sophisticated one. Our emphasis here is on the political implications of this discourse – or arguably, its lack of politics. In the late 1960s, a 'vulgar' Freudianism had currency which seemed to account for how little girls become women. In this version, psychoanalytic theory became not very different from 'socialization' or 'conditioning' theory, according to which the female infant, a blank page, gets stamped with 'the female role'. This corresponded to, and fitted in with, an idea of 'false consciousness' in Marxist terms, which itself began to be discredited. False consciousness, it began to be suggested, implied a vulgar, 'reflexionist' form of Marxism. It was an oversimplified and also an undemocratic model. It implied that the masses did not understand their objective conditions, and that a Leninist vanguard was needed to pull the wool from their eyes and rip apart the veil of their illusions. Increasingly the study of popular culture in particular gave validity and dignity to the idea that women and men invest in particular ideologies for good reasons. Ideology was no longer regarded as false consciousness, but as 'lived relations', as a subjective reality ultimately embedded in the unconscious.

More recently, Juliet Mitchell and Jacqueline Rose (Mitchell and Rose 1983) have argued that psychoanalysis, unlike conditioning theory, is *not* a theory of how little girls become 'feminine' (although it is still easiest to read *Psychoanalysis and Feminism* as such an account); on the contrary, what psychoanalysis is about is how 'little girls *never* become women' (Mitchell and Rose 1983), in other words it is about the failure of ideology. Femininity becomes a structure as flawed and unstable as the ego itself.

This idea, based as it is on a conception of a 'modernist' self that is fractured and ill at ease in the world, has, it has been argued, subversive implications. Some women writers have argued (although not always for the same reasons) that if modernist literature is a literature of estrangement and unease, then women are particularly well placed to be in touch with something that is excluded from the capitalist patriarchal order. Because of the construction of the gender difference, and women's complicated relationship to this, in theory there could be paths opened for the development of new kinds of identity for women.

The concept of the 'fractured self', however, questions the very possibility of a coherent identity, and this process of the deconstruction of the self could also be seen to question the very possibility of women uniting politically around their existence as 'women'. Rosalind Coward, on the other hand, has argued that even if gender identity is ultimately a fiction, there is a basis for a women's movement because the dominant cultural order *does* treat 'women' as a category (Coward 1981).

Juliet Mitchell acknowledges the political questions that have been raised about the implications of psychoanalytic theory. She recognizes, for example, that Lacan's work is often used in a very idealistic way and that what is needed is what was originally being sought, namely a theory of ideology in which to ground psycho-analysis, and she also stresses that while 'the psyche never directly reflects either the biological or the social – it is quite another thing to say that anatomy and society do not figure in the account' (Mitchell and Rose 1983). None the less, in the absence of a theory of the relationship between them, her insistence on the psychic 'necessity' (which is not even invariably borne out empirically) of particularly conservative versions of masculinity, femininity, and heterosexuality has the concrete effect of reinforcing a psychic determinism in which the iron law, in her own words, still holds: 'Phallic potency and maternity for men and women . . . come to stand for wholeness' (Mitchell 1984).

What we further object to about this formulation is the idealism of placing this 'necessity' entirely within the realm of the psychological, thereby depriving it of any material basis. It seems downright perverse to downplay the biological to the extent that Juliet Mitchell does, yet then to recreate a mirror image of biological determinism in the psychic sphere. Her formulation is also heterosexist, implying a negative evaluation of homosexuality on the grounds that it must necessarily constitute a denial of 'difference'. In addition, the 'necessity' of the twin 'ideals' of phallic potency/maternity denies the possibility that homosexuality might have the kinds of subversive implications allowed it theoretically in the whole idea of the 'fractured self' and the necessary incompleteness of gender identification implied in the assertion that we 'never' become feminine (or masculine).

Finally, the feminist enquiry into psychoanalysis does appear largely divorced from political practice, other than at the level of the therapeutic enterprise. We still feel that a questionable assumption has been built into many of the feminist writings and discussions of the creation of femininity, female subordination, and the construction of female sexuality. This widespread assumption is that if the core of women's subordination is sexual experience and sexual identity – *sexual* oppression, indeed – then the way to change that is *necessarily* by an intensified examination of that experience. Without wishing to denigrate the important role that the practice of psychoanalysis, and of 'feminist therapy', can play in helping individual women, we feel that there are other possibilities too, and that this is one of the areas in which radical feminism has been much stronger and has had a more powerful campaigning approach. To argue that the provision of refuges for battered women may do more to change consciousness than theorizations about sexuality is not to 'trivialize' sexuality; on the contrary, Women's Aid is a political response that precisely recognizes the importance of the sexual, of gender identity, and of sexual oppression.

Psychoanalytic theory, then, has claimed to elucidate the construction of ideologies, and it has been argued that it is the account we need of how the dominant ideologies become 'lived experience' or 'lived relations'. This, too, has been an important dimension of feminist theory. Initially the attempt was to account for the persistence of stereotypic constructions of gender and beliefs that women are inferior. This then widened into a cultural enterprise of the exploration of popular culture as it constructed femininity, and in recent years interesting work has been done on girls' and women's magazines and 'pulp romances', on pornography, and on fashion, as well as on film and the novel. A distinct feminist current within 'creative writing' has also emerged more strongly since the mid-1970s, and it is in this area alone that the experience of the lesbian, and of the black and immigrant woman, has been given due place.

The second approach, which treats the family as an autonomous structure within capitalism, has developed into what we describe as a form of materialist separatism. Increasingly the family has been seen by socialist-feminists as a discrete entity structured by specific historical and ideological forces. Such developments are in part the product of an increasing body of feminist work which provides a more complex understanding of the family, but it has also been fuelled at a theoretical level by critiques of Marxist functionalism. Arguments that there is a functional relationship between specific family forms of the privatized nuclear family and advanced capitalism have been criticized as tautological and mystifying in that they assume an idealized or generalized family form.

This criticism has some validity, but the effect of this anti-functionalist critique has been to sever the analysis of family relationships entirely from an analysis in terms of modes of production. As a consequence of this 'materialist separatism' the crucial political issue becomes the redistribution of power and income within the family rather than a challenge to the relations of production, which simultaneously confronts the structure of the family. This emphasis on distribution parallels the tendency we have already described in relation to women's work and the trades unions, that is, a concern with transferring resources from men as a section to women as a section, and is in a tradition of bourgeois economic and social policy which locates the issue as one of distribution rather than one of control of overall resources (ownership of the means of production.

Behind the social democratic policy reforms we have outlined above lurks what Lise Vogel calls the 'dual systems perspective' which, she argues, has been implicit in the socialist tradition from Engels through the Second International onwards:

> 'In essence, the dual systems perspective takes off from what appears to be obvious: divisions of labour and authority according to sex, the oppression of women, and the family. These phenomena are treated more or less as givens, analytically separable, at least in part, from the social relations in which they are embedded. The major analytical task is to examine the origin and development of the empirical correlation between sex divisions of labour and the social oppression of women. In general, it is women's involvement in the sex division of labour, and their direct relationship – of dependence and of struggle – to men, rather than their insertion in overall social reproduction, that establishes their oppression. At the same time, women's oppression and the sex division of labour are seen to be tied to the mode of production dominant in a given society, and to vary according to class. These latter factors enter the investigation as important variables which are, however, essentially external to the workings of women's oppression.'
>
> (Vogel 1984)

The family policy put forward by Anna Coote, for example, does not challenge the separate spheres argument, rather it argues in essence for recognition of these separate spheres and in so doing legitimizes the privatization of familial relations, an aspect of the nuclear family consistently criticized by the earlier women's movement. Criticizing the 'male' character of the AES she writes:

> 'Patriarchal politics begin from and are focused upon one relatively limited area of life: production . . . . Our starting point for an alternative strategy would change. Rather than asking in the

first instance: "how can we regenerate industry in order to create full employment?" we might begin with a different question, such as "how shall we care for and support our children?"'

(Coote 1981)

Whilst this analysis may provide a strong moral critique of existing relations of production and of the sexual division of labour it contains no strategy of class struggle. Indeed it becomes much easier to separate feminism from the labour movement and for the private virtues of family life to be emphasized against the encroachments of an uncaring state and the demands of the labour market.

We do not wish to invoke 'class struggle' as some antidote to the reformism and indeed the latent conservatism of much recent feminist thought. We do, however, believe that to set men against women in this way for a larger slice of the existing, *non-expanding* cake is quite wrong. Without a transformation of the relations of production some gains for women may be made but they will be partial and will reflect existing class and racial inequalities.

This parcelling up of feminism into a number of discrete policy demands has also facilitated the entry of women into the Labour Party. Interestingly, the same process occurred after the Second World War when the British feminist movement was incorporated into the social democratic programme of the Labour Party (Wilson 1980).

Throughout the period we have been discussing, socialist-feminists were searching for an alliance with progressive men, and many men appeared to be of like mind. The influential document of this alliance was *Beyond the Fragments*, published in 1979.

Perhaps the most important effect of this book was that it acted as a bridge for many women between the women's movement and the Labour Party. By asserting the strength of feminism and its relevance to socialism the way was paved for a re-entry into socialist politics. The Labour Party seemed particularly appropriate, as at least by tradition its federal structure could provide an organizational vehicle for the bringing together of the fragments. Of course, in fact the Labour Party was probably the organization on the left most removed from the local grass-roots campaigning that *Beyond the Fragments* extolled. Its emphasis on electoral politics at the expense of any mass, extra-parliamentary action was not only a tenet of faith, but also led consistently to a phenomenon we would call political substitutionalism, that is the tendency to substitute the Labour Party for mass organization. One expression of this has been the hostility to the idea of black sections within the Labour Party. Women have been able to rely on the traditional women's sections, but have so far lost arguments for positive action within the party itself. More significantly, women's activity within the Labour Party either in women's sections or in the growing number of women's committees, has eclipsed activity within the women's movement itself. Of course, part of the attraction of the Labour Party for contemporary socialist-feminists was that the party was enfeebled by its reliance on electoralism and it was possible in many local parties for the 'new forces' to become the majority. This was especially marked in local elections, and for the first time in many years left-wing majorities have gained control of local boroughs, have included at least some women councillors, and have usually had some commitment to women's rights.

Therefore, in perhaps an unexpected way, municipal socialism, something more associated with wash-houses and council housing than with the politics of subjectivity, has become a key area of women's organization and advance.

While women's committees have been able to draw on fifteen years' experience of the women's movement, women involved at councillor and officer level have had to fight for budgets, create forms of organization, and determine priorities on a hand-to-mouth basis, and with no blueprints. This has naturally led to uneven developments and it is difficult at this early stage to detail clear tendencies.

We would suggest, however, that where women's committees have been able to supplement or initiate policies within a strategic framework which has clear class priorities this has been more successful than purely reactive strategies which have conceived the women's committee as merely a source of 'pump priming' for grass-roots organization. So, policies designed to promote equal opportunities in the workforce by measures such as improved maternity and nominated career leave, provision of workplace nurseries, job sharing, and affirmative action programmes have had real success and have, by and large, been actively supported by NALGO, the local government officers' union. Within the community the GLC strategy on child care has resulted in a considerable increase in child-care provision in London which has been of inestimable benefit to all working women. At an ideological level, and at the financial level, the commitment of women's committees to anti-racism has provided an important lead for feminism and has facilitated the mobilization of black women.

In other words, when women's committees have been most sensitive to the articulation of sexual oppression within class relations they have also been most successful in mobilizing women, in meeting needs, and in challenging racist and sexist ideologies. What we seek to emphasize is the importance of always understanding the articulation or relationship between sex and class, and not, as Hobsbawm and others have done, reducing women to an anodyne and undifferentiated mass – 'all women'. The precise nature of this relationship needs to be studied and cannot be deduced *a priori*; it is historically constructed within the laws of capitalist development and can be easily distorted by ultra-leftism and by right-wing reformism, and very often by the two coming in tandem.

The approach we have tried to outline is based on a concept of class unity as against an electoral coalition in which women are but one of many sectional interests. By this we do not mean 'class unity' in the traditional sense in which it was used in the 1930s, to oppose a popular front or broad alliances on principle. What we are arguing is that this populism, as it currently seeks to deal specifically with the challenge posed by feminism, is vacuous, since it has *no* strategy for women. In fact it is idealist, since effectively it can only hope for a change in male attitudes to improve the position of women.

Class unity is not a simple matter of building an electoral alliance around certain policy demands. Unity, and the understanding of difference, is created in the context of struggle. There can be no better example of this than the miners' strike. The mobilization of women from the mining community has made women more visible in political action than they have been for many years. The 10,000 women who marched in the 'Women Against Pit Closures' march on 11 August, 1984 were participating in the biggest women's demonstration held in Britain since the suffragettes. The largest women's rally in recent years was organized by Barnsley women in support of the miners. The accounts of their experiences show very clearly and movingly this unity in action:

> 'As we all stood on the stage the sight and sound of all the women singing, chanting, and shouting filled the hall. Different accents, different banners – rows and rows of them; Welsh, Kent, Durham, Barnsley, Sheffield, Staffordshire, went on for ever it seemed. Both on the stage and off, women were crying with emotion . . . . In this country we aren't just separated as a class. We are separated as men and women. We, as women, have not been encouraged to be actively involved in trade unions and organizing. Organization has always been seen as belonging to men. We are seen to be the domesticated element of the family. This for too many years has been the role expected of us. I have seen the change coming for years and the last few weeks has seen it at its best. If the government thinks its fight is only with the miners they are sadly mistaken. They are now fighting men, women and families.'
>
> (Barnsley Women 1984)

Similarly the specific support amongst the black and the lesbian gay community for the miners has created links and understanding that seemed impossible before the strike began. The NUM was the only large union to support feminist demands for positive discrimination within the Labour Party at the 1984 conference.

It is difficult to summarize the achievements of the women's liberation movement in the last fifteen years, but we believe that the ideological impact of feminism has so far been much greater than any changes in women's material position. For this reason we emphasize the importance of women's economic demands. This is not to say that we disdain the ideological, nor to deny that the dominant construction of sexuality is exploitative of women; rather we suggest that feminism has been more successful in challenging the ideological than the economic contradictions in bourgeois society. Unfortunately the emphasis on ideology and its subjective operation in the individual has too often meshed in with the emphasis on individual change that was always a strand within women's liberation with the result that personal life styles more amenable, at least within the middle class, to change than late monopoly capitalism appear to be the main target of feminism. Of course it is important if individual men clean lavatories and change nappies (and such changes are easiest to effect in better-off, more leisured families) but structural change is required as well. Meanwhile the position particularly of working-class women, both with and without paid work, and of black women is deteriorating rapidly. Women are becoming the new urban poor. (Beatrix Campbell, in *Wigan Pier Revisited* (1984), gives a graphic account of women's poverty in the 1980s, but argues – we believe mistakenly – that women have nothing to gain from working-class movements as presently constructed.) The loss of full-time employment, cuts in social services and public housing, and the decline in the real value of state benefits are restricting the opportunities of many young women in a way not seen since the 1930s. So women are caught in another pinch of the contradiction. While women's right to equality is increasingly (if grudgingly) recognized, the material basis for equality and independence is denied. This perhaps explains how things seem to be getting both better and worse at the same time, and why so-called Thatcherism does not incorporate a clear call for women to return to the home.

In this situation, far from women distancing themselves from working-class movements we would argue that the best conditions for change for women lie in a challenge to capital and mass campaigning for a socialist government. The key issue for women is an expansion of the economy and the creation of secure, full-time jobs for women. To ensure this, the two pillars of a free employment programme for women must be on the one hand anti-discrimination and positive action programmes, and on the other the expansion of socialized services, particularly collective child care and the caring services for the sick and the elderly. This does not exclude demands for part-time work or job sharing, but these will only secure greater rights for women workers if they exist in the context of a right to full, secure employment and also the independent right of women to a 'disaggregated' income within the social security system, instead of the present assumption within the system of female dependence on men.

Such a strategy, we believe, creates the most favourable context for challenging male chauvinism, male violence, and homophobia. It does not mean that these issues have to be left until after the AES is implemented, or until 'after the revolution'. They must be addressed now, but we must also have an understanding of the general conditions which will be most conducive to winning our particular demands. Such demands are in the interests of the working class as a whole. At a material level they will provide for a dramatic improvement in living standards; and in conjunction with particular struggles against expressions of male power and supremacy, they will create the basis for relationships between and within the sexes that are not overdetermined by a vicious system of gender difference, heterosexual supremacy, male domination, and female subordination.

Finally, such changes can only be won through class struggle. It is not and never can be solely a matter of inserting policies into parliamentary programmes; what will be required is a substantive shift in the balance of class forces to pave the way for a revolutionary transformation of society. Women have a unique role to play in this struggle and are in a good position to challenge both the economism and the ultra-leftism which has characterized the left. In fact there is no other option. The intensification of class struggle in Britain will leave the women's movement high and dry on the shores of bourgeois democracy unless we can once again grasp our revolutionary potential.

PART III ◆ Women's Experience and Feminist Consciousness

7 ◆ Gayness and liberalism

Introduction

I dislike this article for what now seems a caricatured account of
parts of my past and of my lover of the 1960s, and am including it
only because it does recall a period when the attitude of many
feminists towards lesbianism was either suspicious or romanticized.
It was a polemic against the radical feminist view that 'any woman
can be a lesbian', but I am still astonished that some women read it
as an argument that bisexuality does not exist (I simply queried it as
a *political* position) or that homosexuals are 'born not made' (I was
arguing that although they are socially constructed, homosexuality is
not *just* a matter of freely willed, conscious choice). The article was
an early, and not very successful, attempt to integrate polemical with
experiential writing.

Gayness and liberalism

Ever since the Bristol Women's Conference it has seemed important
to members of the Red Rag Collective that there should be some
discussion of the role of gay women in the women's movement.
Since I am myself gay it's natural that I should have thought a lot
about this, but although I don't think my personal life gives me any
particular right to speak on the subject, in another way I feel that
perhaps I do have a responsibility at least to try to explain why I, as a
Marxist, am not a radical feminist, and yet do at the same time feel it
is important to see homosexuality as more than a mere matter of
private choice. I decided to begin by describing some of my personal
experiences not because I want to exhibit myself, but in the hope
that this might make clearer why a liberal attitude to homosexuality
isn't enough, and in fact is insulting to homosexuals. There is

increasing liberalism towards homosexuals not only in the whole of society but also in left parties and groupings, and within the women's movement it is at a superficial level very readily accepted indeed, but this makes it harder rather than easier to confront.

I grew up during the late 1950s, the affluent society of Macmillan's 'You never had it so good'. My own home was far from affluent, yet my mother and grandmother with whom I lived, though reduced to genteel poverty and letting rooms by a series of disasters, divorce, ill health, and bad luck, operated on assumptions of privilege left over from the grandeur of my grandmother's past. She lived on memories of country houses, 'servants', the Indian Empire, and a luxurious Edwardian heyday.

Their unhappiness made me ill at ease and peculiar. I couldn't cope with the contrast between them and the liberal, academic, private school I had been sent to, where the other girls came from the families of well off London intellectuals. These girls were sophisticated and many of them had boyfriends when my fantasy life still centred largely around girls and women. Partly because I was a social misfit I came to feel I was a sexual misfit too; and this came to seem very exciting, strange, and evil. To be attracted to another girl seemed unmentionable, horrifying. The theme of the homosexual as damned I also came across in the books I read (for example, French nineteenth-century literature and novels). These seemed to confirm a vision of myself as satanic, doomed, and alone. Yet of course this pose gave me a certain feeling of superiority. At least I would never be ordinary.

Other people sometimes react to homosexuals in this way too. Because homosexuality faces them with something they find threatening they can cease to see you as human, and instead you become sinister; disturbing because you seem, whether purposely or not, someone who doesn't respond or conform to the deep 'natural' laws of family and procreation. To give an example of the way in which homosexuality is still equated with evil and madness, the *Sunday Times* only a few months ago (19 August, 1973) ran a sensational article on terrorism which set out to prove that all terrorists were mad, mentally sick perverts: 'In Britain, more than one member of extremist organizations . . . has been convicted of offences involving sexual abnormality.'

Sexual confusion

I progressed to the ritual-ridden world of Oxford student society. There was a certain amount of furtive sex along with the walnut cake for tea and six o'clock sherry parties (it really was like that). At school I'd been totally isolated; in the more unreal world of Oxford I found it easier to achieve the semblance of relationships, but I could never feel at ease or come to grips with myself because the competition for social and intellectual success made it impossible for me ever to know what I really wanted.

When I first arrived I was shocked to discover that what most of the women wanted was marriage. I was really stunned by this, my brain being the only aspect of myself I'd ever been taught to respect or feel positive about; and also I'd somehow got hold of Simone de Beauvoir's book *The Second Sex*, and she did after all, whatever we think of her now, rightly argue the necessity for women to fight for economic independence. And in a way I was right – though what I wanted, not white tulle and wedding bells, but a vague, imaginary kind of success, to be on a par with the men, was no better. Anyway, I think it was really only possible to succeed in competition with the men if you, as a girl, had terrific self confidence and could succeed both as a man and as a sex object.

I told some of the women in my college that I thought I was a lesbian and was upset and humiliated when they reacted either by brushing it aside as a phase, or else by looking on me as neurotic rather than sinful. This attitude of 'you are sick' rather than 'you are wicked' was actually the more undermining of the two.

This is still the most usual attitude in society today. In this scheme of things the homosexual is an inferior being unable by reason of his or her hangups to achive a relationship with a member of the opposite sex. A homosexual is to be pitied for he or she is less than the 'normal' man or women. As Anthony Storr, well-known psychiatrist and apologist for sexism, puts it: 'Lesbians do not know what they are really missing' (Storr 1964). This view lacks the positive strength of wickedness. I certainly felt I was ugly, awkward, wrong; but I was no longer magnificent and tortured ('Evil, be thou my good') just a squalid social casualty, victim of my socially embarrassing background. If only I'd had a Daddy, everything would have been okay.

Men did take me out, of course, and I told some of them too about my 'problem'. They, understandably, were even less able to help than my friends, for they were either alarmed or aroused by the information – interestingly, they *all* saw it in terms not of me, but of their own virility.

I'd hung the label 'lesbian' round my neck before I came to university because I was so obsessed by my feelings about women, yet what that label did once I was there was prevent me developing any understanding of my feelings towards men. Because I could only have men, I could only want women. Men attracted me sexually, but I hated the relationship they expected to have with me, in which I was expected to be socially passive yet responsive, vivacious and charming, putting on an act or entertainment for them the whole time. I think I should have liked to have men who were friends, but this was not possible, for me at any rate, so I ended up by being what was then called tarty. I could roll about on sofas and in punts with men I hardly knew – and usually didn't want to know – because that was satisfactorily unreal and unimportant. And while I was doing it I was *always* saying to myself inside my head 'I'm really a lesbian' – whatever that meant, since I'd never had a complete sexual relationship with a woman.

When I did finally meet and start an affair with another woman I immediately became very dependent on her, because, believing as I did that homosexuals were all doomed to misery (since that is what you read in all books on the subject) a happy relationship was something to cling to as hard as you could.

Sexual typecasting

We entered the 'swinging sixties' together and became the 'white negroes' of a rather pleasure-seeking, but mildly political, group of academics in the Midlands. What she and I gave each other that was positive (and there was a lot) was always subtly distorted by our living in this liberal, heterosexual world. I did not, in the beginning, see her as male, but everyone else did, largely because she had a higher-status job than me. The men she worked with gave her recognition as an honorary man. She could fancy birds and drink pints, but I remained 'feminine'. Yet I still preferred women, or could only find a woman, so I was the woman's woman, which made me the lowest of the low. This world, where we imagined we were freed from the domination of men, was shot through with male assumptions and male values. And it was the men, I think, who liked our company; most of the wives and girlfriends either saw us as manless and therefore to be pitied, or else a special kind of rival and thus not to be trusted. But we were so grateful for being accepted that we never even noticed the price we were paying (and nor did anyone else, since there was certainly nothing deliberate or malicious about all of this).

This then was our place in the Permissive Society – to make our friends feel liberated and progressive by 'accepting' us, without their having to feel any challenge to their own sexual identities.

We had a second, separate social life centering on the 'gay scene' in London.There we were also typecast, as a stable couple, in a group in which stability was much prized; and here too we were pressured to play the roles of male and female, 'butch' and 'femme', even though in the class-conscious scene such role playing was much more open and exaggerated among working-class than among middle-class women; the more middle-class you were the more you emphasized equality and sharing – but only in the way 'straight' middle-class couples do. That was still the standard we measured ourselves against.

This scene too was drenched in liberalism. That is, we *said* it was OK for everyone to do their own thing; you could sleep with whom you wanted and you shouldn't really be jealous; a good relationship was an open relationship; you shouldn't make moral judgments about sexual behaviour – an extreme of liberalism that clashed violently with the wish to 'succeed' as a stable lesbian couple, and often led to hysterical exaggerations of feeling, while at the same time a kind of shallowness in a world from which children were almost wholly absent so that what is usually the *material* reason for fidelity was missing and gave an air of unreality to the scenes and dramas.

Many of us were obsessed with clothes and our image. There was one particular group of women who seemed to associate together on the basis of all being very rich and beautiful. They all had affairs with one another – a tiny, incestuous clique. I remember a party of theirs we went to in a Dolphin Square flat where there was no furniture at all except an enormous bed surrounded by mirrors and hundreds of bottles and jars of make-up and scent – just like something out of a movie.

For lesbianism, while remaining unacceptable, can still become a mask of assurance to hide behind. I myself did not in fact have many 'extra-marital' affairs. I was on the whole timid and faithful, and hid behind my lover, while feeling more and more resentful of her. We developed many of the worst features of a 'straight' couple. Having lived through this I am suspicious of women in the movement who proclaim lesbianism as a solution to sexism in men, for lesbianism too can be sexist. When either of us did have an affair, these relationships instead of challenging the nature of our coupledom actively reinforced our mutual dependence – sometimes we even ganged up on a lover, whose belittlement or destruction strengthened us. Of course this was never deliberate. But outside affairs are very far from necessarily challenging the dependence of the couple, or encouraging personal autonomy. Indeed, a whole literature has grown up of 'swingers' (couples who exchange partners on weekends or go in for group sex) and 'horizontal enrichment' (i.e. affairs on the side) the *stated* purpose of which is to strengthen the 'open marriage'.

Along with our friends we drifted towards Marxism as the 1960s wore on. This was to begin with a largely intellectual conviction, but when the women's movement arose we at first rejected it as petit bourgeois. This at least was what we said, but I think it must have been more a result of our feeling cut off from the experience of most women, cut off perhaps from ourselves as women. With the gay movement we did on the other hand immediately identify, and this led to great changes in our lives. We separated and formed new relationships and I was somehow freed to be politically active.

I think one reason for this was that in its beginnings the great, explosive, positive thing about gay liberation was the feeling that there were hundreds of homosexuals who were not afraid to assert their homosexuality. It no longer had to be discreetly hidden. That was a truly liberating experience, and although perhaps gay liberation was essentially a liberal movement, its slogans 'gay is good' and 'gay is proud' are important in challenging the oppression and repression of homosexuals. Gay people really are oppressed, although their oppression is a peculiar one since it rests partly on the possibility of always remaining hidden and invisible. This was the reason for the stress on 'coming out' in gay liberation.

The lesson to myself of my life during the 1960s is that I could be tolerated as a homosexual provided I could be stereotyped. That way I did not challenge society, by wanting for instance to bring up children. One of the Dolphin Square women I mentioned earlier did transgress this unwritten rule by privately adopting a baby. The welfare officer concerned discovered her lesbian relationship and it was only because the adoption was a private one and had already gone over more or less all the legal hurdles that it was not reversed, and indeed the welfare officer did try to bring a court action to do this.

Mothers who subsequently become gay not infrequently have their children removed from them. It is as if women are so deeply repressed sexually, that should they themselves try to divorce their sexuality from their reproductive function, they call down a terrible retribution from society. Indeed the whole way in which lesbians are treated illustrates the extent to which women still are not seen as having a sexuality of their own. Even lesbian pornography is produced for men; to see female sexuality as autonomous would presumably be too threatening.

Bisexuality

Occasionally, when we lived in the Midlands, we did sleep with men, and that made us feel even more liberal and liberated.

I want to say more about bisexuality, since to be bisexual is perhaps to reach the high point of sexual liberalism. It's important to recognize that bisexuality is ambiguous politically as well as sexually.

A distinction, in my view, must be made between bisexuality in the 'future society' and bisexuality in the present. If we see sexuality as a line drawn from pure homosexuality at one end to pure heterosexuality at the other (the way Kinsey saw it) we might suppose that in a freer society than ours more people would be nearer the centre of the line and fewer driven to the extremes at either end. And although this two-dimensional view of sexuality perhaps blots out some of its complexities and the differences would be greater than this, even as things are, many, perhaps even the majority of us are capable of being attracted by individuals of both sexes. Ideally perhaps we should all be able to relate sexually to a much wider variety of people of both sexes and all ages, but this remains an ideal for the future, rather than a present reality.

Individuals on the left who do not wish to condemn homosexuals sometimes express the view that people should be free to choose whether they are heterosexual, bisexual, or homosexual, or even say that people are actually able to do so. This is liberal because it is based on incorrect ideas about the possibility of free choice. It is simply not true that these three categories offer the same possibilities and I don't see how they could as things are. Heterosexuality *must* remain the norm so long as we retain the narrow nuclear family. In our society the nuclear family harnesses sexuality and reproduction firmly together. This disciplines men, women, and children, and is one reason why homosexuality, in challenging this, is seen as threatening and subversive. It *is* subversive, it *does* challenge authoritarian gender roles, and gay men or women, sexist though they can be and mystified as they often are, do objectively have less stake in the *status quo* than adults who are harnessed to a family in its present depleted form. The family man is the reliable worker, and homosexuals in spite of increasing tolerance frequently find it impossible to 'come out' at work – i.e. where they depend economically upon capitalism. Who, for example, has ever met a gay health visitor, shop steward, judge, or secretary?

And in spite of more tolerance, gays are still to a great extent relegated to the rather dingy underworld of the 'gay ghetto', where the worst features of straight society are exaggerated – sexual exploitativeness and competition for example – or else exist in secrecy. For secret homosexuality is perhaps the most common of all – married men who 'cruise' when they're away from home; married women who sleep together when their husbands are away – homosexuality as a substitute, as wholly alienated, or as co-opted and contained.

Sexual consumerism

Bisexuality is different again, as it exists at present. It has no social recognition, no 'role', and is often used as a cover-up for something else. It usually means a secondary liking for one sex in the context of a primary relationship with the other sex. It can be a kind of sexual consumerism in individuals who are largely straight but want more and better of everything, orgasms included; or worse, it can be a way of avoiding 'coming out' and confronting the fact that you are actually homosexual; it is often used as a put-down to gay people (if you were really liberated you'd be bisexual). Bisexuality is the permissive society's solution to homosexuality, and the extent to which it can be political is therefore very limited.

I feel that some women who have hitherto been heterosexual do see in an exploration of sexual relationships with other women a way of both personal and political development. While this is not to be put down, I think it would be a mistake to see it as a solution, and it may even be a very different *experience* from that of women who have always felt they were gay. For example, the following quotation is taken from a *Guardian* article on women's liberation (29 November, 1973). The words are those of a young woman being interviewed:

'Not long ago I made the intellectual decision to become bisexual. I've had sexual relationships with two women, both of whom were close friends anyway. It's slower and more relaxed with women – more like a mirror image – with men the emphasis is always on doing so it's different with women . . . . I'm in love with a bloke just now.'

My own experience in no way relates to what this woman is saying, since I have always experienced my sexual feelings for women as more, not less, violent, compelling, and active than my feelings for men.

But obviously, each individual develops differently. I am not saying that one set of feelings is 'correct' or that some gays are more equal than others. Lesbianism cannot, however, solve the problems of women under capitalism. At the Bristol Women's Liberation Conference in the summer of 1973 there was an entertainment on the Saturday night – the Sister Show – which suggested that lesbianism is the highest expression of sisterhood and the ultimate way forward. Some women were upset by this and by a blanket anti-men stance that ignored or rejected class struggle. On Sunday afternoon there was a debate about this. While it was going on, I happened to want a cup of coffee and on my way to the canteen I passed a small room on the doorway of which was pinned a notice saying 'gay women's meeting'. Looking in I recognized women I had seen or known in gay liberation, women who lived out homosexuality before the women's movement decided it was respectable. These women presumably did not see that debate about the Sister Show as relevant to them, and I feel there must be something wrong with this very loudly voiced and ideological gayness if women whose first ident-ification is as gay find it irrelevant.

In any case, the point isn't whether we should be nice to men and help liberate them while we're all fighting capitalism, nor whether we should kick them out of the present and future societies altogether. The real point is the liberation of all women to find their own autonomous sexuality.

Having seen the seamy side of a world in which everyone is officially 'normal', I could never want everyone to be officially gay, so that straight people were hidden out of sight in an underworld, or cut off from their sexuality altogether. Those on the left who assert that this is what all homosexual activists do want are simply wrong, or feeling threatened. In claiming that homosexuality is a form of bourgeois decadence they are confusing cause and effect. The life I led in the 1960s was decadent, not because I am gay, but because all bourgeois life is in a state of decadence, and gay people are the poseurs, the camp jesters, the extreme manifestation of that decadence. And to say that there will be no homosexuals under socialism also seems very unlikely to be true, since a socialist revolution presupposes an upsurge of energy, and a release of all kinds of feeling, as happened in Russia for a few years, not more repression and stultification. Obviously in a truly socialist society there would be a much wider variety of possible relationships, not a blanket imposition of one particular kind.

I'm not sure why the traditional left has got caught up in these puritanical myths, nor why many of them seem to believe that no working-class people are gay, which is very far from being the case. They are just more oppressed and repressed than middle-class homosexuals.

I have experienced homosexuality as a romantic ideal, and as a prison. It is only during the past few years that I have been able even to begin to experience it as a form of freedom. I do not want lesbianism distorted into some kind of ideal in the women's movement or anywhere else. I simply want us all to fight to free ourselves so that we can apprehend our real feelings more fully, whether we are straight or gay.

8 ◆ Psychoanalysis: psychic law and order?

Introduction

I was surprised and distressed that some feminists read this article as an attack on psychoanalysis both in its feminist and its non-feminist manifestations. I had intended simply to raise what I found interesting – and troubling – aspects of the use of Freudian theory by feminists. In retrospect I can see that to question the politics of this project was likely to prove provocative, but I still believe that the questions raised are legitimate, and they remain unanswered.

Again, some of the most interesting questions about the relationships between psychoanalysis and feminism are only touched on or hinted at in this article; in particular the biological basis of gender difference. Janet Sayers's *Biological Politics* (1982) is an important contribution to this question. Like her, while rejecting the position taken up by Ernest Jones, Karen Horney, and others in the psychoanalytic community in the 1920s (for a lucid account of their work, see Mitchell 1974 and Mitchell and Rose 1983), I find strange the complete rejection of biology characteristic not only of Juliet Mitchell but of socialist-feminism generally (see Jaggar 1983). In the work of both Juliet Mitchell and Nancy Chodorow, despite important differences between them, there does seem to be a tendency to develop a social constructionist theory of gender development that becomes as functionalist and inescapable as the biology they reject. In their theories men and women do develop psychically in very different ways, along the lines of conservative gender stereotypes:

'The castration complex is not about women, nor men, but a danger, a horror to both – a gap that has to be filled in differently by each. In the fictional ideal type this will be for the boy by the illusion that a future regaining of phallic potency will replace his totality; for a girl this will be achieved by something psychically the same: a baby. Phallic potency and maternity – for men and women – come to stand for wholeness.'

(Mitchell 1984:308)

It is clear from this passage that these are meant to be ideal types, not 'reality', yet there remains something both odd and profoundly troubling about a theoretical position that emphatically rejects biology yet recreates symbolic universals whose imperatives appear equally inescapable, a peculiar form of philosophical idealism. Also, as Mary McIntosh has suggested (1981), external social pressure as much as, or more than, internalized feminine identity casts women in the role of nurturant carers, and in some circumstances the role may make women feel less, not more, feminine (see Finch and Groves 1983).

Juliet Mitchell's analysis of the demise of the patriarchal family is close to that of 'The British women's movement'. However, she reaches the opposite conclusion in arguing for two separate strategems rather than one integrated one.

Psychoanalysis: psychic law and order?

Introduction

What are the political implications of psychoanalysis for feminists? What follows is an attempt to explore some of my own doubts whether the psychoanalytic path taken by many feminists and Marxists in recent years is really as fruitful as is claimed. Nor am I convinced that the *politics* of this theoretical position have really been thought through in any coherent way.

I am aware that I am taking up an unpopular position in questioning this new orthodoxy, and that my criticisms will be open to the charge that my stance is purely negative – the implication being that there is no point, or one is not justified, in criticizing the use of psychoanalysis unless one has something better to offer in its place. But although I, on the whole, think that a positive view is preferable, this cannnot always be the only or the overriding imperative. In any case the debate around ideas should not be seen as negative, and I see this piece as inviting a debate that I hope will be taken up in the pages of *Feminist Review* and perhaps elsewhere.

Freud

Although I would agree that all accounts of 'what Freud really said' are themselves interpretations – because of the contradictions and gaps in his own writings – I shall begin with a brief outline of some aspects of Freudian theory in order to point up what I see as certain ambiguities. A fuller and far more adequate (although rather densely written) account of the theoretical controversies surrounding Freud and Lacan may be found in 'Psychoanalysis and the Cultural Acquisition of Sexuality and Subjectivity' by Steve Burniston, Frank Mort, and Christine Weedon (1978).

Freud's work offers an explanation of the creation of individual identity based on the child's changing relationship to its own body (and particularly its sexual impulses, or drives), the early discovery of the boundary between 'self' and 'not self', and the limitations imposed on desire by reality. For Freud, the individual is socially constructed, albeit on a biological basis. At the beginning of its life the infant is dominated by the 'pleasure principle' and has virtually no ego or conscious self as we understand it. This initial state is constantly modified by the incessant demands of reality, and it is this that creates what Freud came to call the ego.

Although the ego is the organizing and rationalizing part of the psyche, and although it is the most integrated part of the 'self' it remains the site of struggle between the pleasure demands of the id or unconscious and the reality demands of the external world. It remains defensive, fluctuating and contradictory, and parts of it also remain cut off from consciousness; so that in the adult there is an ego that has in many ways mastered or come to terms with reality, yet this adult psyche still consists also of an id of which a large part consists of childish, repressed desires. These remain infantile because they have not been modified by the demands of reality, but have been dealt with in early life by being repressed – made unconscious – and thus placed beyond the reach of reality. Parts of the unconscious may however 'return' in certain circumstances. This notion of an unconscious hinterland to the 'personality' (for want of a better word), that somehow contains unresolved conflicts and wishes, explains our often irrational behaviour as adults, our own internal sense of conflict and contradiction, inappropriate feeling states, and neurotic symptoms and dreams.

In his discussion of the development of identity Freud placed primary emphasis on the body and the role played in particular by the child's biological sex. For Freud the ego was a bodily ego; and since the infant was for Freud essentially a pleasure seeker, and since the child's bodily and soon enough specifically genital sensations provide him with his greatest sources of pleasure, sexuality and ego must be complexly bound together. In the satisfaction of his needs the child is dependent upon others, usually primarily his mother, and a need for what the mother can give him eventually develops into a feeling with a momentum of its own: love. The relationship between the satisfaction of sensual needs and this love for another being leads directly in Freud's view to that love being eroticized. Indeed it is *because* of this that the child's sexual feelings can be directed towards another human being; otherwise he would remain locked within masturbatory auto-eroticism.

The infant initially loves his mother in a dual and symbiotic relationship. His feeding relationship with her breast was described by Freud as the prototype of all erotic satisfactions, and the bliss of the hunger-satisfied child asleep at the breast as reminiscent of the bliss of the satisfied lover asleep on the breast of his beloved. The crisis of the child's infant erotic life comes later with the Oedipus complex. By the age of three or four the child has realized that he does not have his mother all to himself, but shares her with another, his father, who has more comprehensive and explicitly sexual access to her. Thus he is caught in the most painful of love triangles, since he also loves his father.

Threats of castration as a punishment for masturbation take on a new and terrifying meaning. Not only has he by this time seen the female genital, and thus realized that some individuals *are* 'castrated', but the castration threat is interpreted as an expression of the father's jealousy. The little boy has both a narcissistic *and* realistic attachment to his genital, so in order to preserve it he renounces his sexual love for his mother and instead he *identifies* with his father:

> 'the authority of the father . . . is introjected into the ego, and there it forms the nucleus of the super-ego which takes over the severity of the father and perpetuates the prohibition against incest.'

(Freud 1977:319)

So far, it is the development of the little boy that has been discussed. Freud at first described the Oedipus complex in terms of the little boy and assumed that the little girl's development was the same in reverse. Later he recognized that the development of the little girl is both more complicated and more obscure. The little boy retains the same love object – a woman – throughout his life; his primary sexual organ is and remains the penis. The little girl, on the other hand, has to achieve a change of both organ and object. She, like the baby boy, begins life with an attachment to the breast and hence to the mother; yet she must transfer her affections to her father/men. The only sexual organ of which she is aware (according to Freud, although here he was challenged by other psychoanalysts in the 1920s) is the clitoris: 'the little girl is a little man': yet she must transfer her sexual excitability from clitoris to vagina.

So Freud was forced to the conclusion that the Oedipus complex in girls is different from the boy's experience. The little boy's Oedipus complex is dissolved or 'smashed' when he gives up his love for his mother and identifies with paternal authority in order to avoid the dreaded retaliation of castration. But the little girl does not fear castration because she *is* castrated; this recognition for her initiates rather than demolishes the Oedipus complex. Only then can she move from the dual relationship with her mother into the triangular relationship in which she takes her father as the object of her desire, giving up her wish for the penis and replacing it by a wish for the baby the father could give her.

Three important consequences of this are that the little girl and the woman is dominated by penis-envy; that the female's super-ego is not so developed as the male's because she has not had to internalize the father; and:

'a third consequence of penis-envy seems to be a loosening of the girl's affectionate relation with her maternal object. The situation as a whole is not very clear, but it can be seen that in the end the girl's mother, who sent her into the world so insufficiently equipped, is almost always held responsible for her lack of a penis.'

(Freud 1977:338)

Freud was always careful to insist on the fragmentary, indeterminate, and unsatisfactory nature of his conclusions:

'It must be admitted . . . that in general our insight into these developmental processes in girls is unsatisfactory, incomplete and vague.'

(Freud 1977:321)

At the same time, and this is presumably where Freud's own ambivalence emerges, he often slips into vulgar stereotypic generalizations. He allows himself to talk of woman as 'enigma' (as in his famous question: 'Was will das Weib?' – 'What does woman want?'). He sees women as a problem because they deviate from the male model. For him, women *are* more vain and narcissistic than men; have less super-ego or 'conscience'; less sense of justice; less sexual libido; and less capacity to love another human being.

Yet there is more to Freud's account of women than this. His notorious statement 'anatomy is destiny', which even Juliet Mitchell describes as 'disastrous', is by no means as downright as most feminists have supposed. He was discussing the differences between the Oedipus complex in the little girl and little boy and all he said was:

'the feminist demand for equal rights for the sexes does not take us far, for the morphological distinction is bound to find expression in differences of psychical development.'

(Freud 1977:320)

To say that anatomical differences between the sexes are 'bound to' have some echo in psychological differences does not in itself seem an objectionable statement. Where there is disagreement is when psychological attributes of narcissism, stupidity, frivolousness, and the rest are taken as inexorably and inevitably 'feminine'.

Freud was perfectly clear that to be anatomically 'male' or 'female' was no simple matter. Bisexuality was central to his theory, and moreover he realized that there was no one-to-one correspondence between anatomical maleness and 'masculinity' on the one hand, and antomical femaleness and 'femininity' on the other. Although the male alone produces semen and the female alone ova (except in very rare cases):

> 'Science . . . draws your attention to the fact that portions of the male sexual apparatus also appear in women's bodies, though in an atrophied state, and vice versa in the alternative case. It regards their occurrence as indicators of *bisexuality*, as though an individual is not a man or a woman but always both – merely a certain amount more the one than the other.'
>
> (Freud 1973:147)

So bisexuality itself had an anatomical basis. It was also, for Freud, a part of mental or psychical life. He argues that really, when we speak of 'masculine' or 'feminine' behaviour, we are usually merely making a distinction between 'active' and 'passive'. He goes on to say that this analogy does have a biological basis since:

> 'The male sex-cell is actively mobile and searches out the female one, and the latter, the ovum, is immobile and waits passively. This behaviour of the elementary sexual organisms is indeed a model for the conduct of sexual individuals during intercourse. The male pursues the female for the purpose of sexual union, seizes hold of her, and penetrates her.'
>
> (Freud 1973:48)

We might quarrel with this description, and it has been pointed out that the ovum is just as active as the sperm in biological fact. Yet Freud himself goes on to point out that in some species this active/passive distinction is not assigned according to the male/female division in the expected way, but is reversed, so that the male cares for the young, in others the female pursues the male sexually, and so on. And Freud concludes:

'that you have decided in your own minds to make "active" coincide with "masculine" and "passive" with "feminine". But I advise you against it. It seems to me to serve no useful purpose and adds nothing to our knowledge.'

(Freud 1973:148)

Yet he often slips back into this terminology himself. He did believe that women must give preference to 'passive aims', and in the very paper in which he argues for bisexuality one of his not infrequent digs at 'feminists' reveals how his own thinking remained stamped with the very usages of which he seemed so critical:

'For the ladies, whenever some comparison seemed to turn out unfavourable to their sex, were able to utter a suspicion that we, the male analysts, had been unable to overcome certain deeply-rooted prejudices against what was feminine, and that this was being paid for in the partiality of our researches. We, on the other hand, had no difficulty in avoiding impoliteness. We had only to say:"This doesn't apply to *you*. You're the exception; on this point you're more masculine than feminine."'

(Freud 1973:150)

A final, and interesting, point about Freud's theory of sexuality is his conviction (of which he spoke in one of his last papers, and which applied equally to men and women, although it had different consequences for each) of the existence at the core of the individual of a 'bedrock' that rendered sexual satisfaction and the reconciliation of both men and women to their bisexuality virtually impossible. It is as if men are condemned to protest forever against any kind of passivity, particularly in relation to men, while women must mourn forever the penis they cannot have.

Freud's work is shot through with the consciousness of biology and its importance. This gives his work at times a contradictory and ambiguous character. Sometimes he seems to be addressing the problem of the psychological consequences of biology and how the psyche of the individual is built on a biological base; at others he seems rather to use biological analogies and metaphors. The difficulties that arise sometimes have to do with the absence of an adequate recognized language, and Freud himself refers to the problems of conceptualizing his thought within the then existing scientific language. Richard Wollheim (1971) has suggested that Freud's theory is built round a 'form of biological learning, in which unpleasure is the teacher'. Frank Sulloway (1979), another recent interpreter of Freud, has emphasized Freud's Darwinian and evolutionist legacy. In Darwinian vein Freud was highly teleological (that is, he saw processes in terms of their ends or purposes), and he was constantly mindful of the fact that although sexuality is for the individual simply a source of personal pleasure and the satisfaction or relief of desire, it also serves a racial purpose, the continuation of the species:

> 'Since the penis . . . owes its extraordinarily high narcissistic cathexis* to its organic significance for the propagation of the species, the catastrophe of the Oedipus complex (the abandonment of incest and the institution of conscience and morality) may be regarded as a victory of the race over the individual.'
>
> (Freud 1977:331)

Of course this means that the clitoris becomes a total mystery:

> 'The clitoris, with its virile character, continues to function in later female sexual life in a manner which is very variable and which is certainly not yet satisfactorily understood. We do not, of course, know the biological basis of these peculiarities in women; and still less are we able to assign to them any teleological purpose.'
>
> (Freud 1977:374)

So part of Freud's attitutde to the clitoris may be because for him it served no 'racial' purpose; although it is doubtful whether this kind of socio-biological argument may legitimately be used to explain the development of the individual psyche.

---

* Freud nowhere gave a rigorous theoretical definition of 'cathexis' (Laplanche and Pontalis 1973:63). Broadly speaking, it means the loading with nervous energy of an idea, symbol, or event. We may say that the infant 'cathects' the mother when he invests her with the eroticized love arising out of his sensual satisfaction at the breast. A foot fetishist 'cathects' feet, or shoes. Or we may say that cathexis is the disposition of energy, or its distribution, in relationships with objects and with the self.

Juliet Mitchell

I hope that the above section will have indicated the kinds of ambiguity that arise in Freud's work around the issue of the relationship between the biological and the psychic. Burniston, Mort, and Weedon have gone further than I have done in insisting that in Freud's own work 'the structuring of the Oedipal triangle is . . . based on anatomical rather than social privilege' (1978:111). Richard Wollheim (1971) and Frank Sulloway (1979) have based their readings on the more biologistic side of Freud's work. Juliet Mitchell in *Psychoanalysis and Feminism* (1974) on the other hand sought to retrieve Freud from biologism by using the structuralism of Louis Althusser and the work of Jacques Lacan, a French psychoanalyst who emphasized the importance of language and of the symbolic in his approach to Freud.

Why was it important for her as a Marxist and a feminist, to move away from a biologistic interpretation of Freud? 'Biologism' must be unacceptable to the progressively minded because it denies, or is usually used as an argument to deny, the possibility of change. Women, or the black races, or the Jews are said to possess certain characteristics that derive from their biology. So, for example, women were said to be prone to hysteria *because* they have wombs. Juliet Mitchell effected the rehabilitation of Freud by presenting him as the theorist of the way in which the infant, 'a small human animal', achieves the entry into *culture*. A *social* not a biological process occurs. This process is the social construction of gender, whereby the infant internalizes the characteristics of 'masculinity' or 'femininity'. This gender identity has no one-to-one relation to biological sex differences, and so – to take an extreme example – it is possible for trans-sexual men to experience a fundamental conviction of their 'femininity'.

But, whereas there are many passages in Freud's work that are hard to read as anything other than assertions that the actual little boy is threatened with an actual loss of a real penis, and that the little girl is objectively inferior because her clitoris is actually an inferior penis, for Louis Althusser (following Lacan) and for Juliet Mitchell (following them both) the penis is not a penis but is the symbolic Phallus: 'the very mark of human desire', a phallus that 'represents the very notion of exchange itself' (Mitchell 1974:395). In this way she appears to transform Freud's theory from a theory about how things are biologically *and* socially, into a theory of the way things are in 'patriarchal society'. Yet since she also accepts the view of both Freud and Engels that equates human civilization with this same patriarchy, she does in effect universalize both the theory and women's oppression. Forever and a day 'the phallus' is and must be the dominating *symbol of power* around which the creation of sexual difference is organized.

This is perhaps a difficult concept that deserves further attention. Juliet Mitchell argues that the 'anatomical distinction' between the sexes is not biologically significant. But:

'to Freud society demands of the psychological bisexuality of both sexes that one sex attain a preponderance of femininity, the other of masculinity: man and woman are made in culture.'

(Mitchell 1974:131)

Juliet Mitchell has developed this line of argument in a recent book review (Mitchell 1980) and to me it seems a strange one. Firstly it is *assumed* as something that need not be proven or argued that the biological differences (which do exist) between women and men are somehow insufficient to ensure the reproduction of the species. Secondly 'masculinity and femininity only exist by virtue of their difference from one another' (Mitchell 1980). This statement translates the linguistic theory which Lacan imports into Freud very directly into the realm of the psychic. To see a system (of whatever kind) as a structure is to emphasize the relationship of one part to another. Structural linguistics stresses also the *arbitrary* nature of the linguistic sign. (A word – for example the name for a quality such as 'red' – is arbitrary. Moreover, just as the colour 'red' can be defined only in relation to other colours, yellow, orange, brown, so words have meaning only in relation to other words.) When Juliet Mitchell translates this arbitrary nature of the sign from the sphere of linguistics to that of psychology, the differences between men and women completely float away from biology and become purely social constructs. This happens because society 'needs' it to (a trace of Juliet Mitchell's functionalism here):

'So long as we reproduce ourselves as social beings *through a heterosexual relationship*, human society must distinguish between the sexes. It is because of this fundamental social situation that we need to feel ourselves as predominatly men or women . . . *for human society to exist at all*, men and women must be marked as different from each other' [my italics].

(Mitchell 1980:234-35)

Yet the logic of this locks us as securely within the structures of phallic power as does 'biologism'. Instead of simply accepting certain biological distinctions between the sexes, of which the psychological and cultural consequences are not necessarily very great (we do not really know how important they are) we appear condemned perpetually and for all time to recreate – or to *create* – the distinction *culturally* because otherwise we could not survive *biologically*, or could not survive at least as distinctively human. Thus the touchstone of human culture itself becomes the difference between 'masculine' and 'feminine'. Strangely, this is both wholly arbitrary and absolutely inevitable. It seems odd to demolish the tyranny of biology only to put in its place an imperative equally tyrannical and unalterable. And I question whether the whole of human culture should necessarily be seen as resting primarily and predominantly on the creation of heterosexuality in this way.

Psychoanalysis and Feminism is both a polemic and a theoretical work. Just as Freud deceivingly slips from detailed theoretical investigation to speculative generalization, so Juliet Mitchell fluctuates between polemic and theory in a fashion that masks some of the weaknesses in her arguments. There is a slippage, for example, from her account of the Oedipus complex to a contentious ideological statement when she writes:

'The woman's task is to *reproduce* society, the man's to go out and *produce* new developments. There is an obvious link between the security of Oedipal father-love (the girl's destiny) and the happy hearth and home of later years.'

(Mitchell 1974:118)

To say this is to argue that the sexual division of labour as we know it in an industrial capitalist society has some *permanent* correspondence with the creation of 'masculinity' and 'femininity'.

Both Burniston, Mort, and Weedon (1978) and Cora Kaplan in her brilliant article on Kate Millett criticize *Psychoanalysis and Feminism* on two major points. On the one hand there is Juliet Mitchell's determinism:

'Freudian theory, with its emphasis on repetition and reproduction of ideological positions, emphasizes, perhaps too heavily, the unalterable distance between gender positions so that they remain rather like Marvell's "Definition of Love" stuck at distant poles, "begotten by Despair/upon Impossibility".'

(Kaplan 1982:393)

On the other hand, ideology and the economy are radically separated; the feminist struggle is against ideology, the socialist struggle against the capitalist infrastructure. There is a further point to be made about the political conclusions to *Psychoanalysis and Feminism*: that is, that they are characterized by voluntarism. Juliet Mitchell wrenches an optimistic, 'revolutionary' conclusion from her arguments when they do not support it. She asserts that a cultural revolution is just around the corner – patriarchy like capitalism is in its death-throes. The arguments to support this prediction appear to run as follows: in capitalism the patriarchy is mediated through the nuclear family, which is all that remains of the formerly elaborate kinship structures (in this respect she follows Talcott Parsons and other mainstream – and right-wing – functionalist sociologists). Yet capitalism also hastens the disintegration of the nuclear family. This in turn implies that patriarchy itself is disintegrating since it cannot survive without the structural support of the nuclear family. (This last assumption is never argued through and Mitchell does not explain why patriarchy could not be mediated through other institutions such as schools and the law.) She argues that patriarchy is disintegrating because the exchange of women and the old kinship relations are no longer *needed* and her political conclusion is that therefore the time is ripe for their overthrow in an autonomous struggle of women against ideology.

Yet Juliet Mitchell argues that the arrival of socialism does not necessarily ensure the demise of patriarchy, hence her insistence on the autonomy of the struggle against ideology. At the same time this recognition weakens the logic of the earlier part of her argument which suggested that capitalism and the patriarchy were so intertwined that they would fall together. And this optimistic scenario is supported by 'evidence' from the experience of the Second World War in Britain, which, she asserts, saw the virtual (temporary) cessation of the nuclear family with the socialization of the means of survival. This is just wrong historically. Whatever the heightening of neighbourliness and communal living amongst evacuated work-mates, in the army, and so on, I know of no evidence that family ties were correspondingly weakened. On the contrary, family support (for instance, grandmothers looking after children for mothers who went out to work) was often of vital importance, while the *idea* of family life as something the British were fighting to preserve was a very important one – hence the popularity of the Beveridge Report (Wilson 1980).

The political consequences of psychoanalysis

The underlying assumption never really questioned by feminists who have followed Juliet Mitchell in exploring the relevance of psychoanalysis for feminist theory has been this: since the subordination of women is so heavily mediated through and in the private realm of marriage and other sexual relationships, in the family, in the reduction of women to sexual stereotypes, and in the threat of rape and generalized sexual violence, the overriding political imperative for feminists must be the immediate struggle against these practices. Part of the Marxist heritage is the belief that political struggles have to be informed by a theory that will enable us to understand the nature of our exploitation/oppression/subordination. It is argued by feminists sympathetic to psychoanalysis that psychoanalysis is *the* theory of the construction of the sexual identity and gender relations; since it emphasizes the social construction of gender it must be the theory feminists need.

It is implied that psychoanalysis enables us to understand how we internalize an oppressive ideology. This in turn assumes (and Juliet Mitchell certainly *does* seem to assume) that women are in general *successfully* constructed as 'feminine' in our society. Women, according to her, *do* end up narcissistic, masochistic, and the rest. This is rather curious since Freud himself laid great stress on the difficulty of this process and its incomplete success in many women.

This appears to me an unproven, certainly an under-researched area. Feminists who have talked with young teenaged working-class girls appear to reach contradictory conclusions (McRobbie 1978; Cowie and Lees 1981) but it does seem as if girls experience heterosexuality and marriage as inevitable rather than desirable. Social pressures of a direct kind as much as the internalization emphasized by psychoanalysis seem to ensure heterosexuality, as well as a desire to be 'normal' which is not quite the same as 'feeling' feminine. But I hesitate to interpret the small amount of evidence available, and would simply suggest that it is a more unknown quantity than psychoanalytic theorists allow.

Even to the extent that women *do* internalize 'femininity', psychoanalysis, while of some use in explaining how this comes about, certainly does not give us much idea how we might escape. In this respect, psychoanalytic theory is odd in its mingling of the highly particular (the details of an individual's biography to elucidate an individual's current psychological state) with the universal and general (the general 'law' of the phallus, and the necessity for the individual – and for all individuals – of entering culture via the Oedipus complex enacted in the nuclear family). At both these levels it misses the historically specific; that is, it can be 'true' of one individual and of all human history; it has little to say about one particular historical period. This makes it especially difficult to integrate with Marxism, since Marxism precisely deals with what is socially particular at a given historical period (Burniston, Mort, and Weedon 1978:127). Although many such attempts at integration have been made, this latest feminist one seems, like the rest, destined to failure. The result has often been in recent years an effective withdrawal from or abandonment of Marxism. (I am not making a value judgement on this score; simply suggesting that it has happened.)

Lacanian theory does not confront the problem of what happens to the individual psyche when family patterns change. Freud's work was at least solidly based on clinical studies of the then contemporary, nineteenth-century bourgeois nuclear family. But the family changes constantly. The generalizing abstractions of Lacan simply do not help us to understand these profound changes which must surely have some significance for the social construction of the individual. This appears to me another fascinating area unexplored by psycho-analysis. May we not be living in a period in which the construction of sexed identity is altering in important ways?

More generally feminist interest in psychoanalysis has not in practice led to a sharpening of feminist political struggle. On the contrary it has validated reactionary positions amongst feminists. I've already given an example of how these surface in *Psychoanalysis and Feminism*. It also appears to me that psychoanalysis has been the justification for some feminists to assert anew that the sexual division of labour presents no problems for feminists; that what is needed is to reassert the value of women's work (i.e. domestic labour) rather than seeking to socialize it; that careers for women may be irrelevant to feminism, even a result of penis-envy. I cannot cite written evidence for this. The statement may therefore be open to the criticism that it is unfair, contentious, distorted, or reliant on a kind of gossip of the women's movement to which only some are privy and that it is therefore élitist. But I am anxious to share with others my fear that such positions are returning; to me they seem to remark a return to constricting images of women accepted by feminists and non-feminists alike after 1945 and before women's liberation (Wilson 1980). If my fears are unfounded, I hope that women will refute them. If they are justified I hope that women who hold such views will commit them to paper and argue them out in open debate. So far they have surfaced only as a kind of unease; for example, in discussions of divisions between mothers and non-mothers:

'In the early days of the (women's) movement, feminists with children discovered their oppression and had the support of their sisters in throwing off guilt and finding independence. Those founding mothers were striving to challenge the mystique – and the material realities – that made them prisoners, to live like those of us who weren't hemmed in by maternity. But their counterparts of today appear to be reversing the process, moving away from us and melting back into motherhood . . . . Will we move motherhood back to centre-stage? Bathe it in the glow of that old insidious prestige, that status of "real womanhood" ? Will we again pick up the ideological baggage we've fought for the last decade to discard?'

(Heron 1980:5)

Another rather different yet related problem about the appropriation by feminists of psychoanalytic theory is that it is used to close up further investigation into the construction of gender:

'From a feminist reading of anthropology we learned that the social meaning of maleness and femaleness is contructed through kinship rules which prescribe patterns of sexual dominance and subordination. From psychoanalysis we learned how these kinship rules become inscribed on the unconscious psyche of the female child via the traumatic reorientation of sexual desire within the Oedipal phase away from the mother and towards the father ("the law of the father").'

(Alexander and Taylor 1982:161)

If we have really 'learned' this with such finality, there seems nothing more to be done about it, and further theoretical discussion seems pointless. I, though, hope I have demonstrated that we cannot really give psychoanalysis this doctrinal status. I would also argue that this kind of determinism can only have pessimistic implications for feminism, suggesting as it does unchanging, static patterns of human psychic development.

I suggest that a more interesting point to discuss might be how we *are* to engage in struggle around issues to do with consciousness and its formation. Feminists drawing on a psychoanalytic perspective have had little to say about this. But what forms of political struggle does psychoanalysis suggest for feminism?

Another point, and an important one for feminists, is that feminist theoretical writings drawing on psychoanalysis have had remarkably little to say about homosexuality and lesbianism. If anything, psychoanalysis seems to have been used implicitly to justify heterosexual relationships at a period in the women's movement when women who wanted to relate to men sexually felt under pressure from feminists who were lesbians. It is of interest in this context that Juliet Mitchell fudges the issue of Freud's attitude to homosexuality. In seeking to reassure feminists that Freud's attitude was not one of hostility she quotes this famous letter to the mother of a homosexual son. This is certainly a very kind and sensible letter, in which Freud tries to comfort the unhappy mother:

'Homosexuality is assuredly no advantage, but it is nothing to be ashamed of, no vice, no degradation; it cannot be classified as an illness; we consider it to be a variation of the sexual function, *produced by a certain arrest of the sexual development*' [my italics].

(Freud 1961:277)

But in omitting the significant last phrase Juliet Mitchell might be taxed with evasion of an admittedly difficult issue. Interestingly, Paul Hirst (1981b:112) later used the same quotation, perpetuating the crucial omission.

Another important question not being asked by Lacanian feminists is, what is the role of the orthodox institutions of psychoanalysis; and what is the role of the psychoanalytic therapy, and can it be changed? Another point of interest: there is a strong interest among feminists today in 'radical' and 'feminist' therapy, but this interest and the ongoing work of, for example, the Women's Therapy Centre, has remained apart from the body of theory I have been discussing; indeed the very concept of feminist therapy has been severely criticized by at least one Freudian feminist (Lipschitz 1978; and, in reply, Women's Therapy Centre Study Group 1979). Yet after all, the issue of therapy is an important one:

'The prevalence of psychic distress in our society, which reproduces neurosis on a mass scale – the figures speak for themselves, represent . . . what could be interpreted as a massive "flight into illness". Any political movement struggling to change society has to confront this striking phenomenon.'

(Delmar 1975:21)

Can the iron law of the phallus be overthrown?

Even the most meticulous critics of Freud within the contemporary debate (for example Burniston, Mort, and Weedon) usually back off at the last moment from a wholesale dismissal of Freud. I too believe, following Michèle Barrett (1980:58), that since Freud's work is not internally consistent or coherent, but is, as some would say, a very 'fractured' body of work, we can if we wish retain some of his insights without buying the whole package, although I do feel there are dangers in this eclecticism. I accept the psychoanalytic account of the way in which sexual identity gets constructed – haltingly and with difficulty – and that, as we know it, it is constructed in the context of male power. Freud often describes very accurately the construction of that male power at the psychic level. But in the Freudian, and even more fatally in the Lacanian account, the organization of difference not only does but *must* occur around the dominant symbol of the phallus, which also represents male power; although in many of these discussions, the phallus becomes no more than a metaphor, be it for male power or for desire. Yet it is possible to imagine that personal identity could be, in a society in which male power did not dominate, organized around some other principle. There could be an adult sexual identity that was constructed around a different symbolic differentiator.

In conclusion, I wish to look again at some of the weaknesses of recent feminist psychoanalytic perspectives in a general way; and to suggest some possible political directions the debate might more usefully take.

I suggested earlier that because the subordination of women occurs in a privatized way it has often been assumed that the struggle against it necessarily consists of for the most part private struggles – to change men, to change relationships with men, or (an entirely different but equally problematic solution) to abandon all relationships with men and sexualize relationships with other women. Or else, individual children should be reared differently and/or collective living relationships should be set up. Such attempts represent an important part of the feminist struggle. They will none the less remain privatized themselves unless the women's movement as a political movement socializes and collectivizes this struggle. This would mean a return to the largely abandoned arena of the family and the construction of campaigns to change the family at different levels and in different ways; social policy, income maintenance, child-care provision, obstetric practices are areas in which such a campaign could operate (and campaigns do flourish in these areas, although they are not ideologically linked to the extent that they might be).

The experience of Women's Aid suggests that social provision may often come before individual change, or that certainly the two go together. It's hard even to say it in the current economic climate, but today we need more than ever non-sexist social provision for many needs currently catered for by the family. Unless the family *is* radically changed (not abolished) I do not see how we can develop different child-rearing practices in which a sexual identity is constructed that gives more conscious and creative control to the child than s/he currently enjoys, and which is not so hysterically obsessed with one particular form of difference – an unstable form, moreover, since the cultural construction of 'masculine' and 'feminine' is a massive edifice elevated on an arguably insignificant base. In other words, I am arguing for social solutions to the oppression we experience as private.

This does not mean that I reject in individual, given circumstances the individual solution of psychoanalysis or therapy. Mental disorder is a serious problem. Even those of us who have no crippling 'symptoms' must often experience a loss of energy, a paralysis of the will, and an apathy generated by the kind of society in which we live. But feminists who take psychoanalysis seriously will have at some stage to confront the sexism of the psychoanalytic movement and its institutional practices far more radically than has yet been done, just as feminist doctors have had to confront the medical hierarchy, and feminist social workers the social services hierarchy. One of the most serious weaknesses of the contemporary feminist psychoanalytic debate has been its failure for the most part (so far as I know) to engage in therapeutic practice.

Perhaps precisely the attraction of Lacan's 'law of the father' has been the sense that it *is* inescapable. It has seemed that only through the gate of the Oedipal trauma could we become adult women and men and save ourselves either from a perpetuation of 'polymorph perverse' infantile sexuality; or from the psychotic symbiosis of the pre-Oedipal mother-infant relationship, at best a narcissistic mirroring. There is a sinister ring to the language used by Althusser to discuss this point:

'[the little girl] doubly accepts that she has not the same right (phallus) as her father, since her mother has not this right (no phallus) . . . . But she gains . . . the promise of a large right, the full right of a woman when she grows up, if she will grow up accepting the Law of the Human order.'

(Althusser 1971:197)

There are similarities here to the language used in political debate since time immemorial, whereby anarchy on the one hand and law and order on the other are posed as antagonistic opposites in order to discredit anarchy, i.e. chaos. Feminists should know better than to be taken in by this kind of language which constantly seeks to mask the progressive or revolutionary implications of rebellion; rebellion is always stigmatized as flouting law and order and producing chaos.

The last thing feminists need is a theory that teaches them only to marvel anew at the constant recreation of the subjective reality of subordination and which reasserts male domination more securely than ever within theoretical discourse. Psychoanalysis is of interest in its account of sexual identity and its construction – indeed, in many ways it is fascinating. More useful to contemporary feminists may be theories of social change that speak to aspects of the self not harnessed to the phallic taskmaster. To change the conditions of work – in the world and in the home – might do more for our psyches as well as for our pockets than an endless contemplation of how we came to be chained.

9 ◆ Forbidden love

Introduction

In this article, as in 'Gayness and liberalism', a certain uneasiness results from the attempt to combine an analytical discussion of romanticism with hints of a confessional account. Several different themes are rather confusingly mingled: the romanticization of lesbianism in the women's movement; personal feelings of alienation; a search for an alternative to the sexual discourses available in the early 1980s.

Forbidden love

'Love hurts
Love scars
Love wounds
And mars
Any heart not tough
Nor strong enough
To take a lot of pain. . . .'

(The Everley Brothers circa 1960)

The lesbian is an inhabitant of the great cities, first glimpsed by Baudelaire in Paris, 'capital of the nineteenth century' (Benjamin 1973). A new kind of woman emerges from the restless anonymity of the crowds, aloof from the sullen aimless excitement of the thousands that drift along the pavements and surge through the squares, a figure whose mystery and danger is that she is alone. The lesbian stands outside family, yet is not simply a worker. Her sexuality necessarily defines her. That is enough to make her lurid. She is a mirror image of the prostitute.

This at least was the prevailing romantic, literary image of the lesbian in the late ninteenth and early twentieth centuries, and one that lesbians themselves seem to have accepted. Later the lesbian is defined in Radclyffe Hall's *The Well of Loneliness*, as innately and therefore tragically masculine, a member of the 'third sex'. The erotic love that Radclyffe Hall's heroine, Steven, feels for each of her lovers is of an 'invert' for a 'womanly woman'. She constructs a romantically, narcissistically masculine being about whom there nevertheless remains a haunting ambiguity. The dissonance between Steven's woman's body, no matter how thin-flanked and boyish, and her male personality, creates an aura of the impossible. She is one of the haunted, tormented, and damned who transcend the degradation which is itself their glory.

Steven embodies the masculinity attributed to lesbians – a masculinity that contributes to a sense of their danger and power, but which is also open to ridicule and caricature. This claim to masculinity can be dramatized, the stigmata transformed into the hallmarks of a doomed and *therefore* fascinating personality. In this second guise, the lesbian resembles the archetypal Romantic movement hero, the doomed rebel, often an artist, often sexually ambiguous, of whom Byron, who was really the first modern pop star, is the classic example. This image is different from the first, which tried simply to be manly, for it lays claim to heroism and to a place above the crowd. It can also degenerate into the sometimes vulgar decadence of Aubrey Beardsley, Oscar Wilde, and other *fin de siècle* dandies, who, Ellen Moers suggests, *spoilt* their dandyism by being overtly homosexual instead of glacially beyond sexuality (Moers 1960).

This lesbian's dandyism is androgyny. Colette, who had a six-year liaison with a woman of this kind, writes insightfully – although perhaps also rather maliciously – about the strangeness and possibly the humorlessness of the androgynous poseur.

> 'The seduction emanating from a person of uncertain or dissimulated sex is powerful. . . . Anxious and veiled, never exposed to the light of day, the androgynous creature wanders, wonders, and implores in a whisper. . . . There especially remains for the androgyne the right, even the obligation, never to be happy. . . . It trails

irrevocably among us its seraphic suffering, its glimmering tears. . . . She is the person who has no counterpart anywhere.'

(Colette 1980)

Djuna Barnes also tried to analyse the attraction.

'What is this love we have for the invert, boy or girl? It was they who were spoken of in every romance that we ever read. The girl lost, what is she but the prince found? The prince on the white horse that we have always been seeking . . . in the girl it is the prince, and in the boy it is the girl that makes a prince a prince – and not a man. They go far back in our lost distance where what we never had stands waiting. . . . They are our answer to what our grandmothers were told love was . . . the living lie of our centuries.'

(Barnes 1963:194)

These women writers, who at various times loved women, accepted an understanding of lesbianism that saw the homoerotic as going against the grain of biological sex, yet as still biologically determined. In this they followed sexologists such as Havelock Ellis, for whom 'lesbianism' and 'femininity' would have been contradictions in terms.

In the 1950s the homosexual reform movements in Britain tried to create a more sensible, normalizing image of the lesbian. Lesbians themselves seemed at this time to be divided between those who still saw their condition as innate, and those who accepted a more psychological view that homosexuality is the result of childhood experiences. In practice there tended to be, in England at any rate, a distinction between the adoption of 'butch' and 'femme' roles among working-class lesbians, and an egalitarian insistence among middle-class lesbians that they were really just like everyone else. Then came the 1960s, a period during which the 'permissive society' and the 'swinging scene' emphasized androgyny rather than sexual difference. Many lesbians and male homosexuals found this atmosphere more congenial than a heavy emphasis on roles that began to seem old fashioned and 'naff'. Yet this new androgyny differed from the old. Its imagery was resolutely bright; it was pretty rather than darkly damned.

It was not until the late 1960s that lesbians and gay men began seriously to question the relationship of sexual proclivities to gender roles. Later still, with the publication of the work of Jeffrey Weeks and others (Weeks 1977; McIntosh 1968; Bray 1982), it came as a revelation for gay men that the 'homosexual identity' had existed in Western societies for only about two hundred years. There had been homosexual acts in almost all societies, but only in relatively few were there individuals who came to be described as homosexuals, a 'master' identity that defined all aspects of their lives and behaviour, not just what they did in bed.

The construction of the lesbian identity appeared to be of even more recent origin, not gaining widespread recognition, in Britain at least, until *The Well of Loneliness* was prosecuted and banned in 1928 (Ruehl 1982). So it is not surprising that lesbians, emerging at the same time with a conscious identity, had, during these years, accepted the sexologists' definition of their 'condition' as biologically determined and clinical, one to which masculinity was the key.

The 1970s saw a break with this tradition and a definitive move away from any lingering idea of the lesbian as a member of the 'third sex'. For feminists, a lesbian was now first and foremost a *woman*; and lesbianism became a major theme of the women's movement. The movement itself has grown out of the 'sexual liberation' of the 1960s. The whole new left had taken as central to its project the disruption of repressed sexuality, and this implied a vision of sexuality as energy. Sexual liberation was to be the nuclear fission of radicalism, and would rocket us into a stratosphere of intensity and power. The women's movement took over this view, and similarly assumed it to be revolutionary. Feminism gave it a new twist, however, for women began to understand how their subordination was enacted in the power relationships that heterosexual love so often created and served to perpetuate. They assumed that the key to women's liberation lay in an understanding of the construction of gender and sexuality. But if heterosexuality was the foundation of female subordination, then for some women lesbian sexuality came to be seen as an immediate source of liberation. Many women felt that a relationship with a man involved the collapse of their own identity, and it was to get away from this internalized sense of inferiority that some turned to other women with whom alone an equal relationship seemed possible.

But lesbianism in this context no longer involved the adoption of roles and dandyism was far from their aspirations. On the contrary, lesbianism now came to seem the escape route from the socially constructed gender roles imposed in a particularly rigid way on women. Paradoxically, the role-playing falsity of gender was, according to this scenario, the mark of heterosexuality, while lesbianism by contrast became the arena for the flowering of real womanhood.

Lesbianism in the early 1970s was seen, then, as a *solution* to heterosexuality. I can remember many meetings at which women spoke of their hopes that lesbian relationships would be free of jealousy, possessiveness, and romantic obsessions. Yet even at the time there was for me, and many others, something obscurely unsatisfactory about the terms of the debate. Feminists described a Manichaean struggle between the hell of wrong desires and the heaven of a love devoid of pain. They spoke of their right to orgasm and the thralldom of being in love. Often, to talk about sexuality was to talk not about sex at all, but about relationships, about life styles, about emotions. The word 'sexuality' went wider, in any case, than sex: 'sex' referred to acts and the engagement in practices; 'sexuality' was about identity and gender, about masculine and feminine, about desire, fantasy, and the whole construction of the self. Feminists also took over, unquestioned, from established revolutionary movements and from the new left, a moralism about the meaning of sexual behaviour in relation to politics, even if the moralism had rather different imperatives from stereotypic 'socialist morality'. Monogamy, possessiveness, and jealousy were still taboo, as was romantic love with its aura of repression and exaggeration, its displacement of sexuality into hysterical, obsessive feelings.

Lesbian sexuality assumed a special importance because, if sex *was* the deepest and most potent of all forms of personal communication, then that communication between two women took on a privileged and special role. In a sense, lesbianism became simply the transcendent moment of sisterhood. Moreover, lesbianism was seen as a fundamental political challenge to male domination. And, in a society in which both the familial and the non-kin female networks that had once supported women were breaking down, lesbianism might provide a new and powerful replacement.

Not until the mid-1970s, in Britian at least, did some feminists begin to question the idea that our sexuality expresses the core and centre of our being. They began to suggest that, far from being revolutionary, this essentialism acts as a central ideological support to modern capitalist societies: the culture we oppose itself accepts sexual passion and sexual relationships as the key to selfhood. British feminists used psychoanalytic theory to challenge the view that all women needed to do was 'let it all hang out', unlock their sexuality from patriarchal suppression, and allow 'it' to flower. Juliet Mitchell (1974) and others used psychoanalysis to argue that there is no pregiven 'it' of sexual energy, and that sexuality is largely a social construct. The work of Lacan questioned the very notion of stable sexual identity. For the Lacanians, the sexual self is at best a fragile thing, wobbling on the border between the conscious 'personality' and the formless depths of the unconscious; for the very notion of sexual *identity* becomes to this way of thinking a kind of ideology, almost an example of false consciousness.

Michel Foucault (1979) has been more interested in the social organization of sexuality and in 'sexual discourses' than in the individual. But his challenge to the view that sexuality is coherent and unitary, his belief – to put it perhaps rather simplistically – that sex *is* about practices rather than conditions, has led to a conscious rejection by some feminists and gay men of the very notion of an identity organized around homoeroticism.

From a radically different perspective, other feminists have rejected lesbian identity in favour of a seamless conception of womanhood. The most extreme and best known statement of this position is by Adrienne Rich:

'I mean the term *lesbian continuum* to include a range . . . of woman-identified experience; not simply the fact that a woman has had or consciously desired genital experience with another woman. If we expand it to embrace many more forms of primary intensity between and among women, including the sharing of a rich inner life, the bonding against male tyranny, the giving and receiving of practical and political support . . . we begin to grasp breadths of female history and psychology which have lain out of reach as a consequence of limited, mostly clinical, definitions of "lesbianism".'

(Stimpson and Specter Person 1980)

And Lillian Faderman (1981) has elucidated a history of romantic friendships between women that claims to rescue these from the 'clinical' definitions of lesbianism created by the hated nineteenth-century medical men.

One criticism levelled against this, the lesbian feminist perspective, is that it desexualizes lesbianism. It has also been seen as 'reductionist' in denying the specificity and difference of the diverse experience of women (Zimmerman 1981). I share these criticisms, yet I have always felt that intellectual disagreement was not enough to account for my deeply felt hostility to lesbian feminism, my anger at what I have felt to be its sentimentality and simplistic blurring of a complex reality.

A difference in life experience gave lesbianism for me a different meaning. I too rejected 'clinical' definitions of the lesbian, but I did still see the homosexual as positively deviant, a rebel against the oppressive society of the 1950s. I adopted the identity as some sort of protection against the 1950s' marriage and the 'feminine mystique'. It served that purpose, but for that very reason (because it set me apart) I never did experience it as an identification with other women. Rich has written: 'The passion of debating ideas with women was an erotic passion for me, and the risking of self with women that was necessary in order to win some truth out of the lies of the past was also erotic' (Rich 1983). Not for me, and perhaps I have missed out. I don't know, but I certainly never longed for 'the power of woman-bonding'. That suggested something too maternal, too suffocating; I always wanted my lover to be *other*, not like me. I did not want to be bathed, drowned in the great tide of womanliness.

Yet how sour and mean it seemed that the truth of my experience contradicted the great feminist imperative of affirmation. But it did. The more strongly feminists insisted upon the magnificence of women, the more that love between them, erotic and emotional, was elevated into the highest moment of political consciousness, the more doubtful I became, the more alienated I felt. For a long time this confused me, and I tried not to think about it. It could not be talked about. I did not understand it.

For after all, I had entered the 1970s on a high. I became part of the meteoric glare of London gay liberation. At the time we experienced it as an explosion of energy that blew apart the permissive 1960s. The demonstrations were impromptu street theatre, the politics were the politics of outrage. We dramatized our oppression and in so doing converted subordination into a weapon of attack. Politics was a new kind of good time. We wrenched an optimism and vitality from the menace of the future. We were the urban guerillas of the ideological war. We were the froth on the nightmare of capitalism, riding the breakers of revolution. I experienced more intensely than ever before, or since, my *identity* as lesbian. This wasn't about sexual practices at all, it was about the assumption of a deviant identity, an identity that ran counter to every notion of womanhood, yet wasn't 'mannish' either.

My whole involvement with feminism has been something of a 'morning-after' since this first intoxication. This was inevitable since it involved a much fuller acknowledgement of myself as a woman in a male society, as a woman – ironically – who could desire men as well as women: it was an acknowledgement of many complexities and uncertainties that had been conveniently censored out by my particular 'lesbian identity'.

Yet there was always a lack, an absence somewhere, in my engagement with feminism; at some level I could never identify with the feminist ideal woman: affirmative, woman-loving, positive, strong. A sense of unease grew slowly more pervasive about the sort of person I as a feminist was supposed to be. I'm not talking about media caricatures, but what I perceived as feminist assumptions. In all sorts of ways I retreated: into work, into a relationship that itself became a kind of mask. But I could not ward off the unease, and eventually it became a suppressed depression, which crystallized, rather oddly, around the issue of lesbian sadomasochism. This, and butch-femme roles, have not achieved as much importance in Britain as they seem to have done in North America, but the 'sex issue' of *Heresies* was none the less widely read and greeted with acclaim by many British women. It was also sold under the counter in at least one London feminist bookshop, because other women so deeply disapproved.

Why did it all leave me cold? So far as I was concerned it might as well have been the General Motors catalogue. Was there then something wrong with me? What *did* I want? It was depressing to feel so unmoved, because this role-playing, 'deviant' lesbian sexuality has been the only clearly spelled-out alternative to 'woman bonding', and it seems to be an attempt to put outlawry and sex very much back into lesbianism.

It also seemed however to carry with it its own romanticism about deviant identity. And when I thought about romanticism I grasped the fact that that *did* have an erotic charge for me. Operatic, star-crossed, forbidden loves were the silent movie backdrop to my sexual forays. My secret life was peopled with fatal strangers, vampiric seducers, idealized violators. Nothing so crude as flagellation or bondage, no silly sex games or dressing up for me; rather the refined thrill of psychic pain, the 'real thing' of rows, reconciliations, parting, absence – thrills, tragedy, and drama.

Feminists have dismissed romanticism, yet it has a psychic reality that can't simply be banished. The magic of dominance and submission is written into romance as it is written into pornography; romance *is* actually a sort of pornography of the feelings, in which emotions replace sexual parts, yet may be just as fetishized.

The themes of romance are compulsion and denial. In romantic fantasy, feelings are not entered into freely, they are stronger than oneself; the lover draws one on, yet ultimately denies. When, and if, the moment of final consummation comes, it has to be the end of the story because (or so Freud suggested) sexual gratification destroys the compulsion. New forms of affection, or indeed thralldom, may ensue, but these are distinct from the original romantic longing. Domestic life, after all, is designed (however unsuccessfully) to maximize emotional security, while danger is the essence of romantic love. The romantic hero (or heroine) is 'mad, bad and dangerous to know' as Caroline Lamb said of Byron. Byron's own poems, like the gothic novels of his period, typically rely on the theme of the abducted heroine, victim in the toils of a tormented tormentor.

Why do such fantasies have the power to compel? Is it that the danger of romantic love acts as a drug or a form of escapism in industrial mass society? Is it that we must have our dreams since life in the typing pool or on the assembly line is so monotonous? But even if we were to accept such a tidy fit between fantasy and economy, it would not explain the content of our dreams.

Romance – again like some genres of pornography – approximates to a kind of grail legend in resembling the journey of the questing individual in search of enlightenment. For a woman particularly, so long at least as the 'taboo of virginity' is powerful, romantic passion can be felt as a transformation, and the first night of passion as a chasm between her former and her future life. In a long chapter in *The Second Sex* Simone de Beauvoir (de Beauvoir 1953: part 4, chapter 14) demonstrated with many examples from diaries, memoirs, autobiographies, and novels the importance and significance of this moment, even when the reality is sadly unlike the myth. Sex then becomes a rite of passage and, as such, a kind of rebirth. This may partly explain its association – within the romantic tradition at least – with death.

Like so many other features of modern life, romantic love can be seen as a secularizaton of spiritual impulses that once expressed themselves in mysticism, ritual, and magic. We cannot return to former beliefs, but the insufficiency of nineteenth- and twentieth-century scientism and hyper-rationalism has led rather to a secular irrationalism. Our culture *is* spiritually impoverished, and we therefore have all sorts of emotional impulses and needs that lack real nourishment. Astrology and encounter groups can hardly satisfy these needs.

Freud was a great debunker of romantic love: 'Sexual overestimation is the origin of the peculiar state of being in love, a state suggestive of a neurotic compulsion' (Freud 1948). On the other hand, Freud saw desire as incapable of being fulfilled and indeed as compelling precisely because of the obstacles in its way. 'An obstacle is required in order to heighten libido; and where natural resistances to satisfaction have not been sufficient men have at all times erected conventional ones so as to be able to enjoy love' (Freud 1977). Since Freud perceived erotic love as rooted in the infant's love of its parental figures, which in turn grows, according to him, out of the satisfaction of the baby's bodily needs (ultimately the need for survival), he viewed the state of being in love as a development from narcissism. The individual in love abandons narcissism, but seeks indirect satisfaction for it by projecting it onto the idealized love object, thereby in a sense reappropriating the love of self.

Adult love, for Freud, was always to some extent a re-enactment of the gradiose and unattainable aspirations of the infant. Romantic passion is really, therefore, a longing for the impossible, representing, like so much else in Freud, the wish to escape the confines of reality and return to a former state of pleasure and happiness untinged by compromise.

In this respect, Freud might himself be seen as a part of the very romantic tradition he at one level challenged. The themes of his work are the tragic themes of opera, novel, and film: renunciation, loss, and the suppression of the erotic. Passion is intense because it is forbidden. Such an idea is anathema to modern feminism, built as it is on the belief that female sexuality should be unleashed and no longer taboo.

Thus to identify romanticism as something too important to be merely willed away by the power of positive thinking is to state a problem, not a solution. To state that romanticism has been important to me psychologically is not to 'come out' as a romantic. It is inadequate merely to justify romanticism; in the same way that the previous rejection of it was an inadequate response and just as there is insufficiency in the testimony (however heroic and difficult it may have been) of these feminists who have 'come out' as sadomasochists. We also must pursue the whole issue of the social construction of sexual identity and sexual desire: how we become masculine or feminine; why our desires and fantasies are as they are. Simply to affirm a 'right' to be sadomasochistic on civil liberties grounds is to beg the question of why, for each of us, our longings tend to get channelled into a particular narrow and highly specific range. The justifications for sadomasochism have never seriously tried to answer that million orgasm question. Probably just as many women – feminists – have romantic as have masochistic fantasies (and perhaps the two are linked). Yet it has remained a stifled discourse within the women's movement, the still shameful secret when so many others have been brazenly revealed. To romanticize one's own identity is merely one way of trying to stabilize the fluctuating subjectivity at which Lacan makes us look. To romanticize desire is, perhaps, to try to stabilize the tide of time that rocks the boat of eternal love and fidelity.

For me, lesbianism was not simply about desires and practices, but was also about my *self*. My involvement in my own lesbian identity was itself romantic, and I can see now that the romance is over. The possibility of being a *femme damnée*, a Baudelairean lesbian, disappeared when the women's movement came along, and I was left caught between two – for me – impossibilities. On one side was the 'lesbian continuum' and woman bonding, on the other the fetishistic specificity of key codes, leather, and coloured handkerchiefs. Romanticism was no magical third way. I do believe, though, that it is far more pervasive than we realize, an attitude to life so deeply woven into our culture that it permeates even radical ideologies – even sadomasochist outlawry and woman bonding are ultimately romanticizations.

Psychoanalysis is in one sense a negative process. It challenges us to confront the dark side of ourselves, the negative, the fearful, the destructive. Like the romantic tradition of which it is itself a part, it acknowledges that passion is contradictory, that eroticism is more than a celebratory hedonism, and that part of its cutting edge may be when it is touched with fear of loss and set against the vista of its own impermanence.

Yet psychoanalysis as a theory, although fascinating and suggestive, cannot be *the* theory for feminists. It has its own silences. It has failed to give a convincing account of lesbianism, and none of the contemporary feminists that has used it has seriously attempted to give lesbianism more than a marginal place. Psychoanalysis is itself to some extent romantic as a process and as a method of self-exploration, with its imagery of quest and hoped-for salvation, its tactic of enlightenment by metaphor. On the other hand, its 'negative' aspect is a potential positive; the process is the unpicking of what has gone wrong rather than the affirmation of what always has to be so brightly right – and this may be more supportive in its acknowledgement of failure and disappointment than the feminist ideology of the strong woman. Of course we need strength; but that strength must be built on a recognition and understanding of our vulnerabilities rather than on a censoring out of all unacceptable feelings.

I recognize that my experience runs counter not only to the admissible feminist reality, but also to the experienced reality of many women who discovered lesbian eroticism, if not identity, as a result of their involvement in feminism. Yet whatever my own experience, the haunting image of the lesbian remains. The lesbian was once the woman who stood alone, unprotected by men, in a refusal of male domination that was profoundly challenging. As Lillian Faderman herself acknowledges, nineteenth-century women's romantic friendships as such did not challenge 'patriarchy'. Baudelaire's woman of the metropolis did. She was part of the disorder of great cities, of the underworld, the underground, the unconscious. Because no man protected her, she herself took on 'male' qualities. She still demands from us a response to what we always thought of – and often rejected – as masculine. She still stands as a metaphor of this 'dark side': of the glamour of masculinity in both women and men; of the ambiguities of passion; of the excitement of danger.

This may itself sound romantic, but it isn't just romanticism. Woman bonding and the lesbian continuum enfold us in a sense of strength and support – the positve political contribution of this perspective has been to suggest a basis for women's collective power. However, it specifically evades a threat that the outlaw lesbian compels us to confront. Far from securing gender and womanliness, she destabilizes female and male; for with homosexuality gender runs amok. Both a woman and a homosexual, she elicits a special horror, for in a homophobic society we are all homophobic at heart.

Psychoanalysis is not an answer. It is a method. It can help us ask useful questions. Above all, like homosexuality, it questions the construction of gender, and it is therefore actually rather surprising that the feminists who have explored and developed psychoanalytic theory have paid so little attention to homosexuality. For to insist on lesbianism as a challenge to stereotypes of gender is ultimately more political than the political importance so far given to it in practice by feminists. To see lesbianism as love for women is to widen it too far; it tends to return women to biology without even achieving unity, since most women don't identify as lesbians. To narrow it down to consensual sexual acts and as nothing else but the exploration of new sensuality won't do either. Both neglect the real reason that homosexuality remains taboo: it challenges the very 'rock' on which society is built.

In what is currently regarded as the best and most comprehensive British textbook on pregnancy the following passage occurs:

'The intensely feminine female ought to be the ideal human reproductive machine and such a person will usually attract and also be attracted to the masculine type of male, so that by a process of natural selection at a biological level the ideal reproductive female is mated with the ideal reproductive male. . . . From a purely biological aspect the masculine type of female and the effeminate type of male are not good vehicles for reproduction and the procreation of the human race.'

(Bourne 1972)

No matter what we in our progressive ghettos may imagine, the ideological battle over gender is far from won. We must continue to insist on the complexity of sexuality and sexual identity. The discussion and exploration of lesbianism and what it means must continue. The lesbian still challenges reductive and conformist beliefs about what it means to be human. Feminists still need her.

10 ◆ Yesterday's heroines: on rereading Lessing and de Beauvoir

Introduction

From the point of view of feminist literary criticism this is an unsophisticated account, which tends to fall into the trap of treating the autobiographical as the 'real'. This, though, is one of the problems of autobiography and autobiographical fiction: authorial intention and the element of fiction in the creation of a literacy 'self'. This creation of an ideal self relates also to the use by some feminists of a particular form of psychoanalytic theory that foregrounds the problem of the fractured self. A question underlying all this, which I find interesting, is whether feminism, or at least some feminist writing (possibly that of Adrienne Rich, for example) is still engaged in the attempt to find a unitary self and a noncontradictory identity for women, while feminism's more 'modernist' voice is confined to an academic or *avant-garde* discourse. Can there be a feminist discourse that engages with modernism or are we still stuck in an affirmative mode that simply ducks the question and endorses an ideological resolution which smoothes out contradiction? Particularly in the United States, for example, feminists themselves see feminism as offering women affirmative 'role models'. To me this search for heroines is problematic, and this was highlighted for me by the experience, mentioned in this article, of rereading Doris Lessing and Simone de Beauvoir twenty years on; the way in which my youthful self uncritically accepted and was influenced by their view of the world now shocks me. Valuable as it was in many ways, their work did not push me towards a search for my own solutions; rather I tried to copy theirs. This was not their fault – and may well have been mine – nevertheless feminists should be questioning (and perhaps they are) both the noncontradictory identity and the images of victimization against which it was no doubt a reaction. Indeed, if we define feminism as the exploration of women's experience, rather than as a more traditional kind of political project, the search for strong and positive images of women as a tool against oppression can't be sustained, since women's subjective experience embraces more than the consciousness of oppression, or the discovery of strength.

I tried to explore some of these problems in an autobiographical book of my own (Wilson 1982), but ironically the main criticism levelled at it was that it was insufficiently affirmative!

Yesterday's heroines: on rereading Lessing and de Beauvoir

Who are these women we admired so much? In the strange cultural landscape of 1960 they loomed up, Cassandras of women's experience, an experience that was everywhere silenced, concealed, and denied.

They were, it is true, famous, fêted, ambivalently, as writers. But this almost seemed to be on condition that their 'testimony' was wilfully misunderstood. A generation of women – and men – ransacked their work for 'truths' about the human condition, and, especially, for the truth about women. Yet their work aroused anger and hatred at the same time as they were idealized. As Doris Lessing has said, they were 'reacted to' instead of being simply 'read'. So it is not simply a question of what they wrote, it is also a question of how their audience received it. How was their testimony read? To whom did they speak, secretly and silently? The statements of these women, each isolated in the spotlight of her gift, must have had a slow-release effect on their audience of millions of women, equally isolated, scattered across the globe. To these women they spoke as unique individuals, and yet they raised woman's voice.

In writing of these exemplary women I write as two readers. My impressions of them are blurred by the double vision of having read them as a very young woman and again now. This has modified my view of them, and I have also seen 'myself' (whatever that is) anew. For this reason I confine my discussion largely to the works I also read 'then', and I have ignored the most recent works especially of Doris Lessing. This is partly because I am not approaching their work as a 'feminist critic' but simply as a feminist, trying to chart my reactions to them then and now, and to gauge their political impact. I am not first and foremost concerned to interpret any given literary text within its own terms. I am less interested in the texts than in the writers and what they have come to stand for as feminists.

If I start from the idea of 'heroine' that is because I saw them as heroines twenty or so years ago. Nor was I alone in this. Margaret Walters writes:

> 'When I first read *The Second Sex* – about fifteen years ago, before the present women's movement – it struck me with the force of a genuine revelation. It helped me make some sense of my confused and isolated depression. Since the book appeared in 1949, de Beauvoir has received thousands of letters from women all over the world, grateful for the way her book helped them to see their personal frustrations in terms of the general condition of women.'
>
> (Walters 1976:351)

Margaret Walters insists, too, that: 'there is a very real sense in which [de Beauvoir] presents herself as an *exemplary* figure.' It is true that she was often seen, popularly, as a malignant rather than as an inspiring example. In *La Verité*, a French film of the period around 1960 (directed by Henri-Georges Clouzot), the heroine, played by Brigitte Bardot, is a juvenile delinquent. In court, the judge is persuaded of the girl's moral turpitude when he hears that she had read *The Second Sex*. In Britain, journalists associated Doris Lessing (and Iris Murdoch) for a short time with the Angry Young Men. They were seen, that is, as rebels and social critics, which other young women novelists of the period from the mid-1950s to the early 1960s – say, Edna O'Brien or Margaret Drabble – were not. Both Lessing and de Beauvoir were therefore seen as subversive and as, in some sense, political. But 'political' in those days never meant feminist, and their lives and writings raise questions about the relationship of the isolated woman to political movements.

In contrasting the lives and work of these two women, one sees immediately the similarities. Yet what two women could be more different, given that both were educated, politically conscious intellectuals who lived within Western capitalism?

Both Doris Lessing and Simone de Beauvoir recount their youthful experiences as escape – from stifling environments that would destroy them. Doris Lessing was brought up in what was then Southern Rhodesia and had to struggle to free herself from a backward, racist, uncultured community. There was a jarring contrast between the vastness of Africa and the blinkered narrowness of imperialism. Her escape was a physical as well as a moral and intellectual escape. Yet it brought her only to the Cold War Britain of the post-1945 period. And in Britain she was always an exile. Simone de Beauvoir, on the contrary, grew up as an archetypal Parisian intellectual firmly centred within a cultural tradition rich in art, literature, and philosophy, the height of 'civilization'. A decade older than Doris Lessing, she also none the less felt stifled by the bourgeoisie as represented by her family, by the dusty pieties of Roman Catholicism, and the vulgarity of the middle class. Both of these families, also, were downwardly mobile.

Simone de Beauvoir's parents once had been financially secure but as she grew up they slipped down towards genteel poverty, although they made every effort to keep up appearances and did maintain some kind of 'normal' bourgeois life. Doris Lessing's parents, on the contrary, experienced a far wider gap between self-presentation and 'reality'. And that is the gap through which madness can leak into daily life. Her parents, foundering on a run-down farm, the very roof collapsing, exist, at least as she portrays them, largely in fantasies from the past. Her father harks back to his days in the trenches during the First World War. Her mother attempts to live out a dream of imperial grandeur based on fantasies born in suburban England. In her autobiographical book *In Pursuit of the English* Doris Lessing (1960) constructs her father as verging on the mad, and (here an ambiguity between fiction and autobiography is very clear) *Martha Quest* contains a similar account of Martha's parents. These white settlers, becalmed on their farm in the vastness of the veld, have in a sense lost touch with the reality that should have anchored them to sanity. Theirs is bourgeois life run into a crazy caricature of itself, based on nothing, not even comfortable.

The great fear of Lessing's Southern African heroines is to be somehow lost down that gap where reality, daily life itself, becomes first meaningless and then mad. They fear annihilation in the endless, dusty, empty spaces of the veld. This does open out into madness in *The Grass is Singing* (Lessing 1949).

For Simone de Beauvoir it is the claustrophobia of the *foyer* (the bourgeois home) that threatens the integrity of the self. The young 'self'of her autobiography *The Prime of Life* (de Beauvoir 1965) escapes *into* the solitude and even the dangers of the hills above Marseilles. Martha Quest recognizes not only her own insignificance in the midst of the veld, but also the insignificance of our planet in the vast inconsequentiality of the universe:

'During that space of time (which was timeless) she understood quite finally her smallness, the unimportance of humanity. In her ears was an inchoate grinding, the great wheels of movement, and it was inhuman . . . and no part of that sound was Martha's voice . . . that is, what was futile was her own idea of herself and her place in the chaos of matter.'

(Lessing 1962:62)

For Simone de Beauvoir by contrast the encounter with nature – when she learns to ski, or when she explores the Mediterranean hills – is a test of her own mastery of nature, of an ego that can never be swallowed up in infinity:

'a sheer wall of rock blocked any further advance, and I had to retrace my steps, from one basin to the next. At last I came to a fault in the rock which I dared not jump across. There was no sound except for the rustle of snakes slithering among the dry stones. No living soul would ever pass through this defile: suppose I broke a leg or twisted an ankle; what would become of me? I shouted, but got no reply; I went on calling for a quarter of an hour. The silence was appalling. In the end I plucked up my courage and got down safe and sound . . . . In any case there were certain things, such as accidents, severe illnesses, or rape, which simply *could not happen* to me.'

(de Beauvoir 1965:93)

Each of these young women has a strong sense of her own individual identity, even in the face of this huge, senseless universe. Each has also a strongly *political* sense of the gulf between individual pain and the difficulty experienced by the individual who tries to change or influence events. Simone de Beauvoir writes in *Force of*

Circumstance of the horror of the war in Algeria, the tortures and persecutions:

> 'Beauty, yes beauty remains . . . but often I loathe it too. The evening after a massacre, I was listening to a Beethoven *andante* and stopped the record halfway through in anger: all the pain of the world was there, but so magnificently sublimated and controlled that it seemed justified. Almost all beautiful works have been created for the privileged and by privileged people . . . they are disguising the horror of misery in its nakedness. Another evening, after another massacre – there have been so many – I longed for all such lying beauty to be utterly destroyed.'
>
> (de Beauvoir 1968:669-70)

Doris Lessing's heroine Anna in *The Golden Notebook* (1964) is likewise obsessed with the senselessness and enormity of human suffering. She feels she is going mad as she surrounds herself with the 'senseless facts' from newspapers, pinning them up all over the walls first of one room, soon a second. And – herself a writer – she finds it impossible to write, to assimilate artistically the horrors of the world.

Both Simone de Beauvoir and Doris Lessing assume, tacitly, in their way of talking about their sense of smallness and futility, that human life *ought* to be purposeful, rational, and coherent. This is a feeling that permeates the literature of the postwar period – that Renaissance man, centre of the universe, had somehow fallen from his pedestal, and been decentred. The agony of man's smallness in the universe was a repeated theme of literature in those years. In Britain, certainly, the postwar literary atmosphere was one of romantic pessimism, tinged with a decadent religiosity. In France, existentialism, of which Simone de Beauvoir and Jean-Paul Sartre were regarded as the 'high priests' in the late 1940s, represented in some ways a 'left' version of this pessimism.

Many male writers after the Second World War posed the individual creative man over against the senseless void of the universe – 'man's cosmic loneliness' as Bertrand Russell put it. *L'Homme Revolté* by Albert Camus, once a close associate of de Beauvoir and Sartre but far to the right of them by the late 1940s, is an expression of this tragic humanism.

Doris Lessing and Simone de Beauvoir both rework these problems and move beyond them. Their bulky writings do partially fit into the 'great realist novel' tradition, and they have tried to retain at least that aspect of the nineteenth-century tradition which used the novel as a vehicle for moral and philosophical dilemmas. Yet as they use it, the capacious cupboard of the traditional novel – panorama of society that does not question the importance of our human concerns – bulges and bursts with the 'new consciousness' of these women.

Each appears to be offering a kind of testimony, the subjective voice of experience, catching the flux and flow of life, which pours like a river across the page, and for which the architectonic structure of, say, Proust, would be inappropriate. Each is at the same time explicitly committed to realism in the novel. Doris Lessing makes clear her commitment in her essay in *Declaration*, a collection of essays from the mid-1950s by authors who at that time were corralled under the label of the 'Angry Young Men'. In Lessing's essay 'The Small Personal Voice' she states:

> 'For me the highest point of literature was the novel of the nineteenth century . . . the work of the great realists . . . . I hold the view that the realist novel, the realist story, is the highest form of prose writing.'
>
> (Maschler 1968:14)

It is only through realism that she can get 'under the net' of all theorizations about life, and down to the thing itself. For Anna in *The Golden Notebook* Marxism and psychoanalysis – the theories she has used to try to make sense of her life – in the end mask the formless inner reality. To 'name' things, as she puts it there, is in the end to betray and diminish; so that when she looks round her analyst's carefully arranged consulting room – a room 'like an art gallery' – she feels that:

> 'Nothing in my life corresponds with anything in this room – my life has always been crude, unfinished, raw, tentative; and so have the lives of the people I have known well. It occurred to me, looking at this room, that the raw unfinished quality in my life was precisely what was valuable in it and I should hold fast to it.'
>
> (Lessing 1964:233)

Both art and theory in the end go against this feeling.

Simone de Beauvoir tells us that she and Sartre greatly admired the 'clipped realism' of the styles of American writers such as Dashiell Hammett and Ernest Hemingway, and in *Force of Circumstance* she criticizes the *nouveau roman* then fashionable in France:

> '[Nathalie Sarraute] confuses truth and psychology, while [Alain Robbe Grillet] refuses to admit interiority; she reduces exteriority to appearances, in other words, a false show; for him, appearances are everything, it is forbidden to go beyond them; in both cases the world of enterprises, struggles, need, work, the whole real world, disappears into thin air . . . . On the whole, one of the constant factors of this whole school of writing is boredom; it takes all the savour, all the fire out of life, its impulse towards the future.'

> (de Beauvoir 1968:636-37)

Yet despite their commitment to a 'life' that shall be reflected in all its vividness in their work, neither of these women authors stays within the confines of classical realism as it's usually understood, since both also explore their subjectivity as women in the manner of the twentieth-century psychological novel. But they do not remain within what has been traditionally cast as the appropriate 'feminine' sphere of the woman writer. They are not like Edna O'Brien, Penelope Mortimer, or Gillian Tindall who spend a lot of time exploring 'feminine' dilemmas. Neither do they take the road chosen by Iris Murdoch in her first novel *Under the Net* (1954) where she evaded the problem by making her first-person narrator a man, Jake (who consequently fits more easily into the British 1950s' mould of picaresque 'existential' hero).

Estelle Jelinek (1980), an American feminist critic, has suggested that the autobiographical form, the diary and the letter form are women's forms *par excellence*, reflecting the diffusion, the multiplicity of roles, and the sense of a fractured consciousness experienced by women. She also points out that, contrary to a popular view, these forms are not necessarily confessional in the sense of representing always the exposure of intimate feelings and psychological truths about the 'self' that is portrayed.

These expectations, though, may account for the way in which the writings of Simone de Beauvoir and Doris Lessing have time and again been received as the 'voice of woman'. They are read as 'the truth'. As the blurb on the back of my (1964) Penguin edition of *The Golden Notebook* puts it: 'Doris Lessing scrutinizes the plight of the emancipated woman of today with an honesty and an intensity which most women will find as pitiless as a mirror on a Monday morning.' There is a kind of triple elision, between author, heroine, and reader. The (woman) reader identifies with a heroine who is at once creator and protagonist. This is made all the easier because of the strongly autobiographical elements in the writings of both Lessing and de Beauvoir. For however strongly each may protest that her novels are not simply autobiographical records (and that is clearly the case) the similarities are often so striking that the reader, in a strange double effect is able to identify simultaneously with the heroine and with the creator (woman writer – real, living woman) who has shaped the heroine who is also 'herself'. This curious effect gives a potency to the voice of the woman writer, so that however passive and victimized womanhood is sometimes seen to be in the writings, the identification is not with woman as passive victim or martyr.

Both writers set up multiple mirrors that reflect a variety of identities or possibly comment upon the fragmentation of identity for a woman who refuses to be bounded by what have been the traditional identities for women. Looked at in another way, the work of each of these writers may be read as an exposition of the production of a 'self'. Each attempts repeatedly to construct a self outside the roles of 'wife' and/or 'mother'. ('Mistress' is frequently alluded to, especially in *The Golden Notebook* and *The Second Sex*, and in Doris Lessing's short story 'Between Men' (in Lessing 1965), as a third possible and mutilating identity for women.)

In writing so extensively in the autobiographical vein Simone de Beauvoir does of course make a much less equivocal claim to 'truth' and 'realism' than we would expect from a work of fiction. Yet there is a rigorous limitation to her self-revelations, as Margaret Walters in her fine article demonstrates:

'The superb consistency of her life and work is also its limitation.

In order to keep it up, she has to reject great areas of experience
. . . . I am always bothered by a shadow behind the clear outlines
of her self-portrait, feelings denied or kept strenuously at bay. Her
rigorous self examination can be a kind of self evasion.'

(Walters 1976:354)

Indeed, her autobiographical volumes display just that 'shaping' and
imposition of a pattern on events that writers on autobiography (see
for example Pascal 1960) have traditionally held to be characteristic
of this form but which Jelinek suggested did not hold good in many
cases for women autobiographers. And what Margaret Walters
condemns as a form of self-evasion has to do in part, I believe, with
the project that shapes de Beauvoir's autobiographies: her determination to prove that the unconventional life of an emancipated woman
can be emotionally rewarding as well as a success in worldly and in
intellectual terms. So we might turn the ambiguity of the relationship
between fiction and biography on its head, and instead of seeing
fiction as reflection of reality, might prefer to see autobiography as
equally an ordering of the 'tentative, unfinished' raw material of the
'real' in a metaphoric and symbolic creation of 'self'.

Amongst other things these famous writers, stereotypes of 'liberated'
womanhood, are famous for writing frankly about women's sexuality.
Yet, curiously, sexuality is implicated with madness for them both,
on account of its irrational force.

Doris Lessing's heroine Martha is confident of her sexual
attractiveness and it represents one possible escape from the prison
of the wide-open veld. Her sexuality, and Ella/Anna's in *The Golden
Notebook*, is part of that spontaneous core of self that Doris Lessing
values so much and which men are so greatly to damage as they take
'her' further and further into its depths.

Simone de Beauvoir (1963) depicts the youthful 'self' of her first
volume of autobiography, *Memoirs of a Dutiful Daughter*, as far less
sexually assured than the young Martha Quest. Her first love affair is
with a cousin who seems to be seen as much, almost, as an ideal self
as a lover – and the 'twin' aspect of her relationship with Sartre also
suggests a kind of narcissistic identification with the masculine.

Simone de Beauvoir's father disparaged her looks, but praised her brain which was 'like a man's'. She can learn to find herself pretty as she teaches herself to dress well – epitome of that very 'French' phenomenon, the *jolie laide*. Sexuality remains, however, an irrational and therefore at some level a resented force. Teaching in Marseilles, and therefore often separated from Sartre, she complains of her frustrated sexual desire as a shirt of Nessus, a hideous torment which has grown into her skin, while she not only mocks but is repelled by the advances made to her by a female colleague, whom she cruelly caricatures.

The sexuality of both Doris Lessing and Simone de Beauvoir is resolutely embedded in heterosexuality. Each rejects lesbianism and masturbation as alike pathetic substitutes bringing only disgust and self-hatred. Their sexuality is a response to a man. It must also be a response to love. Ella/Anna bitterly laments the fact that men do not 'really love' women and cannot therefore give them the 'true' vaginal orgasm. She longs only to be swept away by such a love:

'When she loved a man again, she would return to normal: a woman, that is, whose sexuality would ebb and flow in response to his. A woman's sexuality is, so to speak, contained by a man, if he is a real man; she is, in a sense, put to sleep by him, she does not think about sex.'

(Lessing 1964:447)

Menstruating, she washes her body compulsively, hating her own smell, and when she is aroused by a man who means nothing to her emotionally, she catalogues with disgust the physical manifestations of her arousal.

When, in *Les Mandarins* (de Beauvoir 1954), the heroine's American lover abruptly rejects her, she too loses all desire, her body loses all feeling. In general, Simone de Beauvoir retains a considerable reticence about her own sexual feelings, although it may be of relevance to recall Sartre's own loathing of passive femininity. (He expatiates upon this in a celebrated section of *Being and Nothingness* (Sartre 1969:607), likening femininity to the horrible, clinging gapingness of the 'slimy' – *le visqueux* – matter that is neither liquid nor solid.) Where Simone de Beauvoir speaks most frankly of sex and the ecstasies of love, in *The Second Sex*, she speaks through the

voices of other women, their diaries, their memoirs, their autobiographical novels, and not for nothing have her novels and
novellas been described as 'clinical', as 'case studies' – as if this
almost medical distancing could sterilize sexual experience of its
viscous, cloying horror.

The dominant theme in many of Simone de Beauvoir's books is
the theme of men's betrayal and desertion of the women who became
dependent on them, partly because of their children and their
economic dependence, but also through sexual surrender itself. In
her old age Simone de Beauvoir has indeed said that the 'cult of the
orgasm' has made matters worse for women, and forged only a new
link in the chain of their dependency on men (see Smyth 1978). *The
Second Sex* is full of stories of the wives and mistresses of great or at
least successful men, women who sacrificed their freedom and often
their talents to the genius or ambition of men, to reap only
ingratitude. Simone de Beauvoir portrays her own life differently.
She is the woman who has escaped enslavement. She has managed to
create a relationship of equality with a man. Yet she is haunted by
those others, the women who were not so lucky. Indeed – and it is
sinister – *Memoirs of a Dutiful Daughter* reaches its conclusion with
the death of her great childhood and adolescent friend, Zaza. Zaza,
as Simone de Beauvoir describes it, died, to all intents and purposes
from love, and from excessive devotion to her parents. Unlike
Simone she was not determined enough to break away. She was
trapped, and therefore doomed. She is Simone's dark *alter ego*:

> 'The doctors called it meningitis, encephalitis; no one was quite
> sure. Had it been a contagious disease, or an accident? Or had
> Zaza succumbed to exhaustion and anxiety? She has often
> appeared to me at night, her face all yellow under a pink sun-
> bonnet, and seeming to gaze reproachfully at me. We had fought
> together against the revolting fate that had lain ahead of us, and
> for a long time I believed that I had paid for my own freedom with
> her death.'

(de Beauvoir 1963:360)

Simone de Beauvoir's heroines are frequently marked, haunted by
such ghosts, madwomen who have been undone by love. There is
Paule, in *Les Mandarins*, whose aggression turns against Ann. There

is also an American woman who visits Ann's American lover, and conceives an insane jealousy towards Ann. To be sane, to love sucessfully, brings, it would seem, an enormous danger of retribution.

Strangely, given that both Simone de Beauvoir and Doris Lessing are seen and see themselves as exceptional women, their attitudes to sexuality reproduce attitudes current in a contemporary literature of sexuality which constructed female heterosexuality in a particular way. It was a major preoccupation of the postwar period to construct a contradictory amalgam of femininity as highly sexual and yet as wholly anchored within heterosexual marriage. This tied female sexuality and eroticism more securely to reproduction just at the moment when contraception was enabling women for the first time reliably to control their fertility.

Both Lessing and de Beauvoir do insist on a female sexuality that is divorced from reproduction and they refuse the identity of mother (Simone de Beauvoir does this quite explicitly; Doris Lessing simply marginalizes motherhood for her heroines which in the end may be more subversive – they have children but do not make motherhood the centre of their lives). On the other hand they aspire to 'true marriages', Doris Lessing in a very Lawrentian way. (The Lawrentian ideal of relationships between men and women was influential in Britain in radical circles in the late 1950s and early 1960s. The sexual relationship was seen as, in the words of Raymond Williams, being the 'quick of life', while the idea that sexuality was a 'throwing off of repression' gave it a privileged relationship to 'truth' and the reality 'under the net'.)

This 'return of the repressed' is what gives sexuality its power and its danger. Sexual surrender is repeatedly depicted as a threat to woman's identity. The final, and even more devastating threat, in which sexuality is implicated, is the threat of madness. In the work of these writers the great beast of the unconscious lurks in its dark hinterland always ready to spring.

Simone de Beauvoir's deadpan prose style cannot stifle the demons trying to escape. Political and personal betrayal, genocide, and madness burst forth more horribly for being so ordinarily described. Her reactions are the reactions of the 'ordinary', sane person, and despite what she witnesses, she represents, defiantly almost, the clear and transparent gaze of reason. However horrible the atrocities, they do also represent acute *political* problems for herself, and for the French left.

For Simone de Beauvoir (and for Sartre) madness is the ultimate representation of 'bad faith', and there are many examples in their work of women who abdicate 'authenticity' because they cannot confront the realities of their failing sexual attractiveness and their servile dependence on their men. Marcelle, in Sartre's *L'Age de Raison* (1945) is a case in point; and Sartre uses the ploys of such a woman as an example to illustrate bad faith in *Being and Nothingness*. *The Second Sex* has many examples of women who allowed their dependency on men to betray them in this way, and de Beauvoir more than once describes characters for whom this led to madness. There is Paule, in *Les Mandarins*, who goes mad because she cannot bear to admit that she is growing older, losing her looks, that her lover has wearied of her. There is Camille, once the mistress of the theatre producer Dullin, whom in *All Said and Done* (1977) is described in her sordid and crazy old age as yet another example of this 'feminine' failure of women to 'face the truth'. Madness is a state of self-deception, and delusions are a hideous game that women play with themselves. Simone de Beauvoir retains a highly intellectual attitude to madness. Not only that, but in her avid pursuit of happiness and worldly joy she often seems to be frantically denying the existence of the madness and cruelty of which, in fact, she is acutely aware. Significantly, she and Sartre did refer to her optimism and relentless search for experience and sensation as her *schizophrénie*. By this they meant, I imagine, what a psychoanalyst would call a hysterical splitting, the denial of unwelcome aspects of life rather than the schizophrenic dissociation of thought which is more akin to a misrecognition of the meaning of things. For a schizophrenic the world contains too much meaning: the rays of the sun convey a special message; the neighbours are sending thoughts through the wall. For the hysteric, on the other hand, whole tracts of feeling and even consciousness may be simply blocked out or blocked off; in acute cases leading to loss of memory or hysterical paralysis. So, for a long time, Simone de Beauvoir refused to admit that there was going to be a world war; at the age of forty, she refused to admit that her love affair with Nelson Allgren was destined to end in despair, that he would not love her on her terms, because he wanted a woman who 'belonged' to him. So at times her determination to be happy seems almost itself to be verging on the mad.

Yet for Simone de Beauvoir madness is never the entry to another, more privileged state of consciousness. For Doris Lessing, on the other hand, it is. Anna, in *The Golden Notebook*, temporarily driven insane by the horrors of the world judges her madness as the truly sane response – it is the world that is mad. In this respect her work is close to that of R. D. Laing, the radical psychiatrist who was so influential in the 1960s in Britain and who tried to marry psychoanalysis to existentialism.

Existentialism seems something quite different to Simone de Beauvoir. It is the philosophical expression of sane, rational *choice*. An individual can 'choose' liberty without descent into bad faith, provided that s/he recognizes the chance nature of life and the absence of any supernatural plan for human life, or the universe. As Sartre put it, 'Man is condemned to freedom'. Existentialism as interpreted by Laing and the other British radical psychiatrists on the other hand represented precisely a recognition of the paramountcy of the irrational.

In *The Four-gated City* (Lessing 1972) Linda represents madness as a clearer than normal perception of the truth. When Linda is 'mad' she can get in touch with other worlds; her consciousness is not dulled but widened. In *Landlocked* (Lessing 1967) Martha's former lover, Thomas, goes off to live in a native village, and, after his death from fever, a manuscript he had written comes into Martha's hands. This is the testament either of a madman ('He was nuts, wasn't he' a friend comments) or of someone who had broken through some barrier of consciousness to get in touch with other times and other worlds and had begun to chronicle them.

So there they are, so alike yet so different, Simone de Beauvoir asserting the mastery of the will as her way of grasping experience, Doris Lessing valuing immersion in experience. This is why each has a very different attitude towards politics.

Both appear, and make their heroines appear, as politically conscious women, associated with Marxism, close to the Communist parties of their countries. One important theme of the de Beauvoir autobiographies and of *Les Mandarins* is the evolution of the Sartre/de Beauvoir political position after the Second World War, close to, but never in, the French Communist Party, resolutely set against both anti-Communism and mindless pro-Sovietism. Martha Quest, and Anna in *The Golden Notebook*, both traverse the Communist Party, finding in it an inevitable falsity and posturing. For Doris Lessing the Communist Party is, in the end, ideas in the heads of individuals rather then a genuine lived relationship with the suffering of the black Africans in Rhodesia or of the poor women Anna meets when canvassing in north London. For Simone de Beauvoir the taking up and working out of political positions is a wholly valid activity, but for Doris Lessing such manœuvring necessarily distorts the truth of feeling for which she is always looking.

Both none the less saw themselves and their heroines as inevitably and inescapably political. Yet, as political women, they were distressingly isolated.

When I first read these heroine-authors I was only eighteen – then twenty – then twenty four. To reread them now that I am past forty is a strange experience – the double vision of seeing two of each of them and two of myself as well. How differently I now read these famous accounts of women's experience! And how sad in one way it is that I have lost my ability to identify with them as heroines and alternative selves.

Then I was lost in admiration, so that I noticed neither their political isolation (as women), nor their contempt for lesbianism, nor their romanticism when it came to sexuality. Like many others, I took Simone de Beauvoir's 'bohemian' model of the liberated relationship with a 'great writer' as *the* archetype of a desirable 'free' relationship. Now in *The Prime of Life* I encounter a young woman repeating frantically to herself 'I'm happy – I'm so *happy*', when actually she seems tense and lonely, introverted, obsessive, rude, and contemptuous towards her spinsterly colleagues, and riddled with insecurity and terror lest Sartre leave her.

Now in *The Golden Notebook* – which I then read as a manual of womanly experience – I discern attitudes towards both men and women whose ambivalence repels me. *Then* I looked up to Anna/Ella as an experienced 'older woman'. Now I judge her, looking back at

her from a further, perhaps more cynical, possibly more stoical
landmark of experience, as one of *those* women – the ones who cry
'freedom' while hugging their chains.

This experience – of having read these books in my early twenties
and then rereading them twenty odd years later – has raised many
questions for me about the act of reading and about the way in which
the reader may identify with the 'heroine' or 'writer'. Many young
women of today's feminist movement are very critical of Simone de
Beauvoir, rejecting her as excessively male-identified and highly
individualistic (which in many ways she is). Doris Lessing is, I
think, more acceptable because she speaks so exhaustively of feeling
and particularly of painful feeling, and the contemporary women's
movement tends to overvalue feeling, pain, and subjectivity.

Of course, my angry rejection today of Doris Lessing's mystical
vision of life is itself a kind of negative identification. For some
reason, Lessing and de Beauvoir still invite these passionately felt
responses. Had there been a women's movement in the 1950s and
early 1960s women might not have needed to relate to them in the
way they did, as heroines and exemplars, and they themselves might
not have needed to present themselves – sometimes intentionally,
sometimes not – in this way. It falsified their position. Doris Lessing
claims (of *The Golden Notebook*):

> 'Some books are not read in the right way because they have
> skipped a stage of opinion, assume crystallization of information
> in society which has not yet taken place. This book was written as
> if the attitudes that have been created by the women's liberation
> movement already existed . . . . If it were coming out now for the
> first time it might be read and not merely reacted to.'
>
> (Bradbury 1980)

Yet we have to query this. For in some ways what Doris Lessing says
is the antithesis of women's liberation. The situation and consciousness of her fractured heroine, Anna, is precisely the situation and
consciousness the feminists of the late 1960s were in revolt *against*.
They were trying *not* to feel bounded within masculine sexuality.
They were trying to find a voice in politics, to live politics, to take
women into the political arena instead of rejecting the political arena
as an ultimate falsification.

Today, both Simone de Beauvoir and Doris Lessing seem stuck in one-sided representations of womanhood, caught up in the impossible dilemma of being artists at a period when the artist represented the ultimate in individualism, and of having a representative woman's voice at the same time. Exceptional women speaking as women, their audience assumes that they are speaking *for* women – hence the anger they arouse in many feminists today, since we have come to see our dilemmas differently.

This ambiguity between 'truth' and 'fiction' and between the unique and the representative voice still haunts the consciously feminist writers of today. It is interesting – and deserves more analysis – that so many contemporary feminists have turned to imaginative writing in order to express their experience as feminists as well as women. The early works from women's liberation attempted to *theorize* woman's subordination, and, rightly, to make plain the collective nature of the isolated woman's pain.

In returning to individual lived experience, are today's feminists returning to a post-political or apolitical consciousness? Or are they confronting the recognition that political theory in the 1970s still did not give women a new individualized identity, and that although we need as much as ever our collective identity of 'feminist' each of us needs an individual identity as well?

Even if, today, we feel distanced from these pioneers, we should salute two women who were brave enough to risk exposure and to court isolation for having outlined and explored the terrain on which feminists are still struggling: what they are talking about and what we are still talking about today is the relationship between political consciousness and individual consciousness. We may construct our experience differently today, but we are still engaged in the same project, which is to develop a literature of experience (which is what it should be called, perhaps, rather than either 'fiction' *or* 'auto-biography') that both expresses and enlarges our understanding of the Janus face of feminism – which faces towards both the personal and the political.

11 ◆ The Barnard Sexuality Conference

Introduction

This short piece was written as an introduction to 'Seeking Ecstasy on the Battlefield: Danger and Pleasure in Nineteenth Century Feminist Sexual Thought' by Linda Gordon and Ellen DuBois. Published in *Feminist Review* in the spring of 1983, this was one of the opening plenary papers at the Barnard Sexuality Conference. I have included my account of this event because it was such a unique – and somehow such an American – occasion, and because it summarized the state of the sexuality debate in 1982. A difference between American and English perceptions of the event may be illustrated by the objection raised to me by an American feminist to my description of Dorothy Allison's workshop. My English friend at the workshop had experienced it as women 'showing off' and had felt slightly intimidated and alienated; the American feminist adamantly rejected this interpretation: 'Oh *no*! There was so much *pain* in that room.'

The papers from the conference have now been published in book form (Vance 1984) and I am rather more persuaded by the written version of Gayle Rubin's talk than I was by the spoken one. Although I still find problematic her wholesale endorsement of commoditized sexuality, it is possibly necessary for someone to take up a pro-sexuality stance that does not 'draw the line' anywhere.

Since that time Andrea Dworkin and Catharine MacKinnon have been trying to introduce anti-pornography legislation in the state of Minnesota (see *MS*, April, 1985), an enterprise in which they have been assisted by the American new right. This makes it the more necessary for all progressives to sort out their attitudes towards sexuality and especially 'deviant' sexuality, and it is therefore depressing to find both women and men in the British new left supporting the politics of the anti-pornography lobby.

The context of 'Between Pleasure and Danger': the Barnard Conference on Sexuality

Linda Gordon and Ellen DuBois wrote their paper 'Between Pleasure and Danger', which we publish here, to be given at the ninth conference in a series 'The Scholar and the Feminist' held each year in the United States. The series aims to bring feminist research, academic scholarship, and politics together. In 1982 the conference was held at Barnard College, New York City, on 24 April. The theme for the ninth conference was sexuality.

The conference was a major event for feminists on the East Coast of the United States – and many women must have come to it from other parts of the country. Indeed, there were also feminists from Holland, Britain, and France. About 600 women attended in all. (The conference was open to men, although very few attended.)

To a British observer, the conference was both similar to and unlike women's conferences over here. At one level there was greater formality. There was an opening plenary session with papers read by their authors. There was a buffet lunch, and wine and 'hors d'œuvres' at the end of the day. The conference series is funded in part by the Helena Rubinstein foundation, which in itself seems unexpected to a European observer. The cost of the day was $20, or around £10. So in one sense it seemed like a relatively establishment affair. Yet the content of the opening papers and of most of the workshops reflected preoccupations similar to our own.

As it turned out, the coming together of academic respectability and 'extremist' discourses on sexuality blew the whole compromise apart, and events surrounding the conference have created consternation, anger, and uproar amongst American feminists and deepened the already scarring divisions in the American movement. There had already been storm warnings during the planning stages. Each year a conference planning group is gathered together. It is responsible for inviting speakers and also produces a 'conference diary'. From the beginning some groups of what we would call radical or revolutionary feminists active in the New York area were angered by the composition of the 1982 planning group. They felt they were excluded from the planning, and that the planning group was biased and unrepresentative. The organizers of the conference later responded to this accusation by conceding that, for example, feminist anti-porn campaigning groups had been excluded, but they justified this by arguing that the whole of the American feminist debate on sexuality is now dominated by the 'anti-pornography' position. In the United States the power of the 'moral majority' and the strong anti-feminist and pro-family backlash gives the feminist anti-pornography position an importance and credibility it perhaps lacks in Britain where the women's movement and the backlash are much less in evidence. The feminists who organized the conference at Barnard therefore argued that they wanted to have a forum for a diversity of views on sexuality, and that if the anti-porn perspective were included it would overwhelm and swamp everything else. They also felt the divisions were so deep that confrontation rather than discussion would be the result.

The feminist *opposition* to the feminist anti-pornographers in the United States is again rather different from its British equivalent. There, the pornography debate has centred to a greater extent than here on the issue of freedom of speech and the First Amendment. The opposition to Women Against Pornography is libertarian. It foregrounds discussions of types of sexual practice, particularly 'deviant' forms, such as lesbian sadomasochism. There seems to be less concern than here with how sexuality and gender get constructed and with psychoanalysis as a theory of the construction of gender and femininity.

The content of the conferences was already causing Barnard College unease before 24 April. The Conference Diary, usually available to all those who register on or before the day of the conference itself was this year withheld. Then, on the day of the conference, a line of protestors formed outside Barnard and handed out leaflets to participants as they arrived. These leaflets did not seek to dissuade women from going into the conference – and indeed some Women Against Pornography themselves attended – but sought to explain the reasons for their protest. The leaflet objected to the one-sidedness of the conference planning group and content of the conference; signed by 'Coalition of Women for a Feminist

Sexuality and Against Sadomasochism' it included WAP and several groups of lesbian activists. The conference organizers were accused of having invited speakers who supported forms of 'patriarchal' and 'anti-feminist' sexuality such as sadomasochism and paedophilia. No woman was mentioned by name, but it was clear who was being attacked. Feminist organizations were also attacked. For example, a group called 'No More Nice Girls' was accused of supporting pornography and child abuse; during the plenary Ros Baxandall, a feminist historian, exposed the inaccuracy of this allegation and, as a member of 'No More Nice Girls', said that it was a feminist group campaigning for access to abortion.

Readers will judge whether the content of the Gordon/DuBois paper is anti-feminist or 'obscene'. It was not, however, a main target for attack. The more controversial plenary paper was given by Alice Echols and was a critique of 'cultural feminism' – which includes radical feminism and separatism. Speaking as a lesbian, Alice Echols objected to the way in which, she felt, cultural feminism had collapsed lesbianism into 'sisterhood' or being 'woman identified' –arguments familiar to us in Britain. She made a number of telling criticisms, yet her paper offered no positive perspective other than, implicitly, a reassertion of the right of feminists to seek sexual pleasure. This was also the emphasis of the Conference Diary, and although participants did not receive the Diary until weeks after the conference, it is worth mentioning at this point that the Diary raised the following questions, which expressed the ideas behind the whole conference.

'How do women get sexual pleasure in patriarchy?

Given the paradox that the sexual domain is a dangerous one for women, either as an arena of restriction and repression or as an arena of experimentation and resistance, how do women of various ethnic, racial, and class groups strategize for pleasure?

What are the points of similarity and difference between feminist analyses of pornography, incest, and male and female sexual 'nature' and those of the right wing?

Dare we persist in questioning traditional sexuality and sexual arrangement in the current political climate? If not, when is a "good" time for feminists to do so?

What is the political significance of the position outlined by Betty Friedan, which would jettison gay and lesbian rights and sexual nonconformity as issues marginal to feminist goals? What is the nature of the current conflict between the "social purity" and "libertarian" factions in the feminist community? What can be learned from similar debates during the first wave of feminism in the nineteenth century?'

The afternoon workshops were extremely diverse. Gayle Rubin, under attack by the Coalition because of her known views on lesbian sadomasochism (she has 'come out' as a sadomasochist), gave a paper on the legal regulation of sexuality in the United States. She demonstrated that far from being a 'permissive' society, the different states of the Union sanction very little sexual freedom. She ended her paper with a plea for the decriminalization of sexual activity and for all consenting persons to do what they like sexually. During the discussion the issue of what 'consent' means was raised, and this challenged the weakness in Gayle Rubin's presentation, which is that she had tended simply to restate an unreconstructed libertarian position, and although she mentioned the work of Jeffrey Weeks, there was surprisingly little questioning, in this paper at least, of *why* and *how* desire gets constructed in particular ways; surprising because Jeffrey Weeks and others have challenged the idea that one just 'is' a homosexual; so far as I am aware (but this may be ignorance on my part) there has been no similar attempt to 'deconstruct' sadomasochism.

Although on this occasion Gayle Rubin was not speaking on the issue of sadomasochism, the importance this form of sexuality has come to have in the whole debate merits further attention. Again, at the risk of generalizing from a superficial impression, I find it curious that one particular, and arguably rather marginal sexual practice should have come to occupy such a key space in the discussion of sexuality. Why should this be? One argument put forward in support of sadomasochism is that it makes possible the enactment of power fantasies in a safe situation. Also, from the way some sadomasochistic and similar sexual practices are described it is tempting to suppose that individuals find an outlet for the playful in these 'sexual games'. After all, for adults in our society there is no place where they can really 'play' other than in the intimacy of a relationship that is designated 'sexual'. On the other hand sado-masochism sometimes seems to have to do with sexual outlawry and the dark side of self and forbidden desires. This might also be true of butch/femme roles, and Joan Nestlé does defend such roles on precisely these grounds in the *Heresies* 'sex issue'. Perhaps feminism really has done something to lesbianism in confusing it with noneroticized love between women, so that some lesbians have been attracted to other, more deeply 'forbidden' ways of insisting that lesbianism *is* about sex.

A different point made about the focus on lesbian sadomasochism is that it deflects attention away from heterosexuality altogether. Maybe it lets heterosexual women off the hook in making lesbianism seem so outlandish that they feel absolved from engaging with it. Yet after all there is something arbitrary in this coupling of s/m with lesbianism. Where are the closet heterosexual feminist masochists? Are there really *no* heterosexual feminists who have at least had sadomasochistic fantasies about men? I don't believe that. But I suppose it is too 'politically incorrect' even to mention.

One of the afternoon workshops explicitly took up the idea of 'politically incorrect' sexuality. Run by Dorothy Allison it discussed various forms of desire of which feminists have disapproved. Amongst other topics that came up was that of values. One contributor said: 'My values are being good at sex.' I was not present at this workshop, but a British feminist who was commented to me that this remark seemed to sum up in a sense some absence at the heart of the discussion; a discussion that did not relate sexual practices to the social structure – so that there was a latent consumerism about the whole way in which sex was being talked about.

Shirley Walton and Esther Newton ran a workshop of which the title was 'Beyond the gay/straight split: do sexual "roles" (butch/femme) transcend sexual preference?' They described this workshop in the Diary as follows:

> 'The unspoken assumption was that Esther was "butch" while Shirley, because she is heterosexual, was "femme" [the two women are old friends, but not lovers]. But now it appears that

each is most comfortable "initiating" and "orchestrating" sexual interactions. Does this mean that both are "butch"? If so, why does Esther play this out with women and Shirley with men? How and why do homo- and hetero-sexuality complicate, frustrate or facilitate sexual desire and power?

The workshop will attempt to open up the Pandora's box of sexual styles, attitudes and roles banished from the feminist movement as "politically incorrect". Esther and Shirley propose that these styles should be examined and lived.'

There were many other workshops: on pornography, on film, on forms of sexual therapy; Kate Millett ran one on the inability of our society to allow children any sort of sexuality (this workshop was *not* about paedophilia); and the relationship of class, race, money, and disability to sexuality all had a place.

The day ended with a poetry reading. Some of the poems were sexually explicit and the hilarity and excitement of the audience became uproarious – at the same time the euphoria had a slightly hysterical edge to it. Amber Hollibaugh (one of the women attacked in the Coalition leaflet) had already spoken at the final plenary of the struggles women had experienced in the past and the possibilities of passion in the future – if there is a future after Reagan. But the release of tension in the laughter at the end of the day seemed to have more to do with the anxiety and insecurity surrounding sex in the present and of the difficulty – for American feminists more than for British ones – of maintaining a dialogue about sexuality in a society in which sex, the body beautiful, homosexuality – everything – is commercialized to a degree as yet unknown in Europe. The atmosphere of the conference was not so different from that of the Manhattan streets where vividly dressed women and men dramatize their sexual identities in fashion codes and consciously stalk an individualistic ideal of self-fulfilment across an urban landscape of futuristic beauty and immense squalor, where success and despair jostle on every block.

But that is not the end of the matter. Subsequently the Helena Rubinstein foundation withdrew its funding of 'The Scholar and the Feminist' series; and the Barnard Women's Centre has had continuing trouble from the Barnard authorities. This has even further embittered relations between opposing groups of feminists. It possibly means an end to the conferences. Women such as Amber Hollibaugh have been questioned by their employers as a result of the uproar, and some of the conference organizers have spoken of a McCarthyite atmosphere of witch-hunting and purges. So while libertarianism may be insufficient as an analysis of sexuality in our society, the repercussions after the conference have demonstrated clearly how important liberal freedoms are.

The conference was extensively reported and commented upon in *Off Our Backs*, the only American feminist newspaper with a national circulation. Although the *Off Our Backs* reporters had made detailed notes, and while therefore their reportage appeared unbiased, their comment was largely negative. This elicited letters, published in a later edition of the paper, from participants, who alleged that they had been misrepresented. Shirley Walton and Esther Newton, for example, were able to demonstrate that what they had said in their workshop had been seriously distorted in the *Off Our Backs* report.

Petitions were circulated by conference organizers; the conference was widely reported in the New York alternative press; Andrea Dworkin sent out photocopies of the Conference Diary with a letter deploring its obscene and supposedly frightful images. The Conference Diary was finally released and sent to all who had participated in the conference.

There is a part of me that sympathizes with the objections of a lesbian prostitute who wrote to *Off Our Backs*: 'The real, material struggles of women are being ignored while academics debate the niceties of leather and shit.' Am I just a puritan when the (also 'politically incorrect') question bubbles up: is this really so important? But it *must* be important because it has generated so much debate and so much anger; and we need to understand what that is about.

But also, am I really so sunk in the pornographic consciousness that I am unable to sensitize myself to the true frightfulness of the Diary? I am unable to find it offensive. The most explicit image is a reproduction of an Indian erotic painting; it shows a heterosexual couple making love upside down on a galloping horse. Both partners look intensely uncomfortable – and appear to be in some danger –

but to me it doesn't seem objectionable, unless, that is, you find all heterosexual penetration patriarchal. But that of course is the crux of the matter.

Perhaps a contorted coupling on a runaway horse symbolizes rather accurately our wild and desperate attempts as feminists to gain some control over our own sexuality.

References

Adams, P. (1979) A Note on Sexual Division and Sexual Differences. *m/f* 3.

Adams, P. and Minson, J. (1978) The 'Subject' of Feminism. *m/f* 2.

Adamson, O., Brown, C., Harrison, J., and Price, J. (1976) Women's Oppression Under Capitalism. *Revolutionary Communist* 5.

Adlam, D. (1979) Review: The Case Against Capitalist Patriarchy. *m/f* 3.

Alexander, S. (1976) Women's Work in Nineteenth Century London: A Study of the Years 1820–50. In Mitchell, J. and Oakley, A. (eds) *The Rights and Wrongs of Women*. Harmondsworth: Penguin.

Alexander, S. and Taylor, B. (1982) In Defence of 'Patriarchy'. In Evans, M. (ed.) *The Woman Question: Readings in the Subordination of Women*. London: Fontana.

Althusser, L. (1971) Freud and Lacan. In *Lenin and Philosophy and Other Essays*. London: New Left Books.

Amos, V. and Parmar, P. (1984) Challenging Imperial Feminism. In *Feminist Review: Many Voices, One Chant: Black Feminist Perspectives* 17, Autumn.

Armstrong, P. and Armstrong, H. (1983) Beyond Sexless Class and Classless Sex: Towards Feminist Marxism. *Studies in Political Economy* 10, Winter.

– (1984) More on Marxism and Feminism. *Studies in Political Economy* 15, Fall.

Assiter, A. (1985) Review of *Feminist Politics and Human Nature* by Alison Jaggar. *Feminist Review* 19.

Barker, D. L. and Allen, S. (eds) (1976) *Sexual Divisions and Society: Process and Change*. London: Tavistock.

Barnes, D. (1963) *Nightwood*. London: Faber & Faber.

Barnsley Women (1984) *Women Against Pit Closures*. Barnsley, Yorkshire: Women Against Pit Closures, 44 South Road, Dodworth, Barnsley S75 3LQ.

Barrett, M. (1980) *Women's Oppression Today*. London: Verso.

– (1982) Feminism and the Definition of Cultural Politics. In Brunt, R. and Rowan, C. (eds) *Feminism, Culture and Politics*. London: Lawrence & Wishart.

– (1984a) Old Masters of the Left. *New Statesman*, 13 July.

– (1984b) A Reply to Brenner and Ramas. *New Left Review* 146.

Barrett, M. and McIntosh, M. (1980) The 'Family Wage': Some Problems for Socialists and Feminists. *Capital and Class* 11.
– (1982) *The Anti-social Family*. London: Verso.
Beechey, V. (1977) Some Notes on Female Wage Labour in Capitalist Production. *Capital and Class* 3.
– (1979) On Patriarchy. *Feminist Review* 3.
– (1985) The Shape of the Workforce to Come. *Marxism Today* August.
Benjamin, W. (1973) *Charles Baudelaire: A Lyric Poet in the Era of High Capitalism*. London: Verso.
Bennett, F., Heys, R., and Coward, R. (1980) The Limits to Financial and Legal Independence: A Socialist Feminist Perspective on Taxation and Social Security. *Politics and Power* 1.
Birch, K., Plaster, J., Walsh, M., and Young, N. (1979) Pat Arrowsmith – Pacifist. *Gay Left* 8.
Bloomfield, J. (1984) Crossed Lines: Communists in Search of an Identity. *Marxism Today* April.
Bourne, G. (1972) *Pregnancy*. London: Cassell.
Bradbury, M. (ed.) (1980) *The Novel Today: Contemporary Writers on Modern Fiction*. London: Fontana.
Bray, A. (1982) *Homosexuality in Renaissance England*. London: Gay Men's Press.
Brenner, J. and Ramas, M. (1984) Rethinking Women's Oppression. *New Left Review* 144.
Brittain, V. (1953) *Lady into Woman*. London: Andrew Dakers.
Bruegel, I. (1979) Women as a Reserve Army of Labour: a Note on Recent British Experience. *Feminist Review* 3.
Brunt, R. and Rowan, C. (eds) (1982) *Feminism, Culture and Politics*. London: Lawrence & Wishart.
Burman, S. (ed.) (1978) *Fit Work for Women*. London: Croom Helm.
Burniston, S., Mort, F., and Weedon, C. (1978) Psychoanalysis and the Cultural Acquisition of Sexuality and Subjectivity. In Women's Studies Group, CCCS (eds) *Women Take Issue*. London: Hutchinson.
Campbell, B. (1980) United We Fall. *Red Rag*.
– (1984) *Wigan Pier Revisited*. London: Virago.
Campbell, B. and Charlton, V. (1978) Work to Rule. *Red Rag*.
Carby, H. (1982) White Woman Listen: Black Feminism and the Boundaries of Sisterhood. In Centre for Contemporary Cultural Studies *The Empire Strikes Back: Race and Racism in Seventies Britain*. London: Hutchinson.
Chester, G. (1982) I call myself Radical Feminist. In Evans, M. (ed.) *The Woman Question*. London: Fontana.
Chetwynd, J. and Hartnett, O. (1978) *The Sex Role System*. London: Tavistock.
Chodorow, N. (1978) *The Reproduction of Mothering*. Berkeley: University of California Press.

Cockburn, C. (1981) The Material of Male Power. *Feminist Review* 9.
– (1983) *Brothers*. London: Pluto Press.
Colette (1980) *The Pure and the Impure*. Harmondsworth: Penguin.
Coote, A. (1981) The AES – A New Starting Point. *New Socialist* 2, November/December.
Corrigan, P. (1977) The Welfare State as an Arena of Class Struggle. *Marxism Today* March.
– (1979) Popular Consciousness and Social Democracy. *Marxism Today* December.
Cousins, M. (1978) Material Arguments and Feminism. *m/f* 2.
Coward, R. (1978a) Rethinking Marxism. *m/f* 2.
– (1978b) Sexual Liberation and the Family. *m/f* 1.
– (1981) Socialism, Feminism and Socialist Feminism. In Feminist Anthology Collective (eds) *No Turning Back*. London: The Women's Press.
Cowie, C. and Lees, S. (1981) Slags or Drags. *Feminist Review* 9.
CSE London Group (1979) Crisis, The Labour Movement and the Alternative Economic Strategy. *Capital and Class* 8.
CSE State Apparatus and Expenditure Group (1979) *Struggle over the State*. London: CSE Books.
Cutler, A., Hindess, B., Hirst, P. and Hussain, A. (1977) *Marx's 'Capital' and Capitalism Today*. I. London: Routledge and Kegan Paul.
– (1978) *Marx's 'Capital' and Capitalism Today*. II. London: Routledge and Kegan Paul.
Davis, K. (1984) Wives and Work: The Sex Role Revolution and its Consequences. *Population and Development Review* 10, September.
de Beauvoir, S. (1953) *The Second Sex*. London: Jonathan Cape.
– (1954) *Les Mandarins*. Paris: Gallimard.
– (1963) *Memoirs of a Dutiful Daughter*. Harmondsworth: Penguin.
– (1965) *The Prime of Life*. Harmondsworth: Penguin.
– (1968) *Force of Circumstance*. Harmondsworth: Penguin.
– (1977) *All Said and Done*. Harmondsworth: Penguin.
Debord, G. (1973) *La Société du Spectacle*. Paris: Éditions Chantlibre.
Delmar, R. (1975) Psychoanalysis and Feminism. *Red Rag* 8.
Dworkin, A. (1981) *Pornography: Men Possessing Women*. London: The Women's Press.
Echols, A. (1984) The New Feminism of Yin and Yang. In Snitow, A., Stansell, C., and Thompson, S. *Desire: The Politics of Sexuality*. London: Virago.
Ehrenreich, B. and English, D. (1979) *For Her Own Good*. London: Pluto Press.
Eisenstein, H. (1984) *Contemporary Feminist Thought*. London: Allen & Unwin.
Eisenstein, Z. (1979) *Capitalist Patriarchy and the Case for Socialist Feminism*. New York: Monthly Review Press.

Elshtain, J. B. (1982) Feminist Discourse and its Discontents: Language Power and Meaning. In Keohane, N., Rosaldo, M. Z., and Gelpi, B. C. *Feminist Theory: A Critique of Ideology*. Chicago: University of Chicago Press.

Elson, D. and Pearson, R. (1981) 'Nimble Fingers Make Cheap Workers': An Analysis of Women's Employment in Third World Export Manufacturing. *Feminist Review 7*.

Evans, M. (ed.) (1982) *The Woman Question: Readings on the Subordination of Women*. London: Fontana.

Evans, R. (1977) *The Feminists: Women's Emancipation Movements in Europe, America and Australasia*. London: Croom Helm.

Faderman, L. (1981) *Surpassing the Love of Men: Romantic Friendship between Women from the Renaissance to the Present*. London: Junction Books.

Feminist Anthology Collective (eds) (1981) *No Turning Back*. London: The Women's Press.

Finch, J. and Groves, D. (1983) *A Labour of Love: Women, Work and Caring*. London: Routledge & Kegan Paul.

Fine, B., Harris, L., Mayo, M., Weir, A., and Wilson, E. (1984) Class Politics. London (published by the authors).

Firestone, S. (1970) *The Dialectic of Sex; For a Feminist Revolution*. London: The Women's Press.

Foucault, M. (1977) *Language, Counter-memory, Practice*. Ithaca: Cornell University Press.

— (1979) *The History of Sexuality: An Introduction*. London: Allen Lane.

Freud, S. (1948) On Narcissism: An Introduction. *Collected Papers*, Vol. IV. London: Hogarth Press and Institute of Psychoanalysis.

— (1961) *Letters of Sigmund Freud 1873–1939*, edited by Ernst Freud. London: Hogarth Press and Institute of Psychoanalysis.

— (1973) *New Introductory Lectures on Psychoanalysis*. Harmondsworth: Penguin.

— (1977) *On Sexuality*. Harmondsworth: Penguin.

Freud, S. and Breuer, J. (1974) *Studies on Hysteria*. Harmondsworth: Penguin.

Friedan, B. (1963) *The Feminine Mystique*. Harmondsworth: Penguin.

Friedman, S. (1982) Heterosexuality, Couples and Parenthood: a 'Natural' Cycle? In Stanley, L. and Friedman, S. (eds) *On the Problem of Men*. London: The Women's Press.

Gamarnikov, E., Morgan, D., Purvis, J., and Taylorson, D. (eds) (1983) *Gender, Class and Work*. London: Heinemann.

Glyn, A. and Sutcliffe, B. (1972) *British Capitalism, Workers and the Profit Squeeze*. Harmondsworth: Penguin.

Gordon, L. (1976) *Women's Body, Women's Right*. New York: Penguin.

Gramsci, A. (1971) *Selections from the Prison Notebooks*. London: Lawrence & Wishart.

Greenwood, V. and Young, J. (1980) Ghettoes of Freedom: An Examination of Permissiveness. In National Deviancy Conference *Permissiveness and Control*. London: Macmillan.

Greer, G. (1970) *The Female Eunuch*. London: Paladin.

Hall, P., Land, H., Parker, R., and Webb, A. (1976) *Change, Choice, and Conflict in Social Policy*. London: Heinemann.

Hall, S. (1979) Drifting into the Law and Order Society. Cobden Trust Human Rights Day Lecture. Unpublished.

Heron, L. (1980) The Mystique of Motherhood. *Time Out*, 21 November.

Hirst, P. (1981a) The Genesis of the Social. *Politics and Power* 3.

– (1981b) Psychoanalysis and Social Relations. *m/f* 5/6.

Hobsbawm, E. (1968) *Labouring Men*. London: Weidenfeld & Nicolson.

– (1983) Labour's Lost Millions. *Marxism Today* October.

Hunt, J. (1981) Women and the Alternative Economic Strategy. *Economic Bulletin* 8.

Interrante, J. and Lasser, C. (1979) 'Victims of the Very Songs They Sing': A Critique of Recent Work on Patriarchal Culture and the Social Construction of Gender. *Radical History Review* 20.

Jacques, M. (1979) Thatcherism: the Impasse Broken? *Marxism Today* October.

Jaggar, A. (1983) *Feminist Politics and Human Nature*. Brighton: Harvester Press.

Jameson, F. (1984) Postmodernism, or the Cultural Logic of Late Capital. *New Left Review* 146.

Jelinek, E. (ed.) (1980) *Women's Autobiography: Essays in Criticism*. Bloomington: University of Indiana Press.

Jones, K. (ed.) (1978) *The Year Book of Social Policy 1977*. London: Routledge & Kegan Paul.

'Joreen' (1972) The Tyranny of Structurelessness. *The Second Wave* 2: 1.

Joshi, H. (1984) The New Workers. *Guardian*, 17 January.

Kaplan, C. (1982) Radical Feminism and Literature. Rethinking Millett's *Sexual Politics*. In Evans, M. (ed.) *The Woman Question: Readings on the Subordination of Women*. London: Fontana.

Keohane, N., Rosaldo, M. Z., and Gelpi, B. C. (1982) *Feminist Theory: A Critique of Ideology*. Chicago: University of Chicago Press.

Kuhn, A. and Wolpe, A.-M. (eds) (1978) *Feminism and Materialism*. London: Routledge & Kegan Paul.

Lacan, J. (1977) *Ecrits*. London: Tavistock.

Laclau, E. and Mouffe, C. (1981) Socialist Strategy: Where Next? *Marxism Today* January.

Land, H. (1975) The Myth of the Male Breadwinner. *New Society*, 9 October.

– (1976a) Women: Supporters or Supported ? In Barker, D. and Allen, S. (eds) *Sexual Divisions and Society: Process and Change*. London: Tavistock.

– (1976b) The Introduction of Family Allowances. In Hall, P., Land, H.,

Parker, R., and Webb, A. *Change, Choice, and Conflict in Social Policy.* London: Heinemann.
- (1978a) The Child Benefit Fiasco. In Jones, K. (ed.) *The Year Book of Social Policy 1977.* London: Routledge & Kegan Paul.
- (1978b) Sex-role Stereotyping in the Social Security and Income Tax Systems. In Chetwynd, J. and Hartnett, O. *The Sex Role System.* London: Tavistock.
- (1978c) Who Cares for the Family? *Journal of Social Policy* July.
- (1980) The Family Wage. *Feminist Review* 6.
Laplanche, J. and Pontalis, J.-B. (1973) *The Language of Psychoanalysis.* London: The Hogarth Press.
Lefebvre, H. (1969) *The Explosion: Marxism and the French Upheaval.* New York: Monthly Review Press.
Lenin, V. I. (1976) 'Left Wing' Communism – An Infantile Disorder. In *Selected Works,* Vol. III. Moscow: Progress Publishers.
Leonard, P. (1979) Restructuring the Welfare State. *Marxism Today* December.
Lessing, D. (1949) *The Grass is Singing.* Reprinted London: Panther, 1980.
- (1960) *In Pursuit of the English.* Reprinted London: Panther, 1980.
- (1962) *Martha Quest.* London: Panther.
- (1964) *The Golden Notebook.* Harmondsworth: Penguin.
- (1965) *A Man and Two Women.* London: Panther.
- (1967) *Landlocked.* London: Panther.
- (1968) *The Small, Personal Voice.* In Maschler, T. (ed.) *Declaration.* London: MacGibbon & Kee.
- (1972) *The Four-gated City.* London: Panther.
Lewis, J. (1985) The Debate on Sex and Class. *New Left Review* 149, January/February.
Lipschitz, S. (1978) The Personal is Political: The Problem of Feminist Therapy. *m/f* 2.
Livingstone, K. (1984) Fifth Column. *New Socialist* 19, September.
London Edinburgh Weekend Return Group (1979) *In and Against The State.* London: London Edinburgh Weekend Return Group (c/o CSE).
Lown, J. (1983) Not So Much a Factory, More a Form of Patriarchy: Gender and Class during Industrialisation. In Gamarnikov, E., Morgan, D., Purvis, J., and Taylorson, D. (eds) *Gender, Class and Work.* London: Heinemann.
MacCluskie, K. (1983) Women's Language and Literature: A Problem in Women's Studies. *Feminist Review* 14.
McIntosh, M. (1968) The Homosexual Role. *Social Problems* 16.
- (1978a) The State and the Oppression of Women. In Kuhn, A. and Wolpe, A.-M. (eds) *Feminism and Materialism.* London: Routledge & Kegan Paul.
- (1978b) The Welfare State and the Needs of the Dependent Family. In Burman, S. (ed.) *Fit Work for Women.* London: Croom Helm.
- (1981) Feminism and Social Policy. *Critical Social Policy* 1: 1.

MacKinnon, C. (1982) Feminism, Marxism, Method and the State: An Agenda for Theory. In Keohane, N., Rosaldo, M. Z., and Gelpi, B. C. *Feminist Theory: A Critique of Ideology.* Chicago: University of Chicago Press.

McRobbie, A. (1978) Working Class Girls and the Culture of Femininity. In Women's Studies Group, CCCS (eds) *Women Take Issue.* London: Hutchinson.

Malos, E. (1980) *The Politics of Housework.* London: Allison & Busby.

Marks, E. and de Courtivron, I. (1981) *New French Feminisms.* Brighton: Harvester Press.

Marx, K. and Engels, F. (1975) *Collected Works,* Vol. 3. London: Lawrence & Wishart.

Maschler, T. (ed.) (1968) *Declaration.* London: MacGibbon & Kee.

Massey, D., Segal, L., and Wainwright, H. (1984) Stop the Great Male Moving Right Show! *New Socialist* 15, January/February.

Meiksins Wood, E. (1983) Marxism without Class Struggle? In Miliband, R. and Saville, J. (eds) *The Socialist Register 1983.* London: Merlin Press.

Millett, K. (1971) *Sexual Politics.* London: Rupert Hart-Davis.

– (1973) *The Prostitution Papers.* New York: Avon Books.

– (1975) *Flying.* London: Hart-Davis MacGibbon.

– (1978) *Sita.* London: Virago.

Mitchell, J. (1966) Women: The Longest Revolution. *New Left Review* 40.

– (1971) *Women's Estate.* Harmondsworth: Penguin.

– (1974) *Psychoanalysis and Feminism.* London: Allen Lane.

– (1980) On the Difference between Men and Women. *New Society,* 12 June.

– (1984) *Women: The Longest Revolution: Essays on Feminism, Literature and Psychoanalysis.* London: Virago.

Mitchell, J. and Oakley, A. (1976) *The Rights and Wrongs of Women.* Harmondsworth: Penguin.

Mitchell, J. and Rose J. (eds) (1982) Jacques Lacan and the Ecole Freudienne. *Feminine Sexuality.* London: Macmillan.

– (1983) Feminine Sexuality: Interview. *m/f* 8.

Moers, E. (1960) *The Dandy: Brummell to Beerbohm.* London: Secker & Warburg.

Molyneux, M. (1984) Mobilization without Emancipation? Women's Interests, State and Revolution in Nicaragua. *Critical Social Policy* 4: 1.

Morgan, R. (1984) *Sisterhood is Global: The International Women's Movement Anthology.* New York: Anchor Books, Doubleday & Co.

Murdoch, I. (1954) *Under the Net.* London: Chatto & Windus.

National Deviancy Conference (eds) (1980) *Permissiveness and Control.* London: Macmillan.

Oakley, A. (1979) The Failure of the Movement for Women's Equality. *New Society,* 23 August.

Owen, U. (ed.) (1983) *Fathers: Reflections by Daughters.* London: Virago.

Pascal, R. (1960) *Design and Truth in Autobiography.* London: Routledge

& Kegan Paul.

Phillips, A. (1983) *Hidden Hands*. London: Pluto Press.

Phillips, A. and Taylor, B. (1980) Sex and Skill: Notes towards a Feminist Economics. *Feminist Review* 6.

Reiter, R. (ed.) (1975) *Towards an Anthropology of Women*. New York: Monthly Review Press.

Rich, A. (1983) Split at the Root. In Owen, U. (ed.) *Fathers: Reflections by Daughters*. London: Virago.

– (1984) *The Fact of a Door Frame: Poems Reprinted and New*. New York: W. W. Norton.

Rosaldo, M. Z. (1980) The Uses and Abuses of Anthropology. *Signs* 5: 3.

Rosaldo, M. Z. and Lamphere, L. (1974) *Woman, Culture and Society*. Berkeley: University of California Press.

Rowbotham, S. (1972) The Beginnings of Women's Liberation in Britain. In Wandor, M. *The Body Politic*. London: Stage One.

– (1973) *Woman's Consciousness; Man's World*. Harmondsworth: Penguin.

Rowbotham, S., Segal, L., and Wainwright, H. (1979) *Beyond the Fragments: Feminism and the Making of Socialism*. London: Merlin Press.

Rubin, G. (1975) The Traffic in Women. In Reiter, R. (ed.) *Towards an Anthropology of Women*. New York: Monthly Review Press.

– (1984) Thinking Sex: Notes for a Radical Theory of the Politics of Sexuality. In Vance, C. S. (ed.) *Pleasure and Danger: Exploring Female Sexuality*. London: Routledge & Kegan Paul.

Ruehl, S. (1982) Inverts and Experts: Radclyffe Hall and the Lesbian Identity. In Brunt, R. and Rowan, C. (eds) *Feminism, Culture and Politics*. London: Lawrence & Wishart.

Samuel, R. (ed.) (1981) *People's History and Socialist Theory*. London: Routledge & Kegan Paul.

Sargent, L. (ed.) (1981) *The Unhappy Marriage of Marxism and Feminism*. London: Pluto Press.

Sartre, J.-P. (1945) *L'Age de Raison*. Paris: Gallimard.

– (1969) *Being and Nothingness*. London: Methuen.

Sayers, J. (1982) *Biological Politics*. London: Tavistock.

Seed, P. (1973) *The Expansion of Social Work*. London: Routledge & Kegan Paul.

Serge, V. (1963) *Memoirs of a Revolutionary 1901–1941*. London: Oxford University Press.

Smith, J. (1984) The Paradox of Women's Poverty: Wage-earning Women and Economic Transformation. *Signs* 10: 2.

Smyth, R. (1978) The Lost Dream of Simone. *Observer*, 15 January.

Snitow, A., Stansell, C., and Thompson, S. (1983) *Desire: The Politics of Sexuality*. London: Virago.

Stacey, J. (1983) The New Conservative Feminism. *Feminist Studies* 9: 3.

Stimpson, C. and Specter Person, E. (1980) *Women, Sex and Sexuality*. Chicago: University of Chicago Press.

Storr, A. (1964) *Sexual Deviations*. Harmondsworth: Penguin.

Sulloway, F. J. (1979) *Freud: Biologist of the Mind*. London: Burnett Books.
Taylor, B. (1981) Socialist-Feminism: Utopian or Scientific? In Samuel, R.
(ed.) *People's History and Socialist Theory*. London: Routledge & Kegan
Paul.
– (1983) *Eve and the New Jerusalem*. London: Virago.
Thompson, E. P. (1976) Romanticism, Moralism and Utopianism. *New Left
Review* 99.
Thomson, A., Mulvey, G., and Farbman, M. (1977) Bargaining Structure
and Relative Earnings in Great Britain. *British Journal of Industrial
Relations* July.
Timpanaro, S. (1975) *On Materialism*. London: Verso.
Tomlinson, J. (1984) Incomes Policy and Women's Wages. *m/f* 9.
Vance, C. S. (ed.) (1984) *Pleasure and Danger: Exploring Female Sexuality*.
London: Routledge & Kegan Paul.
Vogel, L. (1984) *Marxism and the Oppression of Women: Towards a Unitary
Theory*. London: Pluto Press.
Walters, M. (1976) The Rights and Wrongs of Women: Mary Wollstonecraft,
Harriet Martineau, Simone de Beauvoir. In Mitchell, J. and Oakley, A.
(eds) *The Rights and Wrongs of Women*. Harmondsworth: Penguin.
Wandor, M. (1972) *The Body Politic*. London: Stage One.
Webster, P. (1984) The Forbidden: Eroticism and Taboo. In Vance, C. S.
(ed.) *Pleasure and Danger: Exploring Female Sexuality*. London: Routledge
& Kegan Paul.
Weeks, J. (1977) *Coming Out*. London: Quartet Books.
Weir, A. (1974) The Family, Social Work and the Welfare State. *Case Con:
The Women's Issue*.
Weir, A. and McIntosh, M. (1982) Towards a Wages Strategy for Women.
Feminist Review 10.
Williams, R. (1977) Notes on British Marxism Since the War. *New Left
Review* 100.
Wilson, E. (1977) *Women and the Welfare State*. London: Tavistock.
– (1980) *Only Halfway to Paradise: Women in Postwar Britain 1945–1968*.
London: Tavistock.
– (1982) *Mirror Writing*. London: Virago.
Wollheim, R. (1971) *Freud*. London: Fontana.
Women's Studies Group, CCCS (1978) *Women Take Issue*. London:
Hutchinson.
Women's Therapy Centre Study Group (1979) Letter in Reply to Susan
Lipschitz. *m/f* 3.
Zimmerman, B. (1981) What Has Never Been: An Overview of Lesbian
Literary Criticism. *Feminist Studies* 7.
– (1984) The Politics of Transliteration: Lesbian Personal Narratives.
Signs 9: 4.

Name index

Subject index